ACT FOR BURNOUT

of related interest

Things I Got Wrong So You Don't Have To
48 Lessons to Banish Burnout and Avoid Anxiety for Those Who Put Others First
Pooky Knightsmith
Foreword by Nicola Brentnall
ISBN 978 1 83997 267 6
eISBN 978 1 83997 268 3
Audiobook ISBN 978 1 39980 415 8

What I Do to Get Through
How to Run, Swim, Cycle, Sew, or Sing Your Way Through Depression
Edited by Olivia Sagan and James Withey
Foreword by Cathy Rentzenbrink
ISBN 978 1 78775 298 6
eISBN 978 1 78775 299 3

Challenging Stress, Burnout and Rust-Out
Finding Balance in Busy Lives
Teena J. Clouston
ISBN 978 1 84905 406 5
eISBN 978 0 85700 786 5

Effective Self-Care and Resilience in Clinical Practice
Dealing with Stress, Compassion Fatigue and Burnout
Edited by Dr Sarah Parry, ClinPsyD
Foreword by Paul Gilbert, PhD, FBPsS, OBE
ISBN 978 1 78592 070 7
eISBN 978 1 78450 331 4

Mindfulness for Carers
How to Manage the Demands of Caregiving While Finding a Place for Yourself
Dr Cheryl Rezek
ISBN 978 1 84905 654 0
eISBN 978 1 78450 147 1

Hell Yeah Self-Care!
A Trauma-Informed Workbook
Alex Iantaffi and Meg-John Barker
ISBN 978 1 78775 245 0
eISBN 978 1 78775 246 7

ACT for Burnout

Recharge, Reconnect, and Transform Burnout
with Acceptance and Commitment Therapy

Debbie Sorensen, PhD

Jessica Kingsley Publishers
London and Philadelphia

First published in Great Britain in 2024 by Jessica Kingsley Publishers
An imprint of John Murray Press

1

The information contained in this book is not intended to replace the services
of trained medical professionals or to be a substitute for medical advice. You are
advised to consult a doctor on any matters relating to your health, and in particular
on any matters that may require diagnosis or medical attention.

A CIP catalogue record for this title is available from the British Library and the
Library of Congress

ISBN 978 1 83997 537 0
eISBN 978 1 83997 538 7

Printed and bound in the United States by Integrated Books International

Jessica Kingsley Publishers' policy is to use papers that are natural, renewable and
recyclable products and made from wood grown in sustainable forests. The logging
and manufacturing processes are expected to conform to the environmental
regulations of the country of origin.

Jessica Kingsley Publishers
Carmelite House
50 Victoria Embankment
London EC4Y 0DZ

www.jkp.com

John Murray Press
Part of Hodder & Stoughton Ltd
An Hachette Company

*To Hadley, Piper, and Easan, for giving me love,
support, meaning, and purpose.*

Contents

Acknowledgements

Jane Evans at Jessica Kingsley Publishers approached me with the idea of writing an ACT for Burnout book a few years ago. Jane, thank you for being incredibly patient with me, and I appreciate your guidance on the manuscript. Thank you to Sarah Thomson, Emma Holak, and others at Jessica Kingsley who worked on the book. Thank you to the people who read the book and provided an endorsement. Thank you to Jill Stoddard, Yael Schonbrun, and Easan Drury, who reviewed drafts of my writing and provided me with invaluable feedback (and moral support). Thank you to Vibeke Hansen for helping me understand the Single Item Burnout Measure. Thank you to Leann Harris (who unfortunately passed away before the book ideas we discussed came to fruition), and to Laila Riedell for your assistance.

I have learned about burnout from many people, especially the researchers, clinicians, and writers who came before me, many (but not all) of whom are cited in this book. Thank you to the coworkers, friends, and therapy clients who shared their experiences with chronic stress and burnout with me, for teaching me more about the varieties of burnout than I could ever have imagined on my own.

I would like to thank my former colleagues at the Rocky Mountain Regional VA Medical Center, especially those who worked in the Spinal Cord Injury/Disorders clinic (who were right there with me before, during, and after my lived experience of burnout), the Health Psychology section, the Mental Illness Research Education and Clinical Center, and the Mental Health service. Thank you to my professional communities, especially the Association for Contextual Behavioral Science, the Women in ACBS Special Interest Group, the Psychologists Off the Clock team (past and present), and MEND for racial trauma. The list of individual colleagues to thank is too long to name them all. For now, I would like to offer special thanks to the following people who either collaborated with me about burnout, or taught me something about burnout along the way: Nazanin Bahraini, Sean Barnes, Abbie Beacham, Estela Bogaert-Martinez, Lauren Borges, Lisa Brenner, Bernard Chang, Michael Craine, Elizabeth Holman, Beeta Homaifar, Dale Jones, Kerry Makin-Byrd, Meredith Mealer, Meg McKelvie, Jed Olson, Jennifer Olson-Madden, Sheila Saliman, Geoffrey Smith, Jennifer Shepard Payne, Robyn Walser, and Carynne Williams. Please know that many more colleagues were influential in this work, and I appreciate each of you.

Thank you to all the educators, healthcare workers, mental health professionals, caregivers, activists, and other "do-gooder types" out there, who risk personal burnout to make the world a better place. Take good care of yourselves, please, we need you.

I checked out piles of books from the library almost every week to do research for this book. Thank you to the Denver Public Library for saving me a lot of money, and to libraries and librarians everywhere for the service you provide to our communities. I'm sorry about all the overdue books!

I appreciate the professional and personal support of Meg McKelvie, Kerry Makin-Byrd, Stacey Bromberg, Yumi Perkins, Yael Schonbrun, Jill Stoddard, Diana Hill, Alexis Karris Bachik, Rae Littlewood, Emily Edlynn, Tamara Hubbard, Colleen Ehrnstrom, and Brooks Witter as I was writing this book.

I am grateful for my personal communities of support, without whom I would be burned out beyond repair. Thank you to my parents, siblings, nieces and nephews, extended family, dear friends, and wonderful neighbors. Special thanks to Janet and Gil Geisz, Tom and Sandy Sorensen, Brooke Ditlow, and Amala and Nathan Peruman. And, finally but most importantly of all, thank you to Hadley, Piper, and Easan. How many times did we joke that my burnout book was burning all of us out? Thank you for bearing with me, and for all the love and support along the way.

Hello, I'm Your Burnout Guide

Have you been feeling exhausted and utterly depleted? Disconnected from things you normally care about? Overwhelmed? Stuck? If you feel compelled to pick up this book, I'm guessing you know what I'm talking about. If you are engaged in a stressful work role—whether it's your job, parenting, caretaking, or another area of your life—you've probably experienced periods of burnout. You might be experiencing a period like that right now. And you're here because you're looking for help.

I'm a clinical psychologist with nearly twenty years of clinical experience who specializes in burnout. And I know what it's like to care deeply about my work and yet feel utterly exhausted by it. Several years ago, I experienced a long and difficult period of burnout, which I'll tell you about in Chapter 1, that led me to explore burnout as a passion project. I started talking openly about my burnout with colleagues and friends, many of whom, I discovered, were also struggling with burnout. I thought I knew about burnout before—on the surface it seemed intuitive. But as I explored it more, I learned that it is more complex than I had realized. I read everything I could find on burnout, from books, to research papers, to social commentaries, to news articles about its growing prevalence. I started focusing my clinical private practice on burnout, adding more clients with burnout, and giving talks on methods for navigating burnout in different settings.

Then, in 2020, the Covid-19 pandemic took hold and burnout was everywhere, almost overnight. My practice was inundated with clients who were exhausted and overwhelmed, just trying to keep going. While that might have been good for my private practice, it definitely wasn't good for my clients or the world. My clients were extremely stressed, and they were suffering. Although I was also feeling exhausted with pandemic stress, working as a mental health professional during a difficult time, with two children doing remote learning at home, I had already learned some effective and sustainable ways of coping with chronic stress and burnout. It's these skills I will share with you in this book.

As a therapist, I help people who are struggling to manage stress, keep a healthy perspective on things, and stay connected to what matters to them. Over the course of many years working with a wide variety of therapy clients, I have seen how burnout impacts people across a broad range of professions, ages, and life circumstances. These days, it seems as if burnout is ubiquitous; no one is immune. Clients I work with could include people like:

- A public school teacher who lives with her aging father and has little time to care for herself.
- A sales associate at a large corporation, who is so exhausted from interacting with clients and co-workers, he's been isolating from friends and family.
- A busy ER physician with two young children, who fantasizes about leaving it all behind and living in an apartment at the beach, alone.
- A therapist who works with high-risk clients and is drinking too much alcohol after work to cope with the stress of his job.
- A stay-at-home parent with little support, alone all day with her infant and toddler, who spends hours each day on her phone and feels guilty about being "checked out."
- A worker in the nonprofit sector, who used to be passionate about

the mission of his organization but now feels hopeless that it will do any good.

- A Black assistant professor, tired of watching her less prolific white colleagues get tenure, who is thinking about leaving academia.
- A sleep-deprived college student, who hopes to get into graduate school but procrastinates online instead of studying for his exams.
- An early-career attorney at a demanding law firm, who, under tremendous pressure to make partner, is getting increasingly irritated with her co-workers and lashing out.
- A hard-working executive at a technology start-up, who wants the eventual payout, but is so stressed he feels he can't keep going much longer unless something changes.

Burnout can impact people's lives in many ways. Sometimes people lose interest in a career they've worked hard to attain or get into problematic patterns of procrastination or substance abuse. Or they might become generally dissatisfied with their lives, so they just feel "blah" most of the time. Some people become irritable or disgruntled about their workplace, or start having problems at work or home because they aren't as engaged as they used to be. Some have trouble sleeping, even when they are completely exhausted.

I've seen many people turn their lives around in the face of burnout. One reason I love working with clients with burnout is because I can use my knowledge and personal experience to help them transform burnout and reconnect with meaning. Sometimes burnout can spark important change and growth. That could be big changes, like changing jobs or even professions, or smaller changes, like setting better boundaries or changing daily habits. And sometimes the external circumstances don't need to change. Simply understanding burnout better can help people become more compassionate toward themselves in the face of their struggle.

You can think of this book as a guide to help you in your own struggles with burnout. My goal is to share some of what I've learned, and to help you on your own journey of personal transformation.

What I've learned

I've learned a lot about burnout over the years, and there are a few key take-aways I'd like to share with you.

First, I want you to know that you're not alone! Many people are experiencing burnout these days and are speaking out about the underlying cultural circumstances that lead us there. Burnout has recently been called an "epidemic" (Moss 2021) because it is widespread and on the rise in many places around the world.

Burnout always happens in context. It is a problem of overwork/ chronic stress leading to disconnection and disengagement. To some degree, burnout makes a lot of sense, because it's a natural reaction to chronic stress, and we live in a stressful world! If you are burned out, it's not your fault.

Finally, and perhaps most importantly, I have learned that it *is* possible to transform burnout. I have seen it in clients, and I've experienced it myself. While burnout will sometimes pass on its own, there are things you can do to help yourself. Sometimes, the change you need is an internal one, invisible to others, like a perspective shift or a new way of responding to your thoughts and emotions. Sometimes, you may benefit from a more visible change in your behavior or circumstances.

Some people have argued that efforts to transform burnout must happen primarily at the cultural or organizational level, rather than putting the burden of change on those individuals who are experiencing burnout. I agree with this thinking—burnout is rooted in a cultural context of how we work that needs to be addressed systemically. At the same time, many clients come to my office in a place of deep suffering and want help coping with their own circumstances, even if those big, systemic factors are slow to change. I feel strongly that burnout must be approached at *all* levels—from the broad cultural context, to organizational systems, to helping individuals who are suffering. Much as you would address, say, a pandemic from the high levels of public health and prevention, down to treating individuals who are sick, burnout must be addressed at multiple levels. To truly transform burnout, we must work toward both fixing cultural and systemic problems that contribute to burnout, and helping people (like you!) who are experiencing it now. Indeed, equipping yourself with the psychological skills to manage your own burnout can help you have the emotional capacity to navigate the challenges we all face, and work toward changing the world around us (if you choose to).

Acceptance and commitment therapy: My favorite approach for burnout

In the two decades I've spent practicing as a therapist, I've applied several frameworks to therapy and have found that some approaches are especially helpful in transforming and preventing burnout. My favorite is acceptance and commitment therapy (or ACT, pronounced like the verb "act"). Like a lot of therapists who gravitate toward ACT, I was initially drawn to it, years ago, because it resonated most deeply in my own personal life. Over the years, I have practiced ACT with most of my clients, trained other clinicians in ACT, and co-authored *ACT Daily Journal: Get Unstuck and Live Fully with Acceptance and Commitment Therapy* (Hill and Sorensen 2021), a book that helps people apply ACT in their daily lives. I have found ACT to be incredibly powerful and effective, and the research backs that up. ACT is a cutting-edge and evidence-based form of cognitive behavioral therapy, supported by hundreds of research studies. ACT is frequently used to help clients struggling with a variety of mental health conditions, including anxiety disorders, depression, and chronic pain (American Psychological Association 2022). It has also been shown to help people improve relationships, engage in healthy behaviors, cope with pain, and make positive changes in the world (Hayes 2019).

ACT is a unique form of therapy because, rather than focusing on changing thoughts or feelings, it focuses on helping people relate to their internal experience in a new way—with psychological flexibility. Psychological flexibility involves being open to your experience, with awareness, and engaging wholeheartedly with what matters most. If you do meaningful work, at times it will tire you out. You might lose sleep at night, doubt yourself and perhaps feel frustrated or hopeless at times. And you'll also experience vitality, joy, connection, and meaningful engagement. What matters most is that you are fully engaged in your experience and living a meaningful life.

ACT is a perfect fit for burnout because burnout is a condition of disconnection and disengagement. Leading burnout expert Christina Maslach has stated that engagement is the antithesis of burnout (Maslach, Schaufeli, and Leiter 2001)—and the ultimate aim of ACT is meaningful, values-based engagement with what matters most to you (Hayes, Strosahl, and Wilson 2016). ACT can help you to respond flexibly, with openness and awareness, to life's challenges—including burnout. Evidence-based practice is important, and research has demonstrated that ACT is an effective approach for addressing burnout (Frögéli *et al.* 2016; Hayes *et al.* 2004; Montaner *et al.* 2022; Puolakanaho *et al.* 2020; Reeve *et al.* 2021; Spitznagel *et al.* 2022; Szarko *et al.* 2022).

ACT is thought of as a type of "contextual behavioral therapy," which means that human behavior is always considered within its historical and situational context. This is important with burnout because burnout always happens in the context of chronic stress. ACT is "non-pathologizing," meaning that there's nothing wrong with you for feeling the way that you do, even when you are burned out. Rather, you are having a normal human reaction to a stressful situation. It's *how you respond* to your thoughts, emotions, and sensations that matters most.

About this book

If you're looking for simple life hacks, like "three self-care practices to eliminate burnout today," this is probably not the book for you. There are plenty of life hack options on social media these days and, while some include helpful ideas and practices, quick-fix solutions are not enough to address a complex phenomenon like burnout. In the long run, they often just dig us in deeper.

Applying an ACT framework will give you sustainable strategies for living a more meaningful, fulfilling, and effective life, even though there will always be moments of unavoidable pain along the way (Hayes *et al.* 2016). In this book, we will explore the question of what needs to change in your life, and what needs to be accepted. In the first part, you will learn about burnout and the Cycle of Burnout that keeps you stuck. In the second part, you will learn about psychological flexibility skills that can help you transform your burnout experience internally, like emotional awareness, perspective-taking, and reconnecting with your values. And in the third part, we will explore changes to consider making in your life and your circumstances, including large-scale systemic and organizational changes, that can help to alleviate and prevent burnout.

Burnout is complex, and no two cases of burnout are exactly the same. As you read, you may find that some chapters may resonate more than others for your personal situation. One person reading this book might want to focus on addressing their negative, self-critical thinking patterns, while another may need help with managing time, and yet another may need more social support and connection. I hope everyone who experiences burnout will find something in this book that's helpful for their particular circumstances.

This book is peppered with clinical and personal examples. All of the clinical examples I share are based on my work with clients experiencing burnout. These examples (including the ones listed above) use composites of multiple clients I've worked with over the years, and details have been changed to protect privacy.

In order to grow and make lasting changes, it's not enough to learn about burnout on an intellectual level. We must experience things in a new way. Throughout the book I offer exercises that invite you to try out new strategies, and at the end of each chapter I offer reflection questions to help you apply these ideas to your life. I recommend keeping a notebook or journal to help you explore the material on a personal level. At times, you might feel challenged to try something that might feel a bit uncomfortable. As you read and try the exercises, notice what shows up for you, and what resonates with your experience. You should, of course, take care of yourself as you work through the book by pacing yourself; I'm not trying to add more stress to your life! But nothing changes if we don't grow, and sometimes growth requires some growing pains. I encourage you to find that sweet spot of helpful growing pain for yourself.

My hope is that you will use the ideas in this book to learn, grow, and make lasting changes—maybe big ones or maybe small ones. I want this book to guide you in transforming your burnout-related suffering, recharging your batteries, and reconnecting with what matters most in your life.

Toward new growth

I once went horseback riding near Rocky Mountain National Park in Colorado, through an area that had been burned the previous year by a forest fire. It was sad to see the dead trees and colorless landscape from a distance. But up close, as I rode into a burned area, I was struck by the little bright green plants pushing through the charred earth. After the original landscape was burned, it left scorched earth behind, but it also created space for new growth to thrive. In this book, I will present to you an opportunity for new growth, whatever that means for you. Let's see what can rise out of the ashes of your burnout experience.

PART ONE

UNDERSTANDING BURNOUT

CHAPTER 1

Are You Burned Out?

Who among us has never had a period of feeling exhausted and disconnected from work? It is a normal and common experience to periodically feel disengaged in work or other life roles. However, burnout is different from such fleeting periods of exhaustion. Over time, it can drain satisfaction from life and, when it's severe, can keep us stuck for long periods of time.

We've all heard the term "burnout," but what is it really? The word burnout is used casually and frequently, but sometimes people don't know much beyond an intuitive sense of it. Maybe you know that something has been "off" lately, but how do you know if what you're experiencing is burnout? You may wonder if the rough patch you're going through could be something else, like depression, anxiety, or good old-fashioned stress.

In this chapter, we'll explore the signs and attributes of burnout to help you assess whether you are experiencing it. We'll also explore the severity and progression of burnout over time.

Recognizing burnout isn't always straightforward, even to those who are experiencing it. I am a clinical psychologist, and it took me several months to recognize the signs of burnout in myself.

My burnout story

"I don't even care anymore," I said flatly one day, years ago, to a close colleague and friend of mine. And I meant it. At the time, I was working as a rehabilitation psychologist on a medical team in a hospital. We were in my colleague's office, meeting to discuss some administrative issues we were working on. She looked a little puzzled and asked, "Are you okay, Debbie?" I was struck by her response, and by my own feeling of not caring. My colleague knew that I was typically enthusiastic and passionate about my work. Not caring was just not like me.

That night I reflected on the interaction. What was going on? Why was I struggling so much to engage with work? In a lightbulb moment, I realized I was experiencing severe burnout, and had been for months. I was so overwhelmed, I was feeling disconnected and disengaged. And I was exhausted.

At the time, I was juggling the demands of my job as a psychologist with two young kids and a few side projects (like my new podcast), on top of the usual life tasks and chores. Not only did I feel behind in every area of life, but I seemed to be falling more behind every day. The minute I walked through the door at work, I was busy—seeing patients in clinic, meeting with student trainees and co-workers, responding to emails and instant messages that kept popping up throughout the day, and trying to juggle all the administrative work that comes with working in a hospital setting. Although I loved my work, the demands and stressors accumulated, and due to recent organizational changes, I felt less supported and appreciated than usual. At home, I felt a similar sense of dropping the ball left and right, an overwhelming feeling that I could never catch up enough to feel satisfied and relaxed. I was doing my best to keep going and thinking that if I could only catch up, everything would be okay. But my time was so limited, it was impossible to get there.

After feeling stressed and overwhelmed for a long time, I hit a wall. My interactions with clients, which normally felt meaningful and invigorating, were draining my emotional reserves. Normally very social at work, I stopped taking the time to connect with my co-workers. I would sit quietly during meetings, internally feeling annoyed as valuable time ticked by, and retreat to my office as quickly as possible when they ended. I was starting to feel increasingly frustrated by the little things—finding a parking space, tedious paperwork, the ceaseless email backlog. Tasks that were normally easy to accomplish started to feel as if they would take more energy than I could possibly muster. Rather than giving myself permission to take a real break, I would (begrudgingly) put in just enough effort to stay afloat. I asked my boss about the possibility of changing positions, but that wasn't really an option at the time. I imagined leaving my job, but I felt that I couldn't because my husband was already making a major job transition, and my job was providing us with a stable paycheck and benefits like health insurance. I felt stuck. I wasn't feeling like myself anymore, and I was suffering.

To this day, I'm not exactly sure why it took me so long to recognize that I was experiencing severe burnout. I could spot burnout in my clients and co-workers but, somehow, I missed the same signs in myself. I had been blaming myself for not keeping up with everything, and I didn't recognize what was really happening—that over time, chronic stress had started taking a toll. Looking back, I now wonder if I implicitly thought I was immune from burnout. I like to think of myself as competent and resilient, and I knew about burnout! As a psychologist, I should have the emotional skills to be able to handle high volumes of stress, no problem. Right? Wrong.

Becoming aware of my own burnout was transformational. After that, I was able to gain a new perspective on my situation. I realized I was putting too much pressure on myself in every domain and was being unrealistic about how much I could expect to accomplish each day. I made some changes. I set better boundaries with my time and checked my habit of taking on too much. I started prioritizing activities that recharged me. I reached out for support and made the time and effort to connect with my co-workers. I stuck around after meetings and joined people for lunch instead of closing my office door. I spoke up more about workplace concerns. While workplace factors and culture can be hard (or even impossible) to change, it felt good to acknowledge openly what was going on. Eventually, I was able to re-engage with my work in a way that felt more satisfying. It paid off—my usual energy and enthusiasm returned, and gradually I started to care again.

Of course, I still struggle with similar issues at times—you'll read plenty of anecdotes about my ongoing stress- and burnout-related struggles throughout this book. As with most emotional struggles, coping with burnout is a process. But since that experience, I've learned a great deal about burnout, and I have found it helpful to be able to recognize the signs and impact of burnout. If I can recognize it sooner, and take active steps to recharge, I can prevent burnout from becoming a big problem.

What is burnout?

Although it may seem as if burnout is a new buzz word, psychology researchers have been studying it for about 50 years, dating back to the 1970s. And prior to the formal study of burnout, there were many popular accounts of extreme fatigue and a loss of passion for one's job (Maslach *et al.* 2001).

You've probably heard the word "burnout" a lot and have an intuitive sense of what it means based on your own experiences. But it may be more complex than you realize. Our understanding of burnout has evolved over time, and many questions and controversies remain about what it is (and isn't).

Let's start with the official definition. According to the World Health Organization (WHO):

> Burn-out is a syndrome conceptualized as resulting from chronic workplace stress that has not been successfully managed. It is characterized by three dimensions:
>
> 1. feelings of energy depletion or exhaustion;
> 2. increased mental distance from one's job, or feelings of negativism or cynicism related to one's job; and
> 3. reduced professional efficacy.
>
> Burn-out refers specifically to phenomena in the occupational context and should not be applied to describe experiences in other areas of life. (World Health Organization 2019)

Before we turn to each of the three dimensions of burnout in greater depth, there are a few things to note about the official definition.

First, the WHO defines burnout specifically in the workplace or occupational context, and states that it should not apply to other areas of life. But what counts as a workplace? What about stressful roles like caregiving, parenting, school, competitive athletics, activism, and other areas in which many people experience similar phenomena of exhaustion and disconnection? Many burnout researchers in these and other areas argue that the WHO definition is too narrow. And if you think about it, how do we define "work" anyway? As a parent of two school-aged children, I know first-hand that parenting can be hard work! So can school, competitive athletics, and voluntary or public service work. And anyone in a caregiver role, paid or unpaid, will tell you the same.

For the purposes of this book, we will define "work" broadly, as any task or activity, paid or unpaid, that involves mental or physical effort done to achieve a goal or result. My stance is that burnout can happen in any meaningful yet demanding role in which people are continually exposed to high levels of stress. And while most of the examples in this book are centered on job/professional burnout, the concepts and skills in this book apply across many chronically stressful roles. When you read through the book and see the word "work," you can assume that means any kind of work you happen to be doing—whether in a formal, paid job setting or otherwise.

It is also worth noting that the WHO does not classify burnout as a medical or mental health condition, but rather as a response to situational stress. This is important because people with burnout often get caught in a cycle of self-blame. "What's wrong with me? I shouldn't be feeling this way, I must not be strong enough to handle this. If I could just work harder and catch up, I would be okay..." These are the types of thoughts people with burnout sometimes hold, blaming themselves for feeling the way they do. Consider what it would be like to let yourself off the hook for burnout, and instead recognize the situational and cultural factors that are contributing. We will explore some of these factors in depth in Chapter 3, on burnout in context.

Lastly, the WHO also notes that burnout results from chronic stress that isn't successfully managed. But what does "chronic stress" really mean? Generally speaking, stress occurs when work demands outstrip our resources and ability to cope with them. Some amount of stress is an unavoidable, normal, and arguably even healthy part of life. Some stress can help to motivate us and keep us engaged. But at some point, too much stress over time can take a toll, leaving us overwhelmed and exhausted. Where does the tipping point happen from normal, satisfying, even helpful stress, to the kind of stress and overwork that can lead to burnout? And what does "successfully managed" mean when it comes to stress? Is it possible to successfully manage chronic stress in today's world, where high stress is pretty much unavoidable in many work roles? Is stress always bad? Can we limit it? *Should* we limit it? If so, how do we? These are questions we will consider in the book ahead.

For now, let's take a closer look at each of the three dimensions of burnout.

Energy depletion or exhaustion
"I'm exhausted!" This is the number one comment I hear from my clients who are experiencing burnout. People who are burned out typically report feeling utterly depleted and fatigued. It's not the same kind of sleep-deprived tiredness that usually improves after a few good nights of sleep (although solid sleep certainly doesn't hurt). Rather, it's a state of emotional exhaustion and/or physical fatigue that can be more difficult to remedy. When people who are normally high achieving and enthusiastic about their work experience burnout, their energy level plummets, and each day feels like it requires a great deal of effort just to make it through.

Increased mental distance from one's job, or feelings of negativism or cynicism related to one's job
People with burnout report feeling disengaged from, and negativity toward, their work. They may be feeling irritable and frustrated. They might evaluate their work as mostly negative, even if they normally enjoy it. People in helping roles, like healthcare workers, therapists,

teachers, clergy, and caregivers, might start to experience depersonalization, which means losing contact with the humanity of the people they are meant to be helping. I like to think about this cluster of experiences as disconnection from the meaningful aspects of one's work.

Reduced professional efficacy

People experiencing burnout may feel that they are less productive or effective in their roles than usual. This makes sense—given that people are feeling depleted and disconnected from their work, they probably aren't feeling very satisfied with their performance. Some burnout researchers have argued that this third dimension may not be a component of burnout for everyone (Schaufeli and Taris 2005). Regardless, I have found in my practice that people who experience burnout are often highly self-critical about their own performance. Sometimes people disengage from their work to the degree that they really *are* less effective than usual. For instance, they might be procrastinating on important projects, or spending less time engaged in collaborations. And feeling ineffective can contribute to the experience of burnout, of course, which creates a cycle that goes on and on and on...

Burnout, depression, anxiety, or stress?

Imagine I am talking to a new client named "Monica" who comes in for her first ever appointment with a therapist. She tells me she's reaching out for help with depression and sleep problems. Monica tells me she's had emotional ups and downs over the years, but has never felt this down, for this long. She's so preoccupied by her problems that she's awake for hours every night, even though she feels tired all day. With many stressors in her life, every day feels like a slog, and she can hardly muster the energy to keep going. She tearfully says, "I hate feeling like this. What's wrong with me?"

At first, this does sound like depression and I assume that's what's going on. But then she tells me more, and I wonder whether she might be experiencing job-related burnout, a direct result of the chronic stress of her situation. For the last few months, due to staff shortages and turnover across the healthcare organization where she works as an administrator, her stress level has been much higher than usual. She tells me that her department was reorganized about six months ago, and she does not enjoy working with her new direct supervisor, who micromanages her work more than her previous boss, and whose job she had hoped to move into within the next few years. Work that she feels is beneath her abilities is piled on, and her team is now too small for her to delegate some of her workload. Her supervisor rarely acknowledges how hard she is working but is quick to point out her mistakes. She feels that she can't afford to quit her job right now, and doesn't have time to look for a new one, but she wishes she could leave her job and do something different.

Even though I specialize in working with clients with burnout, and have been researching it for years, I find that it can be difficult to know the difference between burnout and other conditions, like depression and anxiety. They aren't neat little tidy categories that people clearly and simply fall into. And while there are some hallmarks of burnout, it can vary from person to person in its impact and presentation—one person might be feeling bored, another might be irritable, and others might be frenzied and frazzled. Even though that is the case, there are some clusters of experiences that seem to differentiate burnout from other conditions. Here's how I think about the differences.

Depression
Depression and burnout share some overlapping features, like loss of interest or pleasure, low mood and energy, and negative thinking. Some burnout experts have suggested that what we call "burnout" might be just a specific form of depression (Schonfeld and Bianchi 2016). However, most research on this topic supports the idea that burnout and depression are related but distinct conditions (Koutsimani, Montgomery, and Georganta 2019). To complicate things, people are more likely to experience depression if they are burned out, and vice versa—and it is possible to experience both depression and burnout simultaneously. As a general rule-of-thumb, burnout is tied specifically to the chronic stress of your work or productive role, whereas depression involves

feeling generally down across all areas of life. Whereas burnout symptoms might improve if you were to change or take time away from your work role, depression persists and is present across all domains of your life.

Anxiety

Similarly, anxiety and burnout are related constructs, especially as both can result from stressful situations. Anxiety, a tendency to perceive stressful situations as threatening, can certainly arise during times of chronic stress. And people who experience burnout may have higher anxiety, and vice versa. However, like depression, the two seem to be related and overlapping, but distinct experiences (Koutsimani *et al.* 2019). Whereas burnout involves exhaustion and disengagement, there are many forms of anxiety, including excessive worry, tension or panicky feelings, and avoidance of feared situations. While you might feel anxious or worried about your work, anxiety is typically not a feeling of exhaustion stemming specifically from chronic work stress. Again, there can be some overlap and you might notice that you are experiencing some of both at the same time during periods of chronic stress.

Stress

As we have seen, burnout results from "chronic workplace stress." How do we know if we are just experiencing regular life stress, or if we've crossed the line into burnout territory? What we think of as ordinary "stress" tends to be situational and will typically lift when the situation improves. For instance, when you've been working on a demanding project, you'll often feel a sense of relief when you finish it. Burnout, however, tends to be more pervasive, less tied to a specific demand, and typically persists even when the immediate stressors lift. And moderate stress tends to energize us, increasing our motivation and giving us a "charged up" feeling, whereas burnout feels emotionally draining. A reciprocal relationship exists between burnout and stress, where chronic stress increases burnout, and burnout increases chronic stress (Guthier, Dormann, and Voelkle 2020). Stay tuned for more about this cycle ahead in Chapter 4, on the cycle of burnout.

Compassion fatigue and vicarious traumatization

People who work in helping professions may be familiar with the emotional exhaustion that arises from extending empathy to people who are suffering. I've found that terms like burnout, compassion fatigue, and vicarious traumatization are sometimes used interchangeably when the weight of helping others takes a toll. But these are different, albeit related, constructs.

Compassion fatigue (sometimes called empathic distress) is the emotional impact of extending empathy to those who are suffering. The signs of compassion fatigue can look similar to burnout—depersonalization, reduced empathy, numbness, irritability, insomnia, fatigue, feeling overwhelmed, preoccupation, dreading work, and so on. They are slightly different, though. Compassion fatigue is specifically experienced by individuals who are in regular contact with people who are suffering, and usually comes on more quickly than burnout in response to exposure to suffering. Burnout is a response to general chronic work stress, and often develops more slowly over time.

Similarly, vicarious traumatization and secondary traumatic stress can occur when working with traumatized individuals. Vicarious traumatization is a term for the cognitive, emotional, social, and behavioral changes that can occur from repeated exposure to people who have been traumatized. For instance, people who experience this repeatedly hear about the traumatic experiences of others and might begin struggling to trust others or believing that the world is unsafe. Secondary traumatic stress is when hearing about trauma leads to symptoms of post-traumatic stress disorder (PTSD), such as intrusive images, avoidance, and hypervigilance. All of these can be emotionally distressing experiences that can contribute to burnout.

In the end, maybe these subtle differences don't really matter that much. These are all labels and clusters of "symptoms" you may or may not be experiencing. What matters is *your* experience and living your life. If any of this sounds familiar and helps you make sense of your experience, great. If not, don't worry about it. My hope is that our work here will be helpful to you, regardless of which of these categories do or don't apply to you.

Measuring burnout

One of the best ways to measure whether you are burned out is to take a formal burnout assessment. There are several available. The Maslach Burnout Inventory (MBI) (Maslach *et al.* 2017) is a standard and widely used tool for assessing burnout and is frequently used in research and workplace settings. For a fee, you can purchase the MBI online, and take it yourself, or administer it to a group. In addition to the general MBI, there are different versions for certain populations, like medical personnel, educators, and students.

The MBI is not meant to be a clinical diagnostic tool, but rather a comprehensive way of measuring the extent and pattern of your burnout. The MBI asks a series of specific questions, and gives you a burnout profile, with information about where you stand with burnout scales (exhaustion, cynicism, and professional efficacy), along with comparisons to population norms, and personalized recommendations for addressing burnout. I have taken the MBI online and discovered that my biggest challenge is exhaustion caused by being overextended. Your burnout profile might be different from mine.

There are also some much simpler (and free!) burnout measures available that can give you a valid and reliable estimate of your burnout level (Dolan et al. 2015; Hansen and Pit 2016; Schmoldt, Freeborn, and Klevit 1994). You can take one right now!

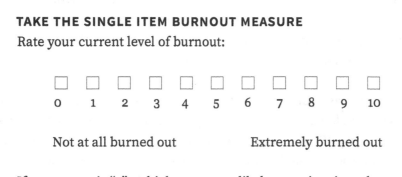

TAKE THE SINGLE ITEM BURNOUT MEASURE
Rate your current level of burnout:

☐	☐	☐	☐	☐	☐	☐	☐	☐	☐	☐
0	1	2	3	4	5	6	7	8	9	10

Not at all burned out　　　　　　Extremely burned out

If your score is "5" or higher, you are likely experiencing a burnout phase (Hansen and Pit 2016).

Although measures like this can be helpful, in the real world sometimes it can be difficult to recognize when you are experiencing burnout. Burnout looks very different person-to-person, and the signs of burnout can be difficult to spot. And burnout, like many other emotional experiences, fluctuates over time.

The severity, duration, and progression of burnout

Like a lot of human experiences, burnout happens on a continuum. It can range from temporary and relatively mild to severe and long-lasting. As I've been paying attention to conversations on burnout, I've noticed that there's a huge range of meaning when people use the word "burnout." While some write about the type of burnout that can be lifted with short, daily breaks or a four-day weekend, others describe it as a severe, chronic condition, reserved only for times when burnout becomes a huge problem that lasts several months or longer. This may lead you to wonder a few things. Are you technically burned out if you've felt exhausted and disconnected a few days a week recently, or do you have to have been continually exhausted for weeks or months? And how severe do your symptoms have to be to consider yourself burned out?

If you go back to the official definition of burnout given earlier in this book, you'll see that the WHO doesn't specify anything about its severity or duration. Part of the confusion is because no discrete cut-off has been established for burnout, and as of the time of this writing, there's no official, agreed-on definition of "severe burnout" (Bianchi 2015). While some formal measures of burnout, like the above Single Item Burnout Measure, offer a cut-off score, others, like the MBI, do not but instead advise looking at your burnout profile and relative degrees of burnout compared to a larger population (Maslach *et al.* 2017).

When looking at the severity and duration of burnout, I think it's most important to look at how much burnout is causing you distress and impairing your functioning. Sometimes, burnout can be a temporary state of disengagement that comes and goes with no major impact. For example, during the period of the Covid-19 pandemic, when my two children were doing virtual school from home, and I was doing challenging work as a mental health professional, I would have hours and even days where I felt utterly exhausted. Suddenly overwhelmed by it all, I wanted to escape for a while, and wondered how on earth I would find the energy to carry on. I think I was experiencing a temporary, low-level form of burnout-type exhaustion now and then. But, unlike my previous and more severe burnout experience, I found that during that period it would come and go relatively quickly.

I'm not very concerned about burnout that comes and goes like that. We *all* have emotions that come and go over time. We might be irritable or down in the dumps for a while. We might go through anxious periods when the world feels a little too scary, or when unfinished tasks wake us up in the middle of the night. The same is true for burnout. If we have a stressful, demanding role, it will hit us now and then. Maybe a period of exhaustion can even be a helpful indicator that we need to take a break, take some tasks off our plate, prioritize sleep, or get some exercise.

At other times, though, burnout can be severe, and can stay severe for a long time—months or longer. When this happens, it can cause a tremendous amount of stress, and impact quality of life and life satisfaction. It can be difficult to function the way we normally would. When this happens, burnout is a bigger problem that can be more difficult to address.

You may be wondering how burnout progresses over the course of time. A few "stages of burnout" models have been proposed over the years (Freudenberger 1982; Veninga and Spradley 1981), and I will occasionally come across infographics and popular press articles that illustrate states of burnout over time. Typically, staged models of burnout show a progression from low-level dissatisfaction and stress that builds up to a crisis state. But do people really progress through discrete stages of burnout like that? While those catchy ideas may be a helpful way to give people a general sense of what burnout can be like, I question the implication that burnout progresses in such a linear way. In reality, as with grief, not everyone progresses through stages of burnout in the same way. Rather, the course of burnout looks quite different person-to-person, and burnout often tends to fluctuate over time, following a circuitous, rather than orderly, path. Sure, for some people burnout builds and gradually increases over time. But that's not always the case—and a lot depends on how you respond to burnout.

The ideas presented in this book can be helpful all along the burnout continuum, from mild to severe. You can take steps to keep mild burnout from getting more extreme, and to help you recover from severe burnout. Recovery typically isn't linear either, but you can take actions that will help you deal with burnout in an effective way.

Before we learn more about burnout, let's pause to reflect on some questions about your personal experience.

REFLECTION QUESTIONS

1. Which of the main dimensions of burnout (exhaustion, disengagement, negative or cynical feelings, reduced sense of effectiveness) resonate most with your personal experience?
2. What do you notice about how you tend to experience burnout?
3. What are some indicators, for you, that you might be starting to feel burned out?
4. Do you think you are burned out now?
5. How severe has burnout been for you recently?
6. How long have you been feeling this way?
7. What has your experience with burnout been over the course of your life?
8. How have stress, exhaustion, and burnout fluctuated over time for you?

CHAPTER 2

More Burnout Basics

We've explored some of the main characteristics of burnout, and how to evaluate your level of burnout. In this chapter, we'll take a deeper dive by learning more about burnout. We'll explore the impact that burnout can have, look at risk factors, and highlight some especially burnout-prone roles.

The impact of burnout

As we learned in Chapter 1, the severity of burnout can vary enormously. Sometimes it can be a temporary state of depletion and disengagement that comes and goes relatively quickly, with no significant impact. Sometimes, though, burnout can stick around longer and take a toll on our wellbeing and quality of life. Severe burnout has been associated with the following (Deligkaris *et al.* 2014; Harvard Business Review 2021; Maslach 2003; Maslach and Leiter 1997):

- Irritability
- Sleep problems
- Tension headaches
- Depressed mood (escalating to suicidal thoughts in extreme cases)

- Poor eating habits and health behaviors
- Substance abuse
- Impaired work performance
- Difficulty with cognition, especially attention, memory, and executive functioning
- Dehumanization of others (such as patients, caregiving recipients, students, etc.)
- Impaired personal relationships
- Impaired relationships with co-workers and team members
- Lower self-esteem.

If this list sounds alarming, don't fret! You've picked up this book, and my aim is to help you get out of the cycle that keeps you spiraling into severe, long-lasting burnout (you'll learn more about the burnout cycle in Chapters 4 and 5). As you progress through this book, and apply these ideas in your life, there's no guarantee that you won't have hours or days of feeling depleted. These feelings will probably resurface now and then when your life gets stressful—you're human, after all! But if you know how to recognize and respond to burnout in a more effective way, my hope is that you won't get as stuck in the Cycle of Burnout, and the long-term impact won't be so severe.

You might be burned out if…: Risk factors for burnout

There's no one-size-fits-all model of characteristics that might make you more vulnerable to burnout or predict who will experience burnout and who won't. There are, however, several risk factors that have been identified (Harvard Business Review 2021; Kaschka, Korczak, and Broich 2011; Swensen and Shanafelt 2020) that are summarized in the list below.

YOUR BURNOUT RISK FACTORS

As you read this list, consider how many apply to you. (Remember that "work" can be defined broadly, depending on which stressful roles you are holding.)

- You identify very strongly with your work role.
- You lack a satisfying balance between your work and personal life.
- You work in a helping profession (such as healthcare, education, social work) or a customer-facing role with frequent and intense interactions with people.
- You do "purpose-driven work" that you care deeply about.
- You are very passionate about what you do.
- You tend to be a high performer.
- You have a high level of education.
- You have a high workload.
- Your workload exceeds your capacity.
- You have high chronic stress in your role.
- You don't have enough resources (such as time, support, money, equipment, staffing) available to meet the demands of your work.
- You feel that the rewards don't match the effort you put into your work.
- There's a mismatch between your personal values and the values of your organization.
- You experience unfair and/or inequitable treatment in your work.
- You have little autonomy and/or lack a sense of control over your work.
- You try hard to be everything to everyone.
- You often sacrifice your own needs for work or caring for others.
- You have high standards and tend to be a perfectionist about your work (Hill and Curran 2016).
- Your workplace community feels unsupportive; you experience behaviors like competition or sabotage, non-inclusive or unethical behavior, demanding or unfair treatment, or abusive management in your workplace (McKinsey Health Institute 2022).

- You are part of a historically marginalized group, for instance a person of color, a woman, a gender or sexual minority, a person with a disability.
- You are a full-time working parent (increased risk for *job* burnout; Mikolajczak, Gross, and Roskam 2019).
- You are a part-time working parent or a stay-at-home parent (increased risk for *parental* burnout; Mikolajczak *et al.* 2019).

Whether you can check a lot of these boxes or only a few, these risk factors might give you a sense of the factors that contribute to burnout. If we zoom out and take a bird's-eye view on this, we can see some themes that may contribute to a higher likelihood of burnout—it usually happens in roles where the emotional load is high, people are highly invested in their work, and there are situational or systemic pressures that contribute to chronic stress.

A closer look: Burnout-prone roles

Burnout can happen to people from all walks of life, throughout the life age span, from a wide variety of roles and professions, and across the entire spectrum of financial compensation. High-earning professionals with demanding jobs can experience burnout, as can people working in the "gig economy" and those doing unpaid labor or trying to make ends meet with minimum-wage jobs. Whether you work full time, part time, or even have a flexible schedule, if you've invested a great deal of your life in your work, you've likely experienced some periods of chronic stress.

While there are far too many examples of chronically stressful work roles to name them all here, some roles do seem to be especially likely to lead to burnout. Let's take a closer look at a few. Each of these could be a book of their own—in fact, there are books specifically about some of these! For our purposes here, I am highlighting here some unique considerations of a few roles that might be relevant to you. Feel free to skim through this section, or just read the parts that are most relevant to you, to see if you learn something about your personal situation.

Burnout in high-pressure job settings

These days, many job settings involve a high degree of pressure, which can contribute to chronic stress. Many jobs can be stressful, but some have extra pressures associated with the work, like the pressure to produce, the pressure of being in high-stakes situations, or the pressure of intense interactions with people.

Some jobs require pressure to produce. For instance, people working in law firms are required to meet their billable hours, and those working technology start-ups are expected to work around the clock. Academic and science jobs can involve competition for grant funding and pressure to publish to achieve career advances, and sales jobs require meeting challenging sales quotas. Some roles come with a great deal of responsibility, such as executives who are responsible for making a profit for the company's shareholders, and leaders who are responsible for managing a large team of people. Some jobs have a high administrative load and expectations of completing volumes of tedious work with a quick turnaround.

Some jobs involve the threat of physical danger, like law enforcement or military service. And some have high stakes in terms of risk taking, sometimes involving life-or-death outcomes—such as air traffic control, emergency response, medicine, and mental health professionals who work with high-risk concerns like substance abuse and suicide.

People working in customer-facing occupations, such as call center and customer service agents, and those working in retail, hospitality, and food service industries, face the pressure of frequent interactions with the (sometimes disgruntled) public. For example, I've recently seen accounts of high burnout rates among hairstylists, who interact with people all day long, and librarians, who support the public in ways that can be stressful. Intense work with people can lead to low workplace morale, and pressure to be "on" at all times, with few breaks to recharge, and lead to feeling drained. Burnout seems to be common in these types of jobs, due to chronic interpersonal stress (Dormann and Zapf 2004;

Grant and Campbell 2001; Maslach and Jackson 1981; McLaren 2021; Zapf 2002).

Workplace culture and other environmental factors in the workplace can make a difference in terms of the toll high-pressure occupations like these take on employees; we will explore some of these factors in depth in Chapter 3. For now, suffice it to say that many types of high-pressure jobs are prone to burnout.

Healthcare

Conversations about burnout have been taking place in the healthcare world for *many* years, and there's a reason why. The highly stressful workplace environment of healthcare is a "perfect storm" for burnout. Many healthcare professionals do life-or-death work that has a direct impact on people's lives. They are expected to reliably show up and perform at a high level, day after day, for the sake of their patients and co-workers, regardless of how emotionally and physically depleted they are. They shoulder the weight of legal risk and ethically complex decision-making. Most people go into healthcare hoping to make a difference in people's lives, but often they are constrained by medical system demands and are too busy to provide the type of care they would ideally like to. Healthcare professionals face long and irregular hours, pressure to see as many patients as possible, lack of control over their workdays, excessive administrative tasks, and the demands of keeping up with charting in electronic medical records (Eckleberry-Hunt, Kirk-patrick, and Hunt 2017; Gupta, Moore, and Neto 2015; Melnick *et al.* 2020; West, Dyrbye, and Shanafelt 2018). Those struggling to keep up with their workload are often unable to provide high-quality, direct patient care to the highest standards to which they were trained (Talbot and Dean 2018), which can lead to a sense of moral injury—the psychological distress that occurs when one's actions don't line up with one's values. And often, work demands lead to less time to spend at home and dissatisfaction with work–life balance.

Healthcare workers are struggling. Burnout rates have been high among these professionals, even prior to the Covid-19 pandemic, as have rates of anxiety, depression, and suicide (Baker *et al.* 2017;

Schernhammer and Colditz 2004). Suicide has even been called "an occupational hazard of practicing medicine" (Poorman 2019, p.181). Statistics on rates of burnout in medicine are alarming. For instance, in a 2019 report that summarized various available research studies, between 35 and 54 percent of physicians and nurses were burned out (National Academy of Medicine 2019).

The challenges of working in healthcare have only been made worse by the stressors and staffing shortages caused by Covid-19. Several studies show that the pandemic significantly increased burnout in healthcare (Leo *et al.* 2021; Ruiz-Fernández *et al.* 2020). Early in the pandemic, already taxed healthcare providers faced increased risk of contracting Covid-19 (Nguyen *et al.* 2020), fearing for their own safety as they also experienced the general pandemic-related psychological distress (Sanderson *et al.* 2020) that many around the world were facing. Several recent research studies have highlighted the acute psychological stressors faced by nurses and other "front-line" healthcare workers during the outbreak phases of Covid-19 (Shechter *et al.* 2020). Over time, some healthcare providers have been impacted by exposure to traumatic events, resulting in experiences of Covid-related moral injury (Borges *et al.* 2020), post-traumatic stress disorder (d'Ettorre *et al.* 2021), and grief (Wallace *et al.* 2020). And healthcare workers have been the target of a political backlash against the pandemic, resulting, at times, in direct animosity. In one study, more than 20 percent of healthcare workers reported being bullied, threatened, or harassed because of their work (Bryant-Genevier *et al.* 2021). In droves, people have chosen to leave their jobs in healthcare in recent years (Galvin 2021; Yong 2021), and those who have stayed have faced the increased demands caused by staffing shortages. It's no wonder healthcare professional burnout has been getting a lot of press recently—it seems to have reached a crisis level in recent years.

Helping professions

"Steve" is a 32-year-old social worker who specializes in suicide prevention in a large community mental health setting. Having lost an older cousin to suicide as a teenager, he was drawn to this type of work because it felt deeply important to him. Although he is experienced with having hard conversations about suicide, and has loved his job for the past three years, he feels as if his work is starting to take a toll. His agency is under-funded and has a waitlist for services. He is often contacted outside work hours to help with urgent situations. He has been feeling less fulfilled by his work lately, and the stress of his job is trickling into his personal life. He has trouble relaxing on weekends and is preoccupied by work. He is considering changing jobs to something that pays better and is less demanding, but he feels guilty when he thinks of the high-risk people who will have to wait even longer for care if he leaves. If he doesn't help them, who will? His work is a matter of life and death for his clients.

Involvement in work with a high level of emotional investment can, over time, take a toll. People are often drawn to human services fields, like social work, teaching, psychotherapy, clergy, and so forth, because they feel they have a calling to help others. While those who have a strong desire to help others may find their work deeply meaningful, they tend to be at risk of experiencing burnout. The high emotional weight of helping professions, especially when the role involves caring for people who are suffering, can feel simultaneously important and emotionally exhausting.

People who are highly attuned to the needs of others may have difficulty turning their back on those in need, even when they are starting to feel overworked and exhausted themselves. Often, helping professionals feel a high demand for their services, but have limited financial and time resources available. It's hard to turn away from someone who is suffering when you have the skills to help them. There can be a tension between other-care and self-care—and although we may have even been trained on the virtues of self-care, putting it into practice is very difficult when people's lives will be impacted if we say no. And like healthcare providers, helping professionals also face the challenge of legal and ethical concerns related to their work.

Caregiving

"Laura" came to see me for therapy for stress, anxiety, insomnia, and irritability. Laura works as an assistant director of a preschool. She has three young children and is married. Her mom, with whom she has always had a very close relationship, has cancer and is going through chemotherapy. Most days, she goes from work to visit her mom, who lives alone in a nearby town, which has required her to be away from her family a great deal. She feels guilty that her husband, who also works full time, has been doing most of the childcare and domestic work. Their marriage has suffered, as Laura and her husband have little quality time together and both have been irritable. She occasionally takes days off from work but is careful not to use up her family leave allotment too quickly because it could still be a long road ahead for her mom. Laura is burned out in multiple roles, including both caregiving and parenting. And although she deeply loves her mother and wants to be there for her in the remaining months of her life, she worries that she can't go on like this—she's just too exhausted.

According to the report *Caregiving in the U.S.* by the AARP (American Association of Retired Persons) and the National Alliance for Caregiving (2020), more than one in five Americans are caregivers who provide care to an older adult, an adult with a disability or medical condition, or a child with special needs. This rate is expected to rise as the baby boomer generation ages. Caregiving duties can include everything from helping with personal or medical needs, to household chores and managing a person's finances, to arranging professional care and medical services. Long-distance caregivers manage care remotely, which can cause logistical challenges and feelings of guilt for not being physically present. Most caregivers have a job in addition to caregiving duties, and many are "sandwiched caregivers" who also have other demanding obligations, such as caring for young children.

Caregiver burnout is defined as:

a state of physical, emotional and mental exhaustion. It may be accompanied by a change in attitude, from positive and caring to negative and unconcerned. Burnout can occur when caregivers don't get the help they need, or if they try to do more than they are able, physically or financially. (Cleveland Clinic 2019)

Caregivers with long-term duties, owing to a chronic condition or disability, are especially vulnerable to burnout.

Parenting

"Josie" is a loving mother who is extremely devoted to her three children, aged nine months, two-and-a-half, and four. She is a full-time parent, having decided to leave her job when her first child was born. Because her spouse works full time and only her oldest child is in preschool, she is on child duty pretty much all day, every day. She loves being a parent and cares a lot about her children's wellbeing. She tries hard to be attentive to their needs and practice the parenting approaches she reads about in parenting books and hears about from podcasts.

While being engaged and hands-on is consistent with Josie's parenting values, recently she's been feeling exhausted. She hasn't been sleeping enough, and has very little time away from parenting to enjoy other aspects of her life. Lately, she's been spending more time on her phone or snapping irritably at her kids, and she feels guilty when she does this. She's been wishing she could take a longer break from her children but feels that she can't. If she did, who would take care of them?

While parenthood is, for most, a meaningful and positive life experience, being a parent can feel like another high-pressure job! Parents are expected to be engaged with and attuned to their children, feed them healthy, homemade meals, not let them have too much screen time, drive them around town to enriching activities, help with schoolwork, plan social events to help them foster friendships, and so on. Meanwhile, many parents lack adequate resources and support. There's no paid vacation from parenting, and it's a job you can't exactly quit (or, at least, not without major consequences). The pressures of modern parenthood can be taxing, leading to missing out on the joy of having children.

Parental burnout is defined as: "A state of intense exhaustion related to one's parental role, in which one becomes emotionally detached from one's children and doubtful of one's capacity to be a good parent" (Mikolajczak *et al.* 2019, p.1319). It occurs when parents lack the resources they need to handle parenting stressors, and as a result become less emotionally engaged than usual with their children.

There are plenty of factors that might increase a parent's risk of burnout. Parents who lack support—both emotional and practical—from a co-parent or broader social network are at higher risk, as are parents who struggle to find effective parenting practices. Parents who are aiming to be "perfect" parents are at risk, as are those who struggle with stress management or emotion regulation skills. Chronic stressors, such as having a child with special needs, single parenthood, economic insecurity, and racial trauma, also contribute to parental burnout risk.

As with job burnout, most parents probably hit a rough patch from time to time when they feel depleted and could use a break from parenting. But when parental burnout is severe and chronic, it can have important and potentially serious consequences. Severe parental burnout is associated with escape or suicidal thinking, and with reduced engagement, increased risk of child maltreatment, and coercive or punitive parenting practices. It's important for parents to have the resources and support they need to deal with stress and burnout, before it takes a toll on both the children and the parents (Mikolajczak *et al.* 2019).

It is worth noting that parental burnout is not the same as job burnout. Some people find themselves exhausted at their job but not at home, and others the opposite (Mikolajczak *et al.* 2019). Working parents are at higher risk for job burnout, whereas stay-at-home parents and those who work part time are at higher risk for parental burnout.

Activism
Whether it's involvement in social justice causes, human rights work, advocacy, or nonprofit work, the do-gooders among us are prone to activist burnout, which is sometimes referred to as "activism fatigue." Activist burnout can be particularly overwhelming because activism work is highly personal; most activists do work that is tied to their identity or a sense of injustice about issues they care deeply about, such as politics, racial justice, feminism, LGBTQ+ rights, disability rights advocacy, animal welfare, environmental or climate change causes, etc. Progress can feel slow, or even as if it's heading in the wrong direction, causing feelings of discouragement and hopelessness.

Activists might feel pressure to have a significant impact and must face conditions that many in society are unwilling to. And activist culture tends to emphasize selflessness (Chen and Gorski 2015). As Devon Price writes in the book *Laziness Does Not Exist: A Defense of the Exhausted, Exploited, and Overworked*:

> If you care about fighting a social problem, it's easy to get swept up in feelings of panic or guilt. When you take a break to rest, to care for yourself, or even to enjoy a vacation, the problem remains, unfixed and looming in the back of your mind. And in many activist spaces—both in-person and online—there's a great deal of pressure to remain focused on pressing, upsetting issues all the time, often to the detriment of our health. (Price 2021, p.199)

Activist burnout can become a barrier to successful movements. Many activist groups have high rates of turnover, and people who leave the movement may never re-engage.

In his research on the topic, Paul Gorski (2019) has identified factors that contribute to activist burnout. Internal, personal factors include deep caring that leads to exhaustion, intense commitment, awareness of structural problems, and personal responsibility to produce change. External factors include backlashes activists experience, such as violence, harassment, and professional vulnerability. And infighting, competition, and tension might occur within activist communities. For instance, within racial justice movements, activists of color might experience white "allies" who exhibit racist behaviors (like usurping organizational power) or who are unwilling to take substantial action. Structural causes of activist burnout have been identified as well, such as feeling that the task of change is too difficult against seemingly unchangeable systems and power structures.

Competitive athletics

In 2021, I watched some of the coverage of the Tokyo Summer Olympics, which had been postponed from the previous year due to the Covid-19 pandemic. At the time, I was preparing to teach a workshop for mental health professionals on using ACT to help their clients with burnout.

45

Simone Biles, one of the greatest athletes in the world, was speaking openly about "the twisties" (a kind of mental block causing disorientation for gymnasts when in the air) and how her emotional struggles were impacting her athletic engagement. I was hearing unfamiliar terms like "overtraining syndrome." Not a sports psychologist, I had been unaware of the degree to which athletes were prone to experiencing burnout. I discovered a whole line of research about athlete burnout.

Within athletic culture, the expectation—implied or even explicit—is that intense training will lead to improvement over time, and that hard work—perhaps at the expense of rest—is necessary to maximize athletic performance. But athletes are prone to burning out from both the physical and emotional stress of training and competitions. Athletes experiencing burnout will often feel a reduced sense of accomplishment and a reduced sense of being able to reach their own goals for training and competitions. Some even start to devalue, or lose interest in, their sports (Moen *et al.* 2017).

What drives athlete burnout? Certainly, the physical load of intense training can contribute. Psychological stress and situational pressures can play a role as well. The cognitive and emotional responses to potential stressors, such as injury, being less competitive, or feeling unable to meet demands, can contribute to the development of athlete burnout. Athlete burnout is influenced not just by the physical demands of training and competition, but by the athlete's perception of their ability to perform (Moen *et al.* 2017). Perfectionism, of both the athlete and the coach, seems to play a role, as well. Athletes who are highly perfectionistic, and those who perceive their coaches to be perfectionists, are more likely to experience burnout (Olsson *et al.* 2021).

While this list of burnout-prone roles is by no means complete, it highlights some examples of the many various stressful roles we might hold, and some of the ways chronic stress can lead to burnout. Perhaps you can identify with some of these areas. Let's now take a moment to reflect on your own experience with burnout.

REFLECTION QUESTIONS

1. Has burnout ever caused problems in your life, or impaired your ability to function at your usual capacity?
2. Go back and look at the list of risk factors for burnout. Are there any that apply to you? Which hit close to home?
3. Are there particular roles you hold (or have held in the past), that are chronically stressful, where you might be likely to experience burnout? What factors do you think contribute to the stressful nature of the roles you hold/have held?
4. As you read about the chronic stress associated with some specific burnout-prone roles, were any relevant to your life?

CHAPTER 3

Under Pressure

Burnout in Context

We often blame ourselves when we are struggling. When we are going through a tough time, we kick ourselves when we're down, becoming harsh and critical toward ourselves. In the case of burnout, we might wonder why we aren't able to handle things easily, or beat ourselves up for not being as engaged as usual. This was true for me. During my most extreme burnout period I blamed myself for not being able to handle everything.

When we think this way, we are "medicalizing" our problems, framing them as medical or mental health issues that are rooted in ourselves, without acknowledgement of the circumstances and environmental factors that contribute to the situation. The underlying message is that we alone are responsible. We will then try to figure out what's wrong with us, and the onus is on us to "fix" ourselves to solve the problem. This can lead to a shame spiral of self-blame, as some of the most important drivers of the problem are ignored. Solutions will not be entirely effective if we discount the importance of addressing the historical, cultural and social contexts in which we live.

The truth is, you are not to blame for experiencing burnout. It's a response that makes perfect sense when viewed in the context of what's happening in your life and in the broader socio-cultural context in which you live and work. That's not just true for burnout. *All* suffering occurs within complex social, political, and economic systems, and to truly understand any aspect of our experience, we must acknowledge these relationships at multiple levels—including biological, psychological, social, and cultural factors.

There are many factors that drive burnout and explain why we are seeing so much of it in recent years. In our modern world, overwork and chronic stress have become the norm and expectation for many of us. People, especially those who live in cultures that emphasize individualism, are increasingly isolated and disconnected. Due to unrestrained capitalism, people around the world are pressured to devote more and more time and energy to their work, to the point where they are chronically stressed and overwhelmed—and we do our work in environments that aren't always good for our emotional wellbeing. Many types of work are undervalued and underappreciated. And in recent years we've faced the extra stress of a pandemic, wars, gun violence, natural disasters and the climate crisis, economic uncertainty and growing financial disparity, as well as systems of oppression against historically marginalized groups, the rise of authoritarianism around the world, and so on. Eventually, all these factors (and more) take an emotional toll on us. No wonder so many of us are exhausted!

This chapter is an exploration of systemic, cultural, and economic factors that contribute to burnout. We will look at some workplace factors that are known to contribute to burnout. I will highlight additional stressors faced by women, people of color, and other historically marginalized groups, as well as some of the pressures associated with modern-day employment, parenting, and caregiving that may contribute to chronic stress and burnout for many of us.

The more we understand the complex factors that underlie burnout, the more we can take a step back and see it for what it is. This helps us take a new perspective and unhook from self-blame. And doing so can help guide our thinking about what we can do about burnout that will make a real, substantial difference for everyone.

The very big picture: Evolutionary, cultural, and economic history

In his comprehensive book *Work: A Deep History, from the Stone Age to the Age of Robot*, anthropologist James Suzman argues that "to live is to work" (Suzman 2020, p.27). Work, the extension of effort and energy to achieve a result, is a fundamental part of being alive, a key difference between living and non-living things. Forms of life have evolved to do energy-efficient work for survival in various environments. We must do work, in its fundamental sense, to keep ourselves, our offspring, and other members of our groups alive. Work is required to feed ourselves, care for children and other vulnerable people, and protect ourselves from the elements and predators. In other words, the basic capacity to work is wired into humans and other animals; it's a critical part of who we are.

We *Homo sapiens* are a unique animal species. Because of the extra-large frontal cortices in our brains, we have become prolific and expert users of tools, enabling our versatile species to work and survive in a wide variety of environments—from the jungle to the Arctic tundra, from subsistence farms to urban office buildings. We are an ultra-social species that can pass skills along through language and social learning. We are well adapted to living together in social groups and working in collaborative, sharing economies for the benefit of mutual survival.

Our ancient human ancestors banded together to forage for food, defend themselves as a group, meet their other basic survival needs (like water, safety, companionship, and shelter), and care for offspring and each other. Over thousands of years—the blink of an eye in the grand scale of life on earth—our species went from the Stone Age to the Agricultural Revolution, the Urban Revolution, the Industrial Revolution, and into the modern technological age. As agricultural societies around the world started to grow food on a massive scale, and feed larger groups of people, we became more urbanized and found new and even more complex ways of living together and dividing up our labor (Suzman 2020). New skills emerged, and we started to be siloed into specialized trades. During the Industrial Revolution, machines and factories were developed that made work more efficient. Then, in the much more recent Technological Revolution, lots of work became automated and conducted via computers.

For the most part, people around the world no longer live in the small hunter-gatherer groups of ancient humans—the types of groups we are so well adapted to as a species. The disbanding of those small, connected groups with a shared survival purpose, and formation of larger, yet more disconnected groups, has led to a reduced sense of community and belonging.

Recently, our standard of living has gone up overall, and we have more and more innovations that should, in theory, help us to work less. But people in power are optimizing for the accumulation of wealth, not having everyone work less, and so as this has occurred, so has further economic disparity, isolation, and overwork. Modern society, while economically prosperous, is more isolated than ever before. I can sit in my house alone, work on my computer, and order food online that will be delivered to my front door by a stranger I will never talk to again.

Over a hundred years ago, Émile Durkheim, sometimes referred to as a father of sociology, wrote about the concept of "anomie," an intense feeling of dislocation and anxiety that arose as people became less connected to a close community. Even though prosperity has increased, so have suicide and social stress (Durkheim 1951, 2014; Olsen 1965). In individualistic cultures, we tend to focus more on our individual success than on the good of the larger social community.

To make a *very* long story short, we are now in the situation of having an "evolutionary mismatch" between how our bodies and brains are equipped and the modern-day world in which we live and work. We are biologically well suited to do work, but not necessarily in the way most of us do these days.

The hustle and grind of modern capitalism

When I grew up, I saw images of multi-millionaires (billionaires weren't really "a thing" yet, it was the 1980s and 90s) in movies and TV shows. They were usually self-made business people who lived in giant houses and were driven around in limousines to important events. In my memory, they were often shown exerting power at work, and then clad in tuxedos or ball gowns, sipping Champagne or martinis and flying around the world, via first-class or private jets. Although these characters were often (but not always) portrayed as cold-hearted, they depicted the most extreme and impressive version of the "American Dream" we were all supposed to be striving for: work hard and do well in school and you can rise up the ranks toward fortune, no matter your humble beginnings. Then you too can have this glamorous lifestyle and the well-deserved respect of your friends and neighbors.

Capitalism offers us this promise—that if you work hard, you can prosper financially, attain a high social status, and live a life of luxury and ease. Most economies around the world today are some form of capitalism, the economic system based on the private ownership and control of trade and industry. The amount of governmental regulation and restraint on capitalism varies by country. The driving force of capitalism is the motivation to earn profit for those in power, who seek continual growth to increase their own wealth and the wealth of their shareholders. In a competitive, free-market environment, business owners compete to gain market share. To do so, they usually employ people who receive wages in exchange for working toward profit on their behalf. But workers are often not personally motivated toward the goal of maximizing profits for business owners and shareholders.

Capitalism has advantages as an economic system, like overall increased standard of living, freedom, and financial independence. But at its extreme, unrestrained capitalism is associated with some problems. It can lead to wealth disparity, social inequities, a conflict over working conditions vs. profits, potential for corruption, and the exploitation of labor. Capitalism is associated with a focus on perpetually maximizing the rate of economic growth (and, incidentally, more economic growth over recent decades has not slowed the goal of maximizing growth— quite the contrary).

Unrestrained capitalism and its promise have contributed to our culture of overwork, hustle, and grind. The average work week has been creeping up in recent decades. Since the 1970s, there has been a gap between productivity, which has been steadily rising, and wages, which have flatlined, comparatively (Mishel 2021). This means that most of us are working harder but without the relative increase in financial benefits to match. If it seems as if you're working harder than previous generations, just to keep up financially...well, you probably are.

This is compounded by narratives about the importance of hard work. Here in the United States, where I live, our history is rooted in a puritanical work ethic, where hard work is valued as a moral virtue (Price 2021). Humans are treated as work machines, and we've been told that we must work constantly if we want to survive (Hersey 2022). Busyness has become a badge of honor, and feels like a necessity for survival. And due to technology, we have access to work after hours, time that would have historically been spent with our families, relaxing, and taking care of ourselves.

Even if we are fortunate enough to have plenty of resources, and our basic survival needs are met, we are still driven by this system to acquire and achieve more. For modern humans, both the accumulation of wealth and work-related achievement are tied to social importance. We seek validation, acceptance, status, and belonging through productivity and achievement. We have been told that we must keep up with social expectations, by working hard to produce and acquire even more resources. Plenty of advertisers will remind you of this, so that you will purchase their products. We are told that buying certain products will fill the emotional void—created at least in part by our way of living—and make us happy. And for a brief period of time, maybe they do fill an emotional void. But that wears off quickly.

Consumption is encouraged by capitalism and, when we buy into it, we associate our financial worth, our high-status possessions, with our worth as humans. To reach our desired lifestyles, or keep them going, we must keep working hard. We have "lifestyle inflation," in which as people earn more money, they tend to increase spending and live a more luxurious lifestyle. This makes it difficult to gain net worth, save money, and stay out of debt. The goal becomes to sustain a certain lifestyle, to show how successful you are. But somehow, we never seem to reach that place of security and ease we imagine. Resources are not distributed equally, but, rather, wealth is held primarily by a privileged few. Some will never experience financial prosperity, but must keep working hard to make ends meet. And even the multi-billionaires keep working hard to increase their net worth and protect their wealth. This keeps us on an endless treadmill of consuming and working to earn money.

A big part of our modern-day chronic stress problem is driven by the pressure to overwork, which has become the norm and expectation. Most of us don't have much choice when it comes to work demands—we must show up for a busy work shift or risk losing our jobs. There aren't enough hours in the day to do all that work, and keep up with other demands, like personal, domestic, and caregiving tasks.

And when this stress affects us to the point where we are no longer able to function at our peak level of performance, when we burn out, we believe we must quickly fix ourselves so that we can bounce back and be productive again. James Davies, author of the book *Sedated: How Modern Capitalism Created Our Mental Health Crisis* (2022), is one of many writers who have offered social criticism of the modern-day economic landscape and how it contributes to our suffering. He writes:

> Since the 1980s, successive governments and big business have worked to promote a new vision of mental health; one that puts at its centre a new kind of person: resilient, optimistic, individualistic and above all, economically productive... We define "return to health" as "return to work." (Davies 2022, p.2)

So here we are. We're hustling, grinding, and working hard in a world that promises us an eventual payout if we do. Some of us do luck out and get the payout, but most of us never seem to reach the promised land. We just keep working as hard as we can in a system that perpetuates this myth, and we are chronically stressed and burned out because of it. It's not healthy for us. Ask yourself this question: who is profiting most from your hard work?

Burnout and the modern workplace environment

In the context of capitalism, many workplaces share certain qualities that can contribute to chronic stress and burnout. These days, when so many people are working in environments that are high stress and unsupportive of worker wellbeing, there's a good chance that at least some component of your burnout is driven by environmental factors in your workplace. Unfortunately, many workplaces are not emotionally healthy environments in which we experience respect and supportive social interactions.

Leading burnout scholars Christina Maslach and Michael Leiter (2022) have identified six categories of key workplace factors that can cause a mismatch between the person and the environment, and lead to burnout:

1. *Work overload:* Workplace has high demands with insufficient resources, like time, tools, and support, available to meet those demands.
2. *Lack of control:* There are problems with power dynamics, like workers being micromanaged or lacking autonomy to do their jobs well. Workers feel ignored and/or excluded from decisions related to their work.
3. *Insufficient rewards:* Workers do not receive adequate financial, emotional, or social rewards for their hard work.
4. *Breakdown of community:* Environment is competitive, and/or people do not feel a sense of trust or support from their colleagues. Effective teamwork is undermined, causing a breakdown of community.
5. *Absence of fairness:* People are not treated with respect, or decisions are viewed as unjust or discriminatory. Workers feel exploited and can develop a high degree of cynicism.
6. *Values conflict:* Employees face conflicts with their values, like when job requirements clash with moral principles, or when an organization's practices are not in line with their stated mission. People are left feeling a mismatch between their work and their integrity.

Often, people feel that their workplaces are reactionary, so that seemingly urgent work is constantly thrown at workers, and communication is poor. People are tracked for productivity, and subjected to pointless meetings and check-ins. People are working extra hard because of budget cuts and low staffing, but still people feel guilty for not working hard enough.

Boxer and activist Muhammad Ali famously said, "It isn't the mountains ahead to climb that wear you out, it's the pebble in your shoe." This metaphor is used a lot in the burnout world, because often those little day-to-day stressors add up and make life difficult. As an example of this, healthcare professionals will sometimes notice that they can perform complicated and intense patient work all day, but are more drained by the ceaseless administrative work, electronic medical records, and being on call.

The pebbles in your shoe can also be thought of as "microstressors," or "the relentless accumulation of unnoticed small events—in passing moments" (Cross and Dillon 2023a). Cross and Dillon (2023a) have identified three overall categories of microstressors. First are those that drain your capacity to get things done, like team demands or increased responsibility at work or home. Second are microstressors that deplete your emotional reserves, like confrontational conversations or feeling responsible for the wellbeing of others. And third are those that challenge your identity and attack your self-confidence or self-worth, like pressure to do something that's not in line with your values.

Microstressors tend to come at us quickly, and each one seems so minor we might barely notice it. But they can "snowball" and create a ripple effect of increasingly stressful consequences (Cross and Dillon 2023b), for example when a last-minute request from your boss causes you to have to race home through traffic and be 15 minutes late to a social event. And when we face too many of these, as we often do, they can accrue and have a big effect on our wellbeing in the long run.

However you slice it, many modern workplace environments are stressful these days. And the chronic stress of working under these conditions can take a toll, and contribute to burnout. It's not in your head—the environment in which you work matters, and has an impact on your wellbeing.

Working in the Covid-19 pandemic era

Daily life is stressful enough. And then the pandemic hit in 2020. In recent years, the stress and burnout situation was made even worse as the Covid-19 pandemic upended the world. The pandemic touched us all. Some entered the strange new world of working remotely, with non-stop Zoom meetings, and without the opportunity for "water cooler" conversations with co-workers. The separation between work and home was blurred, and work hours spilled into our personal lives. Those essential workers who continued working in person risked their own safety and were often in highly stressful situations. For many workers, such as teachers, nurses, grocery store workers, and healthcare and mental health professionals, work stress was extreme during that time.

During and in the aftermath of the pandemic, many jobs became so stressful that people left. Entire professions became short-staffed, like customer service jobs, food service, healthcare, and education. In some industries, economic decline in the aftermath of the pandemic led to mass layoffs or the threat of job loss in industries like technology and academia. Job turnover and labor shortages have contributed to the feeling that many of us are overworked and overstressed in our occupational roles.

Extra pressure: Oppressed and marginalized groups

Members of oppressed and historically marginalized groups face additional stressors that can contribute to burnout. Living in a context of systems of power that favor one group over another, like patriarchy and white supremacy, can be exhausting to people who experience the constant stress of discrimination based on race, ethnicity, gender, sexual orientation and gender identity, disability status, age, economic background, religion, body size, and so on. The degree and impact of this type of stress varies. Many people, unfortunately, experience extreme oppression and trauma, such as violence toward women and gender and sexual minorities, racial trauma (Payne 2022), and systemic racism.

I asked my colleague and friend, Dr. Jennifer Shepard Payne, author of the book *Out of the Fire: Healing Black Trauma Caused by Systemic Racism Using Acceptance and Commitment Therapy* (2022), for her thoughts on the relationship between racial trauma and burnout. She shared that, over time, ongoing racial attacks "can chip away at one's emotional, physical, and spiritual resources. A person of color experiencing these things can begin to feel unsafe in areas that should be safe, such as at their job, in their neighborhoods, driving, going to grocery stores, going to churches, or residing even at home" (Payne, personal communication, September 17, 2023). That experience causes a state of chronic stress and hypervigilance that can, of course, lead to burnout and exhaustion for many.

Sometimes, the stress is more subtle and implicit and goes unacknowledged. People from oppressed and historically marginalized groups frequently experience discriminatory behaviors sometimes referred to as "microaggressions"—those day-to-day interactions, often unnoticed and unintentional by the people who are doing them, against members of a marginalized group. These are the offensive remarks (like commenting on someone's "good English" or focusing on a woman's appearance), slights, non-verbal cues, exclusionary behaviors, being spoken over/unheard/not given space, and other kinds of maltreatment. The aggressors often deny that these are happening, which causes additional stress from the minimization of one's experience. Many antiracist scholars and activists argue that the term "microaggressions" itself is minimizing of these harmful behaviors. As Ibram X. Kendi states, "A persistent daily low hum of racist abuse is not minor" (Kendi 2019, p.47). These experiences tend to happen frequently, are cumulative, and are damaging.

These types of stressors are alive and well in the workplace. To illustrate this, I asked therapist, and cohost of the podcast *Black Girl Burnout*, Kelley Bonner, to describe Black women's experience related to stress and burnout in the workplace. She shared that:

Workplace stressors for Black women are a combination of systematic racism, gender-based discrimination, and microaggressions. Black women may, for instance, encounter prejudice in the hiring, promotion, and performance assessment processes. They are also more likely to be excluded from professional networks and opportunities. Additionally, they might have to deal with pressure to meet Eurocentric beauty standards (e.g., hair discrimination), debunk myths about their intellect and work ethic (the angry or aggressive Black woman trope), and reconcile competing standards for assertiveness and emotional expression. (Bonner, personal communication, 21 March, 2023)

Kelley shared that these pervasive stressors are combined with pay disparity and expectations related to caregiving and emotional labor, and can result in, "feelings of loneliness, irritability, and burnout" (Bonner, personal communication, 21 March, 2023).

Members of historically marginalized groups will often get the message (either subtly or overtly) that they don't fit in to the dominant social group. To make it in a workplace culture centered around a dominant group (which historically has been straight, cisgender, able-bodied, white men in many industries), people may engage in code-switching—downplaying one's membership in stigmatized groups by adjusting one's style of behavior, speech, and appearance for a specific situation. For instance, Black workers may feel devalued while navigating mostly white organizations and feel pressure to avoid stereotypes by adjusting their behavior, perhaps becoming quieter than they would be at home. Gay workers might feel they need to hide their sexual orientation at work, and change the way they dress or act, thereby concealing a key aspect of their identity.

Code-switching comes with a psychological cost. When people cannot be authentically themselves, and must instead hide their true selves and work to fit into different groups and avoid stereotypes, it can be mentally and emotionally exhausting, and contribute to burnout (McCluney *et al.* 2019).

There is a deep history of inequality and patriarchy related to labor and work. Many professional workplaces were historically designed by and catered to white men. The United States, for instance, was built on the labor of Black and Indigenous people, and immigrants, whose bodies were used as machines to do low-wage or unpaid labor. Systems of power and oppression have kept some people rich, and some poor. Generational wealth was built through slave labor and colonialism. Think about who is doing the majority of the unpaid/low wage labor, the domestic work, and the caregiving, in our society. Caregiver positions, often unpaid or poorly paid, are more often filled by women, especially women of color or immigrant women. And parents and caregivers often don't have enough support as they do their difficult and often emotionally draining work.

In heterosexual relationships, women take on the majority of the childcare and routine housework. Even as women have increased their participation in the paid workforce over recent decades, men's participation in domestic work and childcare has not, overall, increased at the same rate. Therefore women, even those who work as many hours as their partners or are the primary wage earners, still do a disproportionate share of unpaid labor at home resulting in a "second shift" (Hochschild 2012, first published in 1989; Moyser and Burlock 2018). In many homes, domestic work and childcare duties fall to women by default, without discussion or agreement (Rodsky 2019). Women are often more responsible for the "emotion work," like providing emotional support, managing interpersonal relationships, and caring for the emotional wellbeing of others through listening and providing encouragement and empathy (Erikson 2005). The same goes for the "mental load" work, like planning, organizing schedules, and keeping track of information (Robertson *et al.* 2019). Much of this extra labor is "invisible" (Daniels 1987) in the sense that it is not appreciated and respected as work, the way paid labor is. As Eve Rodsky has said, "Men's time is guarded as a finite resource (like diamonds) and women's time is abundant (like sand)" (Rodsky 2019, pp.53–54).

For women, it's exhausting. And, as Megan Stack writes, women are in a bind:

> When we are saddled with disproportionate work at home—and studies show that virtually all of us women are, particularly during child-rearing years—we are too embarrassed to say so out loud. We don't want to

complain. We don't want to tax our romantic partnerships. And, in the end, we stand to be blamed. The fact of this disproportionate impact is further evidence of our incompetence. (Stack 2019, p.x)

During the Covid-19 pandemic, these inequities became especially pronounced. Women, even those with paid jobs, were saddled with most of the increased childcare and domestic work caused by remote learning and working from home, and were more likely to become unemployed (Grose 2021; OECD 2021).

The impact of all this stress

Thanks to the many contextual factors mentioned in this chapter, and others, levels of stress and burnout are high around the world. In the US 2021 Work Health Survey, conducted by Mental Health America (2021), 83 percent of respondents indicated that they felt emotionally drained from their work, 71 percent felt that workplace stress affected their mental health, and one in four employees experienced the more severe signs of burnout. And it's not just in the US; chronic stress is happening all around the world. According to the Gallup 2021 State of the Global Workplace poll, 43 percent of people globally report feeling a high level of daily stress (Gallup 2021). The US and Canada reported the highest stress, at 57 percent, followed by 51 percent in East Asia; 50 percent in the Middle East and North Africa; 49 percent in Latin America and the Caribbean; 45 percent in Australia and New Zealand; 44 percent in Sub-Saharan Africa; and 40 percent in Europe. The same survey found that job dissatisfaction is at a staggering all-time high. Similarly, a McKinsey (2022) global survey of nearly 15,000 employers and 1000 human resources decision-makers in 15 countries demonstrated that about 1 in 4 employees was experiencing burnout symptoms.

That's a lot of stress.

The bottom line of this chapter is that it's not your fault that you're so stressed and burned out, and you're not alone. The world in which we are all living and working is increasingly stressful, and everyone is feeling the impact, especially those from marginalized groups. In Chapter 16, I will offer some suggestions for addressing systemic issues that contribute to burnout. In the meantime, as we will see in the chapters ahead, how you respond to that stress matters for your wellbeing. And there are actions you can take to help yourself, even in the midst of this stress.

REFLECTION QUESTIONS

1. What's your workplace environment and culture like?
2. What messages did you receive about work from your family and community growing up? What are some of the cultural messages you hear about work?
3. What world events and economic factors contribute to your experience of chronic stress?
4. Are there aspects of your identity, like race/ethnicity, gender identity, sexual orientation, disability, age, that factor into the stress you experience in the world?
5. What systemic factors—in your organization or workplace—do you face in your position that might be contributing to your burnout?
6. Write about some examples of "microstressors" you frequently experience in your work and personal life. What toll do they take on you?

CHAPTER 4

Fuel to the Fire
The Cycle of Burnout

What if I told you that most of the things you've been doing to free yourself from chronic stress and burnout, even things that seem to make perfect sense, are probably not going to work in the long run? Not because you're doing these things wrong, or because you need to try harder, but because you're likely trying to do the impossible.

With or without realizing it, we often try to change how we feel when we are experiencing stress, overwhelm, exhaustion, or other kinds of emotional discomfort. We may develop coping strategies—like working late into the night responding to emails, unwinding with a few cocktails, scrolling social media, or squeezing time for self-care into our busy schedule—to try to reduce stress and help ourselves feel better for a while. While these strategies make sense on the surface, and might even reduce stress for a little while, they can just add fuel to the burnout fire, making things worse over time.

You may recall from Chapter 1 that the definition of burnout mentions that it is the result of "chronic workplace stress that has not been successfully managed" (World Health Organization 2019). While some of the strategies we use might be helpful, especially in the short term, many don't help us "successfully manage" stress in the long run. And worse, some strategies backfire, increasing our stress over time. When that happens, a Cycle of Burnout is created; our efforts to avoid or control our emotional discomfort lead us into a struggle that makes the problem worse.

The Cycle of Burnout

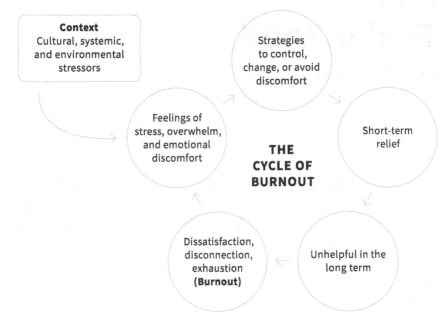

When we are engaged in meaningful yet stressful roles, we will experience discomfort sometimes. It's just going to happen! As we saw in Chapter 3, chronic stress occurs in the context of cultural, systemic, and environmental stressors, many of which are beyond our control. When we don't like feeling this way, or have got the message that we *shouldn't* feel this way, we try to change how we feel. This makes sense, of course. Wouldn't we all want to feel more comfortable when we are struggling? We then use strategies to try to avoid or control our uncomfortable emotions, like disengaging, over-analyzing, procrastinating, doing the minimum, overworking, drinking too much alcohol at the end of the day, and so on. This keeps us stuck in a self-reinforcing cycle, and as the cycle continues, we end up feeling more dissatisfied, disconnected, and exhausted, which exacerbates our chronic stress all over again.

The above figure illustrates the Cycle of Burnout. While this model of burnout is overly simplistic, it can be helpful to "zoom out" and see how the behavior patterns we use to try to cope with stress may dig us even deeper into burnout. To truly understand your own behavior patterns, it helps to break them into small components and take a close look at what happens. By building awareness of your thoughts and feelings, and how you respond to them, you can think about alternative approaches to test out. To illustrate this for you, try walking through an example from your own life.

YOUR PERSONAL CYCLE OF BURNOUT

Think about your own experience with chronic stress that led to burnout. In your notebook or journal, or on a piece of paper, you can either draw your own burnout cycle or write answers to these questions:

1. What cultural, systemic, and environmental context factors added to the chronic stress you were experiencing?
2. Was something stressful going on in the days, weeks, and months leading up to that stressful period? Were you tired or sleep deprived? What else might have contributed to your high stress level?
3. What feelings of stress, overwhelm, or other emotional discomfort did you experience? In detail, describe any thoughts, emotions, and sensations you can remember.
4. List the behaviors and strategies you used to try to manage stress.
5. Which of those behaviors and strategies helped you manage stress in the short term? What was reinforcing about them?
6. What were the longer-term consequences of your stress management efforts? Which were helpful and effective in the long term? Did any backfire in the long term or lead to more dissatisfaction, disconnection, or exhaustion?

Did any "add fuel to the fire" by increasing your chronic stress and burnout?

Now, let's take a deeper dive into the Cycle of Burnout.

The full range of human emotions

Think about some of the important work roles you carry out in your life, like work, caregiving, parenting, athletics, social activism. If you were to track your emotions carefully every two minutes throughout the day as you engaged in those roles, what would you discover?

I am writing this sentence at 4pm, at the end of a workday. Thinking back on my day, I remember feeling excited for the weekend ahead (it's Friday!); touched by a meaningful story a client shared with me; frustrated that I didn't have enough time to get everything done I had hoped to this week; discouraged and a bit hopeless after reading news headlines between clients; tired and bored when I hit my 3pm daily slump time; anxious when I saw a phone call I missed; and satisfied that I made it to the end of the working week. And this was a relatively boring day in my life! (Aside from the Friday thing.)

Any time we engage in demanding, important life roles, we will experience a range of emotions. This will, undoubtedly, include some degree of emotional discomfort. Uncomfortable emotions are an inherent part of life. That is especially the case during periods that are stressful, or when we experience challenges, setbacks, and struggles. We are out in the world doing hard things, and are often overextended without enough support or resources to carry our full load. When stress is high for a long time and we are unable to resolve the source of the stress, we might experience two by-products of stress—overwhelm and exhaustion.

Work is an example, for many of us, of a life domain in which we will feel plenty of emotions—both pleasant (we hope!) and uncomfortable ones. Most of us invest a great deal of time, energy, and effort in our work. We have feelings that rise and fall constantly throughout the day, and those emotions don't shut off during the work hours.

EMOTIONS AT WORK INVENTORY

Let's do a quick inventory of the emotions you typically experience at work or in other burnout-prone roles, like parenting. Check the categories of emotions you've felt within the past week or two. You may need to "dig deep" on some of these. Be honest with yourself.

- Stress or overwhelm (as if you can't possibly catch up; as if you have something stressful looming or an interpersonal problem).
- Tiredness or exhaustion.
- Boredom, numbness, discouragement, or apathy.
- Calm, contentment.
- Happiness, excitement, enthusiasm, or joy.
- Fulfillment, satisfaction, vitality.
- Dread about a task or even about showing up to work.
- Anger or frustration (for example, when interacting with an unreasonable customer, if your child doesn't listen to you, or if working in an inefficient work system).
- Irritation or annoyance, like if dealing with a difficult co-worker or unpleasant task.
- Moral emotions, like guilt, shame, or regret (for example, if your work violates your personal ethics, you question a decision you made, or you struggle to reach your highest ideals).
- Embarrassment (for example, if a project didn't go well, if you've made a mistake, or if you've been uncomfortable in the spotlight).
- Sadness, despair, or hopelessness (this might apply if you work with people who are suffering, if you work for an important cause, or if you are caring for loved ones).
- Empathy, caring, concern.
- Jealousy or envy.
- Rejection or hurt.

- Self-doubt or uncertainty (you might experience these if you are doing something new or challenging, or if you are doing work that's demanding and consuming).
- Other emotions not listed above.

If you're like me, you have felt most of these emotions in just the last few weeks. All of your emotions are perfectly valid, and are part of the human experience. In fact, they are there for a reason. We are wired to respond to our environment with emotions, and our emotions can provide information that can be helpful to our survival. For example, fear prepares us to respond to danger, and anger may help us defend ourselves from harm. However, this may not be the message you've been getting about emotions.

Myths about emotions

Think about what you've been told about stress over the course of your life. Have you heard stressful jobs referred to as "a heart attack by age 50"? You may have been told that stress is harmful and should be avoided as much as possible. Or you may think that you should be able to pile on many stressors and handle them without breaking a sweat—that you are supposed to be "tough" enough to handle a heavy workload without it affecting you emotionally. These types of messages about stress are a trap, because stressing out about stress just increases our stress level!

The way we think about stress reflects some deeply embedded cultural beliefs about how we should respond to our emotions, thoughts, and sensations more generally. We all receive messages, throughout childhood and into adulthood, about which emotions are acceptable to express and which aren't. Phrases like "don't worry, be happy" and "boys don't cry" hint at this message. In many cultures, there's a subtle message promoting what is commonly known as toxic positivity—the belief that no matter how difficult a situation is, our thoughts and emotions should stay positive. The message we get is that feeling happy is good for us, feeling stressed, anxious, or upset is bad for us, and if we do have "negative" emotions, we should try to fix or get rid of them.

Myths like this about emotions are alive and well in the workplace. "Most of us have been fed the absurd idea that the workplace is a rare setting where emotions are unwelcome, illogical, unprofitable, or even unprofessional," argues Karla McLaren (2021, p.5), author of *The Power of Emotions at Work*. "We fooled ourselves into believing that emotions had no value at work...and kicked the emotions out of our factories, our offices, our workplaces, our boardrooms, and our working lives (or we *thought* we did)." (McLaren 2021, p.2). In many workplaces, emotional expression is discouraged and the expectation is that workers will check their emotions at the door.

In environments where this is the case, we may question whether something is wrong with us if we have strong emotions at work. But, despite what society is telling you, it's impossible to do difficult, challenging, demanding work without having an emotional response.

Although having a positive outlook can be a wonderful thing, it can be harmful when over-positivity is forced on us. Whether in the workplace or in other roles like parenting, the belief that we should feel calm and content and have "good vibes only" perpetuates the unfortunate myth that our less comfortable emotions are unacceptable or invalid. We may feel unsupported in our true emotions, which will not always be positive or socially acceptable. We may think there's something wrong with us that needs to be fixed when we experience intense or prolonged discomfort. And believing these myths about emotions can lead us into a pattern of control and avoidance.

Fleeing from discomfort

If we buy into the myth that uncomfortable emotions are harmful, or shouldn't impact us, what happens during the inevitable periods of high stress, exhaustion, overwhelm, and burnout? Likely, we will believe that we shouldn't be feeling this way, and need to do something to fix, change, control, or avoid these emotions and "feel better" before we can move forward.

You've probably found some ways of dealing with stressful events. You might go for a walk or take a few deep, soothing breaths, and feel a little more relaxed. Or you might seek relief by unwinding with comfort food, alcohol, procrastination, or the endless social media scroll. Or you may work harder, trying to work your way out of the stress, thinking that once you do, you will finally, finally catch up and be able to enjoy your life.

These types of stress management behaviors are meant to help us deal with stress, and begin with the assumption that stress is a sign that something is wrong. They often work in the short term by taking the edge off for a while. In moderation, control strategies can be helpful sometimes, at least temporarily, in the face of uncomfortable emotions. There's nothing wrong with taking some downtime with a TV show, finishing up a project that has been lingering, or doing yoga to manage stress. Some emotional control strategies are even values-aligned and healthy for us. But these behaviors can become problematic when we use them to escape from uncomfortable emotions.

The problem with control

My husband has learned *never* to say a few things to me over the years we've been married. One of them is the infuriating phrase, "Calm down." I know I'm not the only one who despises those two words! When you're having an emotional reaction to something, what do those words do to you? Do you think, "Oh, great idea," take a deep breath, and immediately become less tense and more relaxed? I didn't think so—and me neither!

If we had the ability to control our emotions, we would be able to hear the words "calm down" and then calm ourselves right on down. The reason I find those words so annoying in the heat of the moment is that the implication that I can (or should) control my emotions so easily, like flipping a calm down switch, feels invalidating and makes me even more upset.

While emotional control efforts can be fine and helpful in some situations, using emotional control to avoid discomfort can be ineffective or may backfire and make things far worse in the long run! For example, think back to a time when you woke up in the middle of the night and struggled to fall back asleep. What happened when you tried really, really hard to fall asleep, telling yourself, "I have to fall asleep soon or I'll be really tired tomorrow"? Or when you told your overly active 2 a.m. mind to stop worrying and quiet down so you could sleep? Did any of that work? I'm guessing not, because trying to force yourself to fall asleep usually has the paradoxical result of making sleep even more elusive.

The truth is, we can't control our internal thoughts and emotions the way we think we can. When we use these strategies to "feel better," we are attempting to control the uncontrollable. In the ACT model, suffering results from the struggle to change, control, or avoid discomfort. In my opinion, the disconnection that arises from that struggle is the root problem with burnout. We can end up spending so much of our valuable time and energy trying to reduce or avoid our natural experience of discomfort, that we miss out on more important things, and in doing so, lose contact with meaning, purpose, and vitality in our work and our lives.

Engaging in control and avoidance efforts can be especially problematic if they aren't working well, are inconsistent with our values, or are costly to us in some other way. As our suffering grows, this cycle causes burnout-related pain to persist and grow into a bigger problem; control strategies can become endless loops of avoidance that get us nowhere, spiraling us into the Cycle of Burnout.

And...repeat!

Any time we repeat a behavior again and again, there is *something* reinforcing about it. Even behaviors that may not seem to make much sense at face value, like substance abuse or procrastination, serve a function. Often, these types of behaviors are highly reinforcing in the short term, providing temporary relief from discomfort or an immediate dopamine hit that feels good. But in the long term, we may find that we've drifted away from our deeply held values, or we can lose the ability to respond flexibly and effectively to any given situation. We can lose sight of the big picture of what's most important to us and get so locked into life-limiting patterns that we lose a sense of vitality.

Sometimes, we can get so caught up in the Cycle of Burnout that we can't even see that it's happening. Or, we might think that we can successfully beat the cycle. We tell ourselves that when we just finally catch up on things, or if we practice a little more self-care, we'll be okay! So we work a little harder, do more yoga and mindfulness practice, and try changing our attitude to be more positive.

I sometimes like to say to my therapy clients that awareness is the first step. In order to get out of any problematic emotional cycle, we can take a look at it and think about what really needs to change, and what we need to accept. I hope you will consider the possibility that you may have been trying to do the impossible—to control the (understandably) difficult emotions that arise as a response to chronic stress.

In the next chapter, we'll look at some examples of the types of burnout cycles many of us get into. But first, let's pause here to consider some questions about your own personal experience with the Cycle of Burnout.

REFLECTION QUESTIONS

1. What are some of the emotions (both pleasant and distressing) that arise naturally in your work?
2. What did you learn growing up about emotions? Which emotions did you learn were "acceptable" and which were "unacceptable" in your upbringing?
3. What messages have you learned about stress?
4. What is the culture like in your workplace (or other work role) in relation to emotional expression?
5. What are some of the strategies you tend to use to manage stress or control emotional discomfort?
6. How well do those control strategies work in the short term? What's reinforcing about them?
7. How do they work in the long term? Are they adding fuel to the burnout fire?

CHAPTER 5

Burnout Cycles
The Ten Types

B urnout is complex, and no two people experience it in the same way in their day-to-day lives. There are as many flavors of burnout as there are people who experience burnout. And yet, I've observed some common burnout patterns over the years—in myself, my clients, my colleagues, and my friends and family.

In this chapter, I will shine a spotlight on some common burnout cycle patterns I've seen. I'm calling these "The Ten Types": the busy bee, the perfectionist, the people-pleaser, the do-gooder, the marching soldier, the avoider, the cynic, the over-analyzer, the comfort-seeker, and the wellness warrior. These are all examples that illustrate how the Cycle of Burnout works. They're patterns that many of us get into (often without realizing it) in response to chronic stress, that can exacerbate it and contribute to the burnout cycle.

Some of these types might feel very familiar to you. As you read, please reflect on whether you engage in any of these patterns and take note of any insights you might have about yourself. You may notice that you identify strongly with one, or several, of these cycles. Or not—perhaps your flavor of burnout is a little different from these examples. Either way, we will take a close look at these types of patterns, see what's driving them, and help you identify what's helpful and harmful about them. Doing so can help you to be more intentional about your own behavior patterns, and to better understand whether they are helping you to manage chronic stress effectively, or not.

Type 1: The busy bee

I don't know about you, but when I'm too stressed I long to take a beach vacation or lounge around in a hammock all day with a good book. And yet, when I look at a mile-long "to-do" list, I tend to do the opposite— instead of taking a break, I double-down on hard work as a solution to my stress. My internal logic is that I think I will eventually outrun my stress, with hope that someday soon I'll finally conquer my enormous workload. Only then will I be able to take that day in the hammock I've been longing for. Once I catch up on things—which always seems to be right around the corner—my chronic stress will finally subside forever. (Or so I tell myself.)

I call people who use this strategy (like me) busy bee types. In his book *Four Thousand Weeks: Time Management for Mortals*, Oliver Burkeman writes that many of us "deploy the strategy that dominates most conventional advice on how to deal with busyness: we tell ourselves we'll just have to find a way to do more—to try to address our busyness, you could say, by making ourselves busier still" (Burkeman 2021, p.39).

Many high-achieving people are prone to this pattern. In the beginning, overwork has some upsides. Hard work comes naturally to many of us, and it can be highly reinforcing! The buzz of working hard and accomplishing tasks feels good. In her book *Dopamine Nation*, Anna Lembke writes, "I've found it difficult at times to stop myself from working once I've begun. The flow of deep concentration is a drug in itself, releasing dopamine and creating its own high" (Lembke 2021, p.169).

Overworking and busyness are also socially reinforced. The busier we are, the more important we feel. As we saw in Chapter 3, many of us live in cultures where hard work is praised as a moral virtue. We want to keep up with the high-achieving Joneses next door. Workplaces and organizations love seeing hard work from employees because they benefit by having productive workers. The message within many workplaces is that we should be highly productive at our jobs, all the time. When we fall behind on things, we assume it's our fault and that we should just work harder to catch up again. We grind and we hustle, and the idea of taking a break can feel impossible.

When you are already stressed, the busy bee strategy of working harder and harder may be the opposite of what you really need in the long run. In other words, overworking doesn't get us out of the burnout cycle; instead, it can lead to burnout and keep it going. We might be able to fool ourselves into thinking we can outrun stress, but we can't.

Instead of making hard choices about what needs to change, we often try to be more productive and more efficient. As you are making progress on that long "to-do" list, more tasks will appear. The work just keeps getting added, and never really gets completed, which of course makes us more stressed. When we stay busy, we feel as if we are making progress, even if the progress isn't toward the things that are most important to us. When we are overworking, we often neglect our own needs, like caring for ourselves or taking that downtime we've been craving. And (managers and leaders take note!) hustling away without a break can backfire by causing us to be exhausted and even less productive in the long run.

Type 2: The perfectionist

"Amanda" is a recent college graduate who started her first job out of school about six months ago. Each Wednesday she presents a brief report to her team at their weekly staff meeting. Although Amanda did well in school, she isn't so sure of herself in her new job. Everyone else on her team seems confident and has more experience than her. Her boss, Jeanne, keeps telling Amanda not to spend much time working on the presentations, because the meetings are informal and she has other priorities that are more important at work. Amanda prepares her presentation from home on Tuesdays after work hours, so that Jeanne doesn't think she's wasting time on her preparation. Sometimes Amanda will spend hours, staying up until the wee hours of the night, double checking her data and her spelling, and making sure her presentation looks effortlessly polished. She fears that if she makes a mistake, or isn't well prepared, her team will question her competence. Amanda is a perfectionist type.

Sometimes we convince ourselves that our one-way ticket out of Stresstown is to do everything perfectly and avoid mistakes. It feels great to be on top of everything, and have it all "just right," and we sometimes turn to that as a solution for dealing with stress and anxiety. Working hard to ensure that we reach (or exceed) high standards gives us a sense of control. Jennifer Kemp, author of *The ACT Workbook for Perfectionism*, writes, "Perfectionism offers a false promise that you can gain control of your life by working harder, preventing mistakes, attaining more things, or accomplishing difficult tasks" (Kemp 2021, p.60).

Underneath perfectionistic behavior there often lurks an underlying fear of failure or of losing control. We may worry that we will be humiliated or judged if we make a mistake. Especially when we are surrounded by high-achieving people, we may be ashamed and highly self-critical if we don't measure up to high standards and expectations. So, we strive to meet or even exceed them—by simply doing everything very well and never allowing mistakes or shortcomings. If we can just be extremely competent and keep up, we assume that perhaps we can keep feelings of anxiety and uncertainty at bay.

Of course, it's not quite so simple. Efforts to do things perfectly can perpetuate the burnout cycle, because perfectionism is a game we can never win (Ong and Twohig 2022). We can run ourselves ragged trying to avoid mistakes and putting pressure on ourselves to be perfect, but never get there. It can be exhausting to try to keep up with our impossible-to-meet high standards. Sure enough, perfectionism has been linked to burnout and chronic stress (Hill and Curran 2016), and perfectionism about parenting practices has been tied to parental burnout (Mikolajczak *et al.* 2019).

The cost of perfectionism can be especially high in terms of taking us away from our values. If we are working hard to do everything perfectly and meet every deadline, we won't have time or energy to enjoy our lives and do other things that are important to us. Like Amanda, who on a Tuesday night would rather be enjoying her life but is instead working on her report for tomorrow's staff meeting.

Type 3: The people-pleaser

In their book *Burnout: The Secret to Unlocking the Stress Cycle*, co-authors and sisters Emily and Amelia Nagoski (2020) write about "Human Giver Syndrome," an idea based on the work of feminist writer Kate Manne (2017). Human Giver Syndrome means believing you have a moral obligation to be "pretty, happy, calm, and attentive to the needs of others" (Nagoski and Nagoski 2020, p.62). Human givers are expected to be generous. Acting otherwise can result in self-criticism and feelings of failure. People who believe this are oriented toward pleasing others, at the expense of their own personal needs. "Human givers have a moral obligation to *give* their whole humanity, and give it cheerfully" (Nagoski and Nagoski 2020, p.62).

People-pleasers are giving and caring people, who feel good when they attend to others and make them happy. They often receive praise and appreciation for being giving and caring, and prefer to avoid conflict and the uncomfortable feeling of potentially disappointing people. It can be easier (in the short term at least) to say yes to everything, and they fear that saying no or setting boundaries will result in being disliked. And sometimes, "I'll just do it myself" feels far easier than delegating or asking someone for help. Whether it's a family member, boss, or client, it's often easier in the short term to be pleasant and giving to others than otherwise.

When we say yes by default, in order to make others happy, we can end up being chronically stressed from constantly bending over backward. We might take on more responsibility than we really want to or take on the emotional weight of being overly attuned and empathic toward others. In doing so, we can end up without enough capacity left to care for our own needs. When this pattern persists for years, we can lose touch with our own needs completely, having long forsaken them as if they weren't important. And we can end up feeling resentful of the people we are doing things for, which can damage our relationships—the very outcome we were trying to avoid.

There's a reason customer-facing and caregiving roles are at high risk for burnout. In some "helping" or people-oriented professions, pleasing others and meeting their needs is part of the job. People-pleasers are in a bind, because they end up feeling "exhausted when saying yes, guilty when saying no" (Skovholt and Trotter-Mathison 2016, p.4).

Type 4: The do-gooder

Do-gooder types, close cousins of people-pleaser types, are caring people who want to do the right thing. They tend to be engaged in purpose-driven work and derive meaning from having a positive impact in the world. Their hearts are in the right place—they want to make a positive difference, behave ethically, and do the right thing. There's nothing wrong with this; in fact, it's an admirable quality! Do-gooders are some of the best people we have.

While it is usually values-aligned and feels good to have a positive impact, over time caring so much can start to have a heavy emotional weight. We can overextend ourselves with empathy and feel pressure to always do the right thing. We can go overboard in how we engage with purpose-driven work, feeling that we must always do more than we're doing. We can feel worn out from taking on so much personal responsibility for the world's problems. And we can feel hopeless that things will ever improve.

Do-gooder types can easily slip into what Joan Halifax (2018) calls "pathological altruism"—when we go too far with doing good, from a place of trying to fill an internal need. We can get caught up in our own ego, become martyrs to a cause. We can neglect time to care for our own needs, because we are so focused on trying to help others.

Do-gooders also face the possibility of moral injury—the psychological distress that occurs when we feel that our actions are not living up to our own high ethical standards. People in professions like social work, healthcare, activism, and teaching repeatedly bump up against situations that conflict with their values, or that don't allow them to do the highest quality work they can. For instance, healthcare providers can experience moral injury, not just when they make a medical decision that results in a moral violation, but also when they're unable to provide high-quality care to patients in overtaxed medical systems.

An elementary school teacher I know personally described a situation like that to me. One year, she had a child in her classroom who had some severe behavioral issues. Daily, the child would disrupt the class by pushing over furniture, leaving the classroom and yelling. Once, the child even threatened her with a pair of scissors. Trying to teach a room full of seven-year-olds is enough to exhaust the average person in even the most peaceful of situations, and this child made teaching far more stressful for her. On top of her usual teaching duties, she had to find effective ways to manage the child's behavior, attend frequent meetings about him with his parents and school administrators, and write up behavioral plans and reports. Due to teacher shortages, she didn't have enough support in the classroom to help her both manage the child's behavior and teach the rest of her students effectively. One of the things she struggled with most that year was feeling that she was unable to give the other students in her classroom enough attention and support. She went into teaching because she cared about children and education. Because she was unable to teach all of her students to the best of her abilities, she was left feeling guilty, stressed, and dissatisfied.

Type 5: The marching soldier

You've likely seen merchandise featuring the motto "Keep calm and carry on," which was used in motivational posters produced by the British government in preparation for World War II. Going through tough times? Don't get upset about it, just carry on! Keep going! It seems like a lovely idea. So lovely that many of us have adopted this philosophy as an approach to dealing with stress.

Marching soldier types have become experts at tuning out their emotions, ignoring them to carry on and be tough, stoic, and invincible, even in high-stress situations. They have learned to ignore their body's cues that they could use a rest (or a meal, or even a bathroom break). They feel that they can't stop marching, instead, working non-stop all day until they collapse in exhaustion late at night. They think they can just ignore their emotions and bodily sensations and carry on through the stress.

Marching onward can be effective in some ways and is often

culturally reinforced. When we have a job to do, and there isn't time to slow down and feel our feelings, sometimes it makes sense to just keep going. And of course, many employers love it when we do this, because it prioritizes productive action over pausing to make room for one's feelings—at least until we are so burned out we lose productivity! While anyone can get into "carry on" and "power through" mode sometimes, men may be especially conditioned to take this approach, because of cultural messages that their emotions should be hidden away.

While this approach sounds good in theory, the problem is that when we ignore our emotions and just carry on, bottling them up, they fester away inside, unexpressed, which can then contribute to burnout. We've talked in the previous chapter about how avoiding emotions often backfires because we are trying to control the uncontrollable. And we will see in the chapters ahead how, in doing so, we miss out on some important information.

Healthcare is an example of a highly stressful industry in which you often see this approach, especially in recent years with the Covid-19 pandemic. Sometimes, healthcare professionals have to keep seeing patient after patient, in the face of tremendous trauma and stress, and have been taught to never let their patients or colleagues see them struggle emotionally. As Cynda Hylton Rushton writes about her experience as a nurse, "In a culture of 'power on,' I had no words to articulate the impact of my own suffering. This was the job; there was no time for sadness or despair" (Rushton 2018, p.1).

People who feel they must keep calm and march on are often highly competent and capable people, who think that they can and should handle anything that comes their way. When they feel stressed or overwhelmed, they try to hide it, thinking they should be immune from feeling this way, and experiencing shame about the distress they are really experiencing deep down inside.

Type 6: The avoider

"Brian" has been working in the same position for years, with little opportunity for promotion or new responsibilities, and he is dissatisfied.

Although he is busy, many of the tasks on his plate are menial and unchallenging to him. He is largely overlooked by his boss, who pays little attention to him because he is competent and never has any problems getting his work done on time. Like many, Brian was sent home to work remotely during the Covid-19 pandemic and continues to do so. On the one hand, he loves working from home. He can turn his camera off and scroll through the news during staff meetings and take long breaks to nap or exercise in the middle of the day without anyone noticing. On the other hand, although no one seems to pay much attention to what he's doing, as long as he does the minimum, he has become terrified of annual performance reviews, because he feels it is obvious that he's been "phoning it in" for so long. He doesn't want to take on more responsibility—why would you take on more work if you don't enjoy your job? But at the same time, he's self-critical about not meeting his potential to do something more meaningful that really utilizes his skills. Often, when he is supposed to be working, he daydreams about other career paths, or researches early retirement plans. Brian is an avoider type.

A hallmark of burnout is detachment from a work role, even one you normally feel emotionally invested in. In her book *Burnout: The Cost of Caring*, Christina Maslach (2003) writes about a typical pattern of emotional overload leading to burnout, in which a person gets overly involved emotionally, overextended, and overwhelmed in a stressful role, which leads to exhaustion. In response to that exhaustion, the person attempts to save energy by cutting back, doing the bare minimum, and disengaging.

There are many different flavors of avoidance and detachment. Sometimes people procrastinate by putting off projects, getting easily distracted, or focusing on unimportant things, like checking social media (and checking it again), doom scrolling, or playing video games when there is something more important to do. Sometimes they cut back, by doing the minimum or just going through the motions without much effort. Or, they might become overly bureaucratic and rigid, focusing on unimportant aspects of their work instead of the harder stuff that involves more emotional engagement. Some people fantasize or engage in "mental time travel," for instance by thinking about 5pm all day long or imagining a vacation or a new job. For people in caring professions, it can look like depersonalization, or a loss of empathy for people's suffering.

If caring too much feels exhausting, detaching might seem to make sense on the surface. Avoiding emotional engagement can feel like an improvement for a while, because it numbs out the painful emotions. But detachment leads to a lost sense of meaning and vitality. While the implicit goal of this is to reduce pain, the avoider starts to perform worse than usual at the task and experiences guilt, dissatisfaction, and a reduced sense of accomplishment.

Of course, it is completely fine to rest and relax with non-productive activities sometimes! None of these avoidance behaviors are inherently problematic when we do them occasionally. And some forms of pro-crastination can even be good for us, like when we put off work for a while to make time for a fun side project. But procrastination and distraction can be problematic when they're used as avoidance strategies to the point where they interfere with meaningful activities. You might breathe a sigh of relief when you dodge the hard stuff for a while, but a chronic pattern of avoidance and detachment usually does not feel very satisfying in the long run.

Type 7: The cynic

When I worked in healthcare, there was a pattern I would see sometimes among myself and my co-workers (even some of my all-time favorite co-workers!). We would start out enthusiastic and engaged in our work. Fast forward five or ten years and we were cynical. One day, back when I worked in a hospital setting, I was sitting in a meeting with my team and we were brainstorming ideas for how to solve a workflow problem we kept having with patient communication. The newer members of the team had some creative and perfectly logical ideas for what to do. I found myself repeating, "Yeah, we did it that way five years ago and it didn't work," and "We've already tried that." I realized I was being the team nay-sayer. I wasn't contributing anything helpful to the conversation, just shooting people's ideas down. Was that the kind of person I wanted to be on my team? Definitely not!

In her book on transforming moral suffering in healthcare, Cynda Hylton Rushton writes about high-stakes situations:

> When a sense of personal deficiency, frustration, or failure is in the mix, it can lead to attempts to divert attention from one's own suffering and to focus on the failings of others—for example, blaming the patient or family for choices that are at odds with clinical recommendations, vilifying the surgeon for his aggressive efforts to sustain life despite overwhelming complications, or blaming "the system" for one's inability to bring about the outcome one regards as optimal for one's patient. (Rushton 2018, p.15)

This doesn't just happen in healthcare. In any type of work, it's all too easy to focus on everything that's wrong with the world and other people. Cynicism is one of the dimensions of burnout, and many people with burnout experience cynicism (Maslach and Leiter 2022).

Cynic types deflect their more vulnerable feelings with blame, negativity, sarcasm, irritability, and righteous anger. It can feel better to dwell on what's wrong with everyone and everything, rather than feeling all the painful emotions underneath our cynical exterior. This often happens without much awareness; we don't realize we are stuck in unhelpful narratives, but rather we just truly believe that others are to blame. And, unfortunately, our cynicism can spread to others around us.

In my experience as a therapist, I've found that people in the throes of burnout often experience a high degree of irritability—it can be the main problem people come to therapy to address. And when we unpack what's happening in those irritable moments, I find that people are often dwelling on everything that's wrong with the world and other people, stuck in righteousness and stewing on unhelpful negative beliefs.

It's easy to see how being stuck in a place of blame and cynicism can be unhelpful in terms of the burnout cycle. When we dwell on those types of thoughts, we exacerbate our stress in the long run. Doing so can impact our sense of agency and deflect from the real problems at the root of burnout. We can start to feel that we are helpless, unable to see possibility for hope or change.

Type 8: The over-analyzer

Humans have magnificent brains and minds (if we do say so ourselves!) and are thinking machines. As a species, we are great at using our big fancy brains to solve our problems. Broken appliance? Grab your screwdriver! Need a new idea for work? Brainstorm and see what you come up with! Dealing with a relationship problem? Analyze it from all angles until you figure out what to do!

Because our minds can help us with so many of our problems, we often try to analyze things as a strategy for solving our problems. In the case of chronic stress and burnout, there can be a tendency to use thinking as a strategy for solving the painful problems we have. We might ruminate, dwell, or spend hours at night worrying about the problem. We might try analyzing our childhoods, doing research, reading self-help books (a-hem) or learning-everything-there-is-to-possibly-know-about-burnout (oh, is that just me?) to try to fix this problem we're having. Often, clients will come in for therapy, saying in the first session that they want to figure out *why* this is happening, so they can feel better. The assumption is that they'll be able to figure it out, and once they do the problem will go away.

Overthinker types feel productive when they are thinking about their problems. Even if we aren't doing anything, our minds feel as if they are trying to help us. And, the truth is, sometimes it kind of works! If you do stumble on a helpful idea, it can be beneficial.

But...(of course by now you knew this was coming) over-analyzing doesn't always work, and can keep us stuck in the burnout cycle. We can easily end up overthinking, preoccupied by our thoughts, and we can lose sight of what's right in front of us (we'll learn more about this in Chapter 8). Too much worry and overthinking can increase our distress and lead to self-criticism. And, in my years as a therapist, I have never seen someone "figure out" their problem and then immediately everything is resolved. I'm not saying it's never happened before, just that I've never really seen it work that way. Insight can be helpful, sure, but insight by itself doesn't really change much of anything. The truth is, it's difficult to think our way out of a complex internal problem like chronic stress and burnout, no matter how magnificent our brains are.

Type 9: The comfort-seeker

"Megan" is a divorced mom of 15-year-old twins. At the end of a long day at her busy and demanding job in university administration, followed by a few hours driving the twins around to their activities, she pours a glass of wine with her late dinner to help her unwind from the stress of her day. Most nights, she then pours one or two more while she unwinds and watches TV or scrolls through social media, too drained to do anything else. Eventually, she treats herself to a snack and maybe a little chocolate for an energy boost. Although she's exhausted, she stays up too late, usually falling sleep sometime around midnight with the TV still on in her bedroom. When 6am rolls around, she wishes she had slept more, and vows to go to bed earlier, only to repeat the pattern the next night.

Comfort-seeker types seek immediate stress relief through habits that feel good right away. It might be a few too many drinks around cocktail hour, or a nightly marijuana habit to unwind and de-stress at the end of the workday. It might be some "emotional eating," using comfort foods to numb out, or to pep up when we're feeling tired or bored. We might shop online, spending too much money on things we don't need, for the surge of excitement when we hit the purchase button, and the second surge when the box arrives on the front porch. It might be tuning in to our favorite show instead of getting ready for the week or getting a good night of sleep.

Some comfort-seeking habits are more about what we *aren't* doing. We might neglect our own self-care or engage in the kinds of self-care that aren't what we really need. We might put exercise on the back burner when we're busy, even though we know very well it helps us to release stress and tension. Let's face it, it feels much more comfortable to sit on the couch and scroll away than to venture outside for a walk or head to the gym.

None of these comfort-seeking habits are necessarily a big problem in and of themselves. We all probably do some version of this sometimes, and it's okay! You want to eat a few cookies before bed, have a glass of wine at the end of the day, or spend some time on Netflix to unwind? Don't be too hard on yourself—these aren't morally bad or unreasonable things to be doing.

But, as with the other cycles we've seen, most of them don't help with stress in the long run. And they may come at a cost if they are used excessively or inflexibly, or if they are keeping us from our longer-term goals. One of the potential costs of comfort-seeking is that these kinds of habits can escalate our stress levels in the long run. Staying up too late or having a few cocktails might feel good in the short term but, like Megan, we often pay the price later. Comfort-seeker types, please stay tuned for more about burnout-prevention habits in Chapter 12!

Type 10: The wellness warrior

Do you spend a lot of time, money, and energy on self-care and wellness activities, only to find that after the blissful feeling fades you are still just as miserable, stressed, and burned out as you were before? Do you constantly aim for self-improvement, only to find that you still don't feel "good enough"? If so, you might be a wellness warrior type.

The wellness warrior's strategy is a sneaky one. With this strategy, we focus on self-care activities and self-improvement methods to reduce stress and feel better. Why is it sneaky? Because these activities often *do* help us with stress, are aligned with our health goals and values, and look on the surface as if they should work. But I've found that self-care methods can have some shortcomings when we look to them as a longer-term solution to stress and burnout.

Rina Raphael, author of the book *The Gospel of Wellness: Gyms, Gurus, Goop, and the False Promise of Self-Care* (2022), writes that wellness is often marketed to us as an "exit strategy" from the stress and overwhelm we face, particularly for women:

The carrot it dangles in front of women is the one thing they desperately desire: control. Women are promised that they can manage the chaos ruling their life by following a laid-out plan: eat right, exercise, meditate, then buy or do all this stuff. This mass consumerism is a vehicle for harnessing everything that feels turbulent in their lives. (Raphael 2022, p.272)

The multi-billion-dollar wellness industry sells us on the idea that we can have a sense of control over our stressful lives by making time for the yoga, spa treatments, positive thinking methods, and whatever exercise and nutritional programs they happen to be selling. If you improve yourself (by buying their products and services), your problems will be solved. And if those don't work, you must be doing it wrong, or not doing enough of it.

One problem is that wellness often results in feeling good right away, by attaining a blissful or more relaxed state, but without solving the true underlying problems that contribute to stress. Wellness is marketed to fill the emotional voids left in our lives because of the isolation and loneliness of the modern world and its consumerist "grind culture." Western wellness culture places the burden of systemic and cultural problems on the individual person, and often falls short as a longer-term solution. And it can emphasize individual wellbeing for the privileged few, while neglecting the greater good. A similar concept is sometimes referred to as "spiritual bypassing," a term coined in the 1980s that describes an avoidance of the root of a problem through hiding behind spiritual practices. Individual self-actualization is the goal, even if it means overlooking real problems in the world that may be contributing to suffering—yours and everyone's.

Accepting yourself, just as you are, tends to be an overlooked option in the wellness world. And the pressure of constantly trying to improve yourself can add to chronic stress. How many times have you felt guilty because you "should" have been taking more time to relax, meditate, exercise, look attractive, or sleep more, in the middle of an already stressful period? Pressure to engage in more wellness efforts is more pressure! Self-improvement is an elusive goal that requires ongoing effort to maintain, and time and money that may have been better spent doing something else. And while it might feel good, often it doesn't address the real fundamental problem—the stress and overwhelm of living in today's world, with too much demand and not enough support.

To be crystal clear, I am not at all opposed to practicing self-care. It's important, and I will offer some ideas for taking care of yourself throughout this book. If meditation, yoga, exercise, sleep, or spa days give you an enjoyable break to recharge, that's wonderful! And if they enhance your life and fit within your time and financial reality, I hope you will keep on doing those activities.

The distinction between helpful and unhelpful self-care efforts can be subtle. If you tend to engage in a lot of self-care efforts and are still feeling chronically stressed and burned out, ask yourself if you might be using those self-care activities as a control or avoidance strategy, whether the things you are doing are truly aligned with your most important goals and values, and whether something else in your life might need to change—something bigger that more self-care won't fix for you.

I have offered you ten types—examples of strategies and patterns that can lead to the Cycle of Burnout. It is likely that you will identify with more than one of these types. They aren't meant to label you as a person, but rather to help you understand some patterns you might be engaging in.

Let's take a pause here to consider whether you have learned anything you can connect to your own personal experience. Use the questions below to understand more about your own version of the burnout cycle.

REFLECTION QUESTIONS

1. Which types do you identify most with, in your own experience, from this chapter?
2. What ideas and examples resonated most for you?
3. What did you learn about your burnout patterns by reading through these examples?
4. Are there any types or burnout-related patterns missing from this list? Is there anything you didn't see here that would have represented your experience better? If so, write about it.

PART TWO

TRANSFORMING BURNOUT INTERNALLY WITH PSYCHOLOGICAL FLEXIBILITY

CHAPTER 6

Breaking the Cycle with Openness and Acceptance

The poet-philosopher David Whyte has written, "The antidote to exhaustion is not necessarily rest... The antidote to exhaustion is wholeheartedness" (Whyte 2001, p.132). This is one of my favorite quotes on burnout because it captures this chapter, and the ACT model, beautifully. As an alternative to the burnout cycle, it is possible to reconnect with our emotions, be more open to our full experience of living, and move into a place of more vitality and meaning.

Emotional discomfort is part of life, and some degree of it is unavoidable if you are engaged in anything that's important to you. Rather than struggling against our burnout-related thoughts and emotions, we can willingly experience them by letting them come and go naturally, approaching them with a stance of openness and acceptance. We will undoubtedly still experience emotional pain at times, but our relationship to that pain will change. We won't be as consumed with the efforts to get rid of discomfort that perpetuate the Cycle of Burnout. Instead, we can allow discomfort to be there, and be gentle toward ourselves for feeling what we feel. We can choose a wholehearted and meaningful way of living—even as emotional discomfort comes and goes.

Transforming our inner experience of burnout requires approaching our thoughts and feelings in a new way. In this chapter, we will explore how to stop struggling and be more fully open to your emotional experience—the joy *and* the pain. You'll learn how you can break the Cycle of Burnout and move instead toward a stance of wholehearted openness. You'll learn to be in the presence of your inner experience, without focusing so much on controlling it. Once you break free of the burnout cycle, you will be able to respond more flexibly to life's challenges and move forward in new ways.

First, stop struggling

Have you ever been caught swimming in a rip current? Swimmers getting pulled out to sea by rip tides will instinctively try to swim directly toward the shore, hoping to reach safety. But in doing so, they can exhaust themselves by struggling hard against the current without making forward progress.

If you're ever caught in a rip tide, the experts say that first you must stop struggling against the current and let yourself go with the flow of the water a little bit. Once you stop struggling you can swim perpendicular to the current, until you're out of it and can swim directly toward the shore again. This feels counterintuitive because it feels scary to stop struggling and let yourself flow along with the current.

Trying to beat burnout by controlling your thoughts and emotions can feel like being caught in a rip current (Stoddard and Afari 2014). The first instinct is often to keep doing the things you've always done to reach "safety" by heading directly toward comfort and away from painful thoughts and emotions. But doing so can be exhausting and keep you struggling without getting anywhere. Once you let go of the struggle, and float along with your emotions—by letting yourself feel them rather than struggling against them—you can get out of the cycle you've been stuck in. Then you will have the freedom to try something new and different. Until then, you're stuck and exhausted.

We are so used to automatically struggling against our emotions, that we often don't even notice we're doing it. Awareness is a solid first step. Here are some examples of ways you might be struggling against your experience (also known as experiential avoidance):

- Tensing up or bracing yourself against physical and emotional pain.
- Bottling up feelings of anger.
- Holding back tears.
- Trying hard to relax or calm your anxiety and fears.
- Trying to clear your mind of racing thoughts.
- Trying to only think certain kinds of thoughts or get rid of other kinds.
- Attempting to distract or numb yourself from your feelings.
- Over-analyzing or trying to problem-solve or "fix" your emotions away.
- Wondering what's wrong with you for feeling what you do.
- Wishing you could stop having the emotion you're having.

Once you've noticed these or other internal struggles, you can try easing up and instead go along with the flow of your inner experience. I'll walk you through the steps of how do this later in this chapter. For now, let's see what it's like to stop struggling.

STOP STRUGGLING

Just for a moment or two, allow yourself to experience your thoughts, feelings, and bodily sensations without struggling against them. Allow yourself to fully experience all of these, fully, in this moment. If you feel any pull to struggle against your experience, let it go. Try letting your mind roam free, simply allowing it to do its thing effortlessly. See what shifts when you try this. What happens? What do you notice?

In my clinical practice, I've had some clients who are reluctant to try letting go of the struggle for emotional control. This is perfectly normal; for many people this is a new way of experiencing emotions. You've been struggling like this for a reason—because you've learned along the way that this is how you should respond to your emotions and thoughts, to keep them under control. If you do find it a bit scary to stop struggling, try it for just ten seconds the first time, no more. You can do it for ten seconds, and after that, you can go right back to struggling against your emotions if you want to. I promise you, trying this will not harm you, it's just a small internal shift. In fact, let's be honest, you're feeling everything you're struggling against anyway! Try it briefly the first time, just as a starting place, and see what happens.

The nature of emotions

Underlying this reluctance to let go of control, there is often a deep and unspoken fear of emotions. People sometimes worry that their emotions will be so strong and overpowering they will lose composure or be too overwhelmed to function.

Years ago, I had a client, let's call him Jim, who was upset about the recent death of his grandfather, with whom he was very close. Jim worried that if he let himself cry or slow down to feel his grief, he would fall apart. He thought he might stay in bed all day, unable to function, or sob uncontrollably and embarrassingly at work. He didn't know for sure—he had been avoiding the grief by distracting himself and burying his grief inside—but he feared he would.

I've seen similar fears of other emotions. Sometimes people worry that if they don't bottle up their anger, they will fly into a rage, or turn into a crazed maniac, causing damage or harm to people or objects. Other times, they suspect they might have a heart attack from extreme anxiety, or actually "die of embarrassment" that feels intolerable.

Within these fears lie some common misconceptions about emotions. Let's set the record straight. All emotions, even the ones we sometimes don't enjoy, or consider to be "weak" or harmful, are important and necessary, wired in for survival purposes. Every single emotion evolved over time to help our species, usually by helping us to protect ourselves from danger, bond with other humans, or fit into protective social groups. For instance, guilt and embarrassment, often looked on as problematic negative emotions, help us behave in morally and socially acceptable ways with others. And, despite popular misconception, emotions aren't the enemy of rational thought. In fact, they help us pay attention, process information, and make good decisions (Brackett 2019). Emotions, while sometimes uncomfortable, are not dangerous. If we behave in an unsafe way in response to them, I suppose that could be dangerous, but the emotions themselves are harmless. Emotions are just your body's way of responding to your experiences.

In certain contexts, we even purposely seek out the very same emotions we might typically avoid. I cried the first five times I heard the sad and touching Adele song "Easy on Me," which Adele wrote as a message to her child about her divorce. Rather than avoiding that song that made me feel sad, I played it on repeat (to the dismay of the other members of my family, who don't love the song the way I do). And I'm not the only one—Adele's heartbreaker of a song was one of her biggest hits, with nine weeks as a number one song. Similarly, we buy expensive tickets to amusement parks so we can ride scary roller coasters. We return again and again to news sources that fuel our righteous anger.

Like ocean waves, our emotions naturally fluctuate, rising and fading in intensity all the time. A panic attack, which can feel quite scary, will naturally fade on its own. Acute anger will eventually subside in intensity. An urge will pass. If you observe your emotions closely, you will notice that they are ever-changing, and in fact it's nearly impossible to keep feeling any particular emotion non-stop for longer than a few minutes. If you don't believe me, try it. See if you can hold on to an emotion, any emotion, continuously for an hour. You'll see that it's difficult.

Our emotions don't have to drive our actions. If we act with intention, at times we might *choose* to act according to our emotions, when it's helpful to do so. But we don't *have* to. Our emotions don't control our behavior, we experience our emotions and can choose how to respond to them. (Stay tuned for more on responding wisely and effectively to your emotions in Chapter 7.)

We can't discover what our emotions will really be like, or how long they will last, until we allow ourselves to feel them, fully and openly. I talked to Jim, who was afraid to feel grief about his grandfather, about the nature of emotions, and encouraged him to try an experiment to see if his fears were true. They weren't. He let himself feel sad and tried opening up to his grief instead of suppressing it. He continued to live his life, function, and do his work without sobbing uncontrollably all day. Allowing himself to feel his feelings helped him to move through grief. Sure enough, his sadness came and went over the course of time, in waves.

Don't fight your feelings, feel them

When I was first learning about ACT, I started to notice something in my own life. Each weekday morning, I felt stressed as I rushed to get to work. I would dread the busy, non-stop day ahead. My dread would hit its peak as I walked from the parking garage at work, down a long basement corridor, and then up three dark, dingy flights of stairs to my office. This five-minute walk was often the low point of my workday, my anticipation of the day ahead far worse than the work itself. I started a practice I had just learned about, as I rushed up the stairs each morning. I would use that moment to tune in to my emotions and let myself feel, fully and openly, whatever emotions were there. I would usually notice a sense of urgency to get to work, mild anxiety about the day ahead, and irritation with the slight hassle of lugging my work bag, lunch, and full water bottle up the dingy stairs.

Did this small acceptance practice make my emotions go away? Absolutely not. But something did shift inside me each time, by simply allowing myself to tune in to my inner experience and feel my feelings, instead of trying to push them away.

Acceptance and burnout

The concept of acceptance is not new. It's everywhere from Eastern religious traditions, to Alcoholics Anonymous, to models of the stages of grief. Recent research supports acceptance as a more helpful and effective way to respond to emotions than trying to control or change them. In one study (Ford *et al.* 2018) involving a combination of lab experiments, journal descriptions, and survey data, for example, the participants who were more accepting of their "negative" emotions, rather than judging them negatively, handled daily stress better, and had a higher level of psychological health six months later.

This is the case with burnout—when we allow ourselves to feel the emotions underlying burnout, instead of trying to reduce those emotions, we can exit the burnout cycle and transform our experience into one of less long-term suffering. The feeling of being stressed, as we have seen in previous chapters, is a normal human reaction that helps us respond to environmental demands. Stress is not inherently bad, and even has some upsides—we need some stress to keep us motivated and productive! But a lot depends on the stance we take toward it. In her book *The Upside of Stress: Why Stress Is Good for You, and How to Get Good at It*, Kelly McGonigal (2015) writes that compared to people with a "helpful mindset" toward stress, people who view stress as harmful tend to distract, focus on reducing the feeling of stress, and try to escape or withdraw their energy and attention from the problem. When you try to avoid stress, paradoxically, "you end up creating more sources of stress while depleting the resources that should be supporting you" (McGonigal 2015, p.84). In other words, when you stress about stress, you feel more stressed! If you don't view stress as harmful, but rather accept stressful events as part of life, you can find ways to deal with the situation and rise up to life's challenges.

Any of the burnout cycle types from Chapter 5 will involve some version of emotional discomfort, as you move toward acceptance. For example, perfectionist types might have to confront that unsettling feeling of uncertainty that mistakes may have been made. Avoiders might need to face whatever discomfort they are distracting themselves from. Busy bees might need to sit with boredom or stillness. Wholeheartedly opening up to our underlying emotional discomfort, whatever that discomfort may be, helps us to break the burnout cycle and offers a new path forward.

How to fully experience your experiences

Sometimes when I work with new therapy clients, they have struggled for years to suppress and avoid their emotions, thoughts, and other internal experiences. When they come to me, they are usually still trying to do this, but it's not working. With clients like that, I consider my work to be helping them reconnect with their inner experience in new, more effective ways. Gradually, I help them to notice, label, observe, and connect with their internal experience.

Earlier in the chapter you tried letting go of the struggle to control or eliminate thoughts, emotions, or sensations for a moment. Now you can go a step further, by taking a stance of openness and acceptance. Doing so will allow you to re-engage and reconnect wholeheartedly to all the emotions that come along with life's challenges.

PRACTICING OPENNESS AND ACCEPTANCE OF YOUR INNER EXPERIENCES

Here are the steps you can take:

1. Look for emotional discomfort. Be attuned to your emotional experience by focusing your attention inward. When you discover discomfort, notice it and pay attention to what it feels like.

2. Label and describe your emotions. See if you can put words to your experience.

3. Tune in to sensations in your body that are tied to your emotions. Where in your body do you feel them? Outline them. Do they have a shape? A heaviness or lightness? Do they move? Do they feel warm or cold?

4. Be aware of your thoughts. Notice the quality of your mind in this moment. Let your mind roam free, simply allowing it to do its thing effortlessly, without trying to control your thoughts.

5. Be curious. As if you are watching an animal in the wild through binoculars, see what you can observe and notice about your emotions and thoughts.

6. Try loosening up, instead of fighting against discomfort, and see what happens.

When you open up to your inner experience, a little shift will likely happen. Sometimes doing so gives you space between yourself and your emotions, making them less powerful and overwhelming. But not always. And there's a paradox; the minute you aim for this to happen, you are no longer truly accepting, but rather are using this strategy to try to control your experience.

Loosen up (emotionally)

As a Colorado mountain girl, I, like many in my home state, love to ski. I've been skiing a long time, but I'm not a great skier who can gracefully speed down the hardest runs like the athletes in the Winter Olympics. I wish! I've noticed that when I ski on steep mogul runs that are too hard for me (like the backcountry run with the large "Caution: Expert Skiers Only" warning sign my husband tricked me into taking a few years ago—don't get me started on that topic!), I immediately tighten up out of fear. I get tense, clenching my fists around my poles, and try to muscle my way stiffly around the bumps and down the slope. And, of course, my skiing ability immediately gets significantly worse. I lose balance and flexibility, so that every turn I take, even a fairly easy one, feels like a huge effort. In videos of myself skiing (yes, I do have one of that fateful backcountry run, in which I am mostly seen yelling at my husband as I inch down the slope), I can see how stiff and tense my body looks.

Sometimes, when the emotional bumps of life occur, we feel we must endure our emotions stoically, with gritted teeth. Approaching them in this way has a tight, "muscle through" quality, much like how I tense up while skiing down a difficult run. Sometimes, when people are experimenting with openness and acceptance, it might feel this way at first—like something you must brace yourself for. True openness is more like skiing in a loose posture, like the flexible Olympic mogul skier who looks balanced and relaxed as she bounces down the bumps. It involves being gentle and open, rather than harsh and tense, with your emotional experience.

When I get close to the bottom of a difficult ski run like that, and the end is in sight, I loosen up, even if the terrain is still steep and bumpy. As soon as I do, my skiing is back to normal again. If you catch yourself tensing up as you practice openness to your emotions, think of me struggling down the hill, body stiff and fingers clutched tightly around my poles. Try loosening up with your emotions instead, like an Olympic skier bouncing flexibly over the bumps of life.

What acceptance is and isn't

Sometimes the idea of acceptance gets a bad rap. Honestly, I'm a little reluctant to use the "A word" with my clients and right here in this book. People sometimes have negative associations with the word acceptance, assuming it means either giving up, tolerating bad circumstances, or telling yourself things are fine when they're not. Let's clear up a few misconceptions about acceptance.

On acceptance, control, and change

When I write about acceptance, as it relates to burnout, I am referring specifically to acceptance of that which we cannot control anyway— including our thoughts and feelings. There are plenty of things in life we *can* control, but we are wasting our energy when we try to control the uncontrollable.

Accepting your emotions absolutely does not mean you don't make changes in your life. To be very clear about this, I do not think you should accept every situation passively without changing anything. Sometimes you need to speak up, make a change in your life or in the world, or stand up against the status quo. The third section of this book is entirely focused on making changes, big or small. Change is especially important if a situation isn't working well for us, and in situations where we do have some agency for control.

Indeed, acceptance and openness toward our emotions can *help* us change what needs to be changed, in our lives and in the world. Accepting discomfort can foster change by helping us face our problems head on. For instance, leaving an abusive partner requires a great deal of courage, as it can be scary (and potentially dangerous) to do so. Those who aren't willing to experience that fear will never leave.

Openly allowing ourselves to feel the discomfort and hold the uncertainty of our current existence gives us the capacity to navigate the challenges of our stressful lives effectively. The more you can allow yourself to feel what you feel, the more you will be able to make the changes that will be helpful to you.

What acceptance isn't
Acceptance is not the same as tolerating, resignation, or giving up. Rather, acceptance is allowing what's already there anyway, to be there. You can still be unhappy about a circumstance, even vocalize your unhappiness if you want to. Your dissatisfaction is, in fact, another experience that can be accepted.

Being willing to feel your feelings also doesn't mean you have to *like* them or *want* to feel them. Given the choice, most people would rather feel happy and peaceful most of the time, not stressed, anxious, exhausted, and so on. Acceptance means you make room for all emotions, but it doesn't mean you will necessarily enjoy feeling them.

Acceptance also isn't wallowing or indulging in your emotions. It doesn't mean your emotions control your life. You don't have to always "wear your heart on your sleeve" and put your emotions on public display (although you might be inclined to share them sometimes, and that can be beneficial).

Finally, acceptance is not a "one and done" situation, but rather a life-long process. You will always slip back into a struggle against your emotions. I do this work for a living, and still get caught in an internal struggle, pretty much daily. When I do, I try to catch myself and let go, again. The more you practice this, ideally the more quickly you will notice the next time.

What acceptance is
Acceptance is a skill you can practice and get better at. Acceptance can start with small steps you can take outside your emotional comfort zone. Once you learn and practice it, it's always available to you when you need it. That doesn't mean you'll always use it—you will slip back into your old struggles, forget, or even choose not to practice acceptance sometimes. And if another approach works well for you, that's great too! Taking

an accepting and open stance is a choice, and you can always choose openness and acceptance whenever you want to—or not. At times, you might waver back and forth between choosing acceptance and choosing control. But even a moment of feeling your feelings, instead of struggling, is a moment of acceptance.

Sometimes you won't *want* to choose acceptance, but you will anyway, because you care enough about something that requires it. Often the most important things in life, the hard things we truly care about, can be the most uncomfortable. Stepping outside your comfort zone and toward pain is inherently courageous. While this can feel vulnerable, when you practice acceptance, your life will expand and have more vitality. You will feel all there is to feel. You will live wholeheartedly. And that, to return to the poetic words of David Whyte, just might be the antidote to exhaustion.

REFLECTION QUESTIONS

1. How do you know when you are struggling against your inner experience (emotions, thoughts, sensations)? What are the signs?

2. What messages did you learn growing up about emotions? Which emotions were acceptable or unacceptable to feel or express?

3. In what types of situations do you tend to struggle most with your emotions?

4. What's it like when you try letting go of the struggle, even for a moment? Is there a shift?

5. Have you ever worried that your emotions would be dangerous, too intense, or cause you to lose control of your behavior?

6. In your life, how might acceptance and openness to your experience be helpful?

7. What does acceptance mean to you? How might you practice acceptance in your own life, and how might that practice shift something related to burnout for you?

8. What values are tied to your discomfort? Are you willing to have painful emotions in order to do the things that matter most to you?

9. What would it be like to live wholeheartedly?

CHAPTER 7

Dealing with Feelings

Emotional Intelligence and Self-Compassion

A few years ago, back when one of my daughters was in preschool, she threw a tantrum after I said no to her, and she called me the "worst mom ever." There are plenty of ways I could use improvement as a parent, believe me, but I can assure you that I'm far from the worst mom ever! And there is one area I'm especially proud of as a parent: I'm proud of what I've taught my children about their emotions. I ask them questions about how they feel and help them notice and describe their emotions. I label my own emotions out loud for them—intentionally sharing with them when I feel embarrassed, anxious, sad, angry, or excited. I help them tune in to the emotions of others by asking them what they think people (in books, movies, and real life) might be feeling.

Why am I emphasizing emotions so much? I'm trying to help them learn a vocabulary for talking about their feelings, to role-model emotional awareness and openness, and to teach them to be kind and compassionate to themselves for having emotions, even the hard ones. These are the same emotional intelligence and self-compassion skills I teach my therapy clients! For children and adults alike, the better we can understand our emotions and respond to them effectively, the better we can handle life's inevitable stressors. You aren't either born with these skills or not; they can be learned and practiced over the course of your lifetime.

When my daughter called me the worst mom ever, I said to her, "Are you mad at me for saying no?" She paused and said yes. Her tantrum subsided and instead of insulting me again, she talked to me about how mad she was about not getting what she wanted.

In this chapter, we will learn about skills for cultivating emotional intelligence and self-compassion in the face of stress and burnout. What if you could learn how to navigate your stress- and burnout-related emotions more effectively? And what if, instead of being harsh toward yourself, you could be kinder and more compassionate?

Emotional intelligence and burnout

There are many definitions of emotional intelligence out there. I think of it simply as the ability to recognize and understand emotions (your own and the emotions of others) and respond to them effectively. Or as Kristin Neff states, it's "being aware of your feelings without being hijacked by them, so that you can make wise choices" (Neff 2011, p.122).

High emotional intelligence is associated with all kinds of good stuff, such as positive social and academic outcomes in children, high-quality personal and professional relationships, work success, and higher psychological wellbeing and life satisfaction (Mayer, Roberts, and Barsade 2008). As Marc Brackett, the founding director of the Yale Center for Emotional Intelligence and author of the book *Permission to Feel*, writes, "if we can learn to identify, express, and harness our feelings, even the most challenging ones, we can use those emotions to help us create positive, satisfying lives" (Brackett 2019, p.11).

You might be wondering how this is relevant to burnout. Well, lo and behold, high emotional intelligence can help protect us against burnout! In research studies from around the world, with everyone from Greek lawyers (Platsidou and Salman 2012), to Iranian medical students (Shariatpanahi *et al.* 2022), to teachers in Hong Kong (Chan 2006), higher emotional intelligence is associated with lower burnout. This makes sense as emotional intelligence skills can be helpful for managing stress (Wiens 2017). We can use our awareness of emotions to notice that we are starting to struggle, and take active steps to deal with stress effectively.

Emotional intelligence at work

Back in Chapter 4, we learned about the myth that emotions don't belong in the workplace. As workplace culture expert Karla McLaren writes in *The Power of Emotions at Work: Accessing the Vital Intelligence in Your Workplace*, "we kicked out emotions out of the workplace, and in doing so, we created an inhumane and emotionally unlivable environment that doesn't truly work for anyone" (McLaren 2021, p.2).

Healthy workplace environments do not perpetuate the stance that emotions don't belong at work. We tend to do much better in environments that recognize that employees are human, support their emotional wellbeing, and encourage and foster emotionally intelligent behavior. McLaren writes that it's less useful to suppress, distract, or meditate our way out of emotions, and far more useful to "listen to emotions, respect them, work directly with them, and access their irreplaceable information so that we can build healthy structures that work—whether we're working from home, in a business with three workers, or in an organization with thousands of workers" (McLaren 2021, p.14).

Emotionally sustainable workplace environments often have emotionally intelligent leaders who are attuned to this. Marc Brackett, describing his own role as the director of a large center, writes:

> Do you know the one thing that keeps me up at night? How my employees feel. That should haunt the sleep of every CEO, supervisor, manager, and boss in the world. It's the prime determinant of virtually everything that will happen in an organization—good and bad. If we're an emotionally intelligent workplace, most challenges (though not all) are manageable; if we're not, everything is a struggle. (Brackett 2019, p.229)

Workers and leaders can learn to use emotions to be *more* effective at work, inform ourselves about what needs to change, and possibly even improve workplace culture for everyone. Most of us have not received professional training in how to do this; but emotional intelligence skills can be learned.

Emotional intelligence skills

I hope by now I've "sold" you on why emotional intelligence skills are helpful in addressing burnout. I've stated that emotional intelligence skills can be learned and practiced. But how can we do this? Here are some skills you can practice to increase your emotional intelligence.

Describe your emotions

Emotional intelligence begins with awareness. This can mean noticing our emotions, labeling and describing them, and understanding them. I often find that people aren't used to putting words to their emotional experience. Emotions can feel fuzzy, vague, overwhelming, and hard to describe. Sometimes I'll ask, "How do you feel right now?" and the response that comes back is not an emotion, but rather more thoughts and opinions.

If you struggle with finding words that capture your emotions, I highly recommend going online and finding a list or chart of emotion words. There are plenty of them out there. Some have just a few primary emotion words. Others, like most emotion wheels, have dozens of complex and nuanced emotions. I'd recommend starting with a basic one, and for next-level emotional intelligence, try a more complex one. With the tool you like best, practice finding words that best describe how you feel in moments throughout your day.

Tap in to the wisdom of emotions

Our emotions, including sadness, fear, anger, and even emotional exhaustion, can be an important source of information and can teach us something about ourselves. While emotions may seem to occur quickly and out of the blue (and sometimes maybe they do!), they are usually in response to experiences we are having, our history, and our environment. They can point toward aspects of our experience we would otherwise miss. We can gain insight and wisdom by paying attention to our emotions in a particular way.

BE CURIOUS ABOUT YOUR EMOTIONS

To practice this, try approaching your emotions with curiosity. Tune in to them and see what you learn. Ask yourself some questions:

- What is the strongest emotion I feel right now? What label would I give to my emotion?
- Why am I feeling this emotion? Is it telling me anything important? Does my emotion have a helpful function, like trying to protect me or help me respond to a situation?
- Is this emotion in response to something that's happening in my life or inside me? Does this emotion tell me that something is wrong about this situation?
- Can it give me information about what I need, or what would help?
- What do my emotions tell me about what I care about?

When it comes to burnout, exhaustion might be telling us that we need to rest, or that we don't have enough support and resources to manage the responsibilities on our plates. Or it could mean that things are off balance in our lives. Philosopher Valerie Tiberius writes:

Burnout is another way that experience tells us something is amiss in our web of values. Feeling burned out is often evidence that we are putting too much of our energy into one goal—typically work, childcare, or eldercare—and ignoring everything else. (Tiberius 2023, p.41)

If this is the case, burnout might be a reminder to pace ourselves and think about how we are using our time and energy.

Of course, there's not just one emotion underlying burnout. Each emotion we feel is unique, and there's an opportunity to learn something from all of them.

LEARNING FROM DIFFERENT TYPES OF EMOTIONS

Here are some examples of specific questions to consider, depending on the family of emotions you are feeling:

- **Anger or irritation:** Is there something unfair or unjust happening in this situation? Is one of my needs unmet, or has a boundary been violated? Am I getting rigid or righteous about the way I think things "should" be?
- **Envy or jealousy:** Is someone else doing something I would love to do myself? Am I feeling insecure or threatened in a relationship? What do envy and jealousy tell me about what's important to me?
- **Guilt, regret, embarrassment, shame, or disgust:** Was there a moral violation? Did I do something against my values? Did I do something against social expectations or cultural norms, and if so, was there an intentional reason for doing so?
- **Anxiety, stress, pressure, or overwhelm:** Do I have too much on my plate? Do I have all the resources I need? Am I concerned about my performance because this matters to me? Is my anxiety going to help me stay reasonably safe, or is it misleading me?
- **Sadness:** What have I lost? What's not working for me? What do I need to let go of? What does sadness tell me about what I care about? Do I need comfort or support right now?
- **Longing:** What is missing from my life?
- **Joy, excitement, interest:** What about this is sparking vitality and enjoyment for me?

There are many other emotions, of course, and these are broad categories. Regardless of which emotions you are experiencing, try checking them out and see what you learn.

Respond effectively to emotions

The ability to respond effectively to your emotions is an important aspect of emotional intelligence. No matter what you're feeling inside, you can respond to your emotions with intention. You can use emotions as a source of information and respond to them according to your values. Sometimes this means letting an emotion guide your behavior. Other times, when emotions guide you in a less helpful direction, it means overriding them and doing the opposite of what your emotions compel you to do. Either way, it's all about wisely choosing an effective response in that situation.

As an example of this, I often work with burned-out clients who are experiencing extreme irritability and frustration. These emotions are in the anger family, which range all the way from mild annoyance to full-blown rage. The feeling of anger itself is not necessarily a problem. It's an important emotion, the "fight" part of our fight-or-flight system, wired in to help us defend ourselves when we are threatened. However, it's all too easy to react impulsively in problematic ways that damage relationships when we are angry. Yelling, snapping, and stewing away inside are some examples of responses that are not usually effective.

Instead, we can pause, notice our irritation, and use our values as a guide for what action to take. Sometimes that might mean speaking up against injustice or setting a boundary (see Chapter 15 for more on boundary-setting). Other times, it means choosing not to act out of anger, but rather to let it go, or intentionally act with kindness and respect. It can be difficult to respond effectively when our anger is "hot," at a temperature of 95 degrees out of 100 on the anger scale. At that point, the emotion feels so powerful, there's a tendency to react impulsively. While this quick response may keep us alive in dangerous situations, it can be problematic in many others, like when we impulsively yell, break something, or say something we don't mean, before thinking twice about it. But if you can learn to catch anger as it is rising, and pause before acting, you can be more effective.

No one on planet earth is going to respond "perfectly" to their emotions every time. The good news is that you don't need to! Even your mistakes can be a source of information about what to do differently next time.

Pause to let your values be your guide
What does it mean to call a response "effective," you may wonder (with good reason!). It's not the case that there is always one perfect or best way to respond to an emotionally charged situation. To know what to do, you can look toward your values. We'll explore your values in more depth in Chapter 10. In the meantime, ask yourself:

- How can I respond in a way that I will feel proud of later?
- What words would I use to describe my "best self" in emotionally charged situations?
- Who do I admire, in terms of their emotional intelligence? How would they handle this situation?

Responding intentionally and according to our values can be difficult in the heat of the moment when we tend to react quickly. There is a simple framework I like to use to slow down and be less reactive, called "Pause, Notice, Choose."

PAUSE, NOTICE, CHOOSE
This practice is easily embedded in the lives of busy people (like you!) because it's an internal shift you can use in any situation—you don't need to stop doing important tasks, take up much extra time, or go to a special place. It does take practice, though, to get better at it.

Here's what you do. In a moment when you feel an emotion arise:

1. **Pause:** When you notice an emotional shift, pause and create a little space for yourself before reacting. Step back from your emotions and take a breath.
2. **Notice:** Check in with your experience and ask yourself some questions. What are you reacting to? What sensations do you notice in your body? What thoughts are you having? What emotions are you feeling? Are your emotions telling you anything important, or not?
3. **Choose:** What would your "best self" do in this moment? Now, choose to respond by acting as your best self would.

Opposite action

In an episode of the 90s TV show *Seinfeld*, Jerry Seinfeld's friend George Costanza tries to turn his life around by doing the opposite of what he would normally do. He realizes that all his natural instincts have been wrong, and that's why nothing has worked out for him. He changes his lunch order from his usual tuna on toast with coffee to the complete opposite: chicken salad, on untoasted rye, with tea. Instead of being too intimidated to talk to a beautiful woman, he walks right up to her and boldly tells her he's unemployed and lives with his parents.

This is similar to a concept from dialectical behavior therapy (Linehan 2015) called opposite action. Sometimes, our immediate, instinctual response to an emotion is ineffective. Our reactions are often automatic, driven by a desire for short-term relief, but not so helpful in the long term. For instance:

- *Sadness* might compel us to stay isolated in bed when we would be better off being active and engaged.
- *Fear* can drive avoidance, which is life-limiting and tends to lead to more fear.

- *Shame* drives us to hide when we could benefit from support.
- *Self-doubt* holds us back from taking a courageous step, even if it's something we'd like to do.
- *Anger* can lead us to react impulsively and aggressively, when a more measured approach would be better.

When our emotions are guiding us in less effective directions, instead of following them in the wrong direction, we can follow George Costanza's lead and choose to do the opposite. Sometimes this isn't easy, as it usually requires pausing and acting in a way that is less pleasant temporarily given your current emotional state. But your emotions aren't in charge of your behavior—you are! Just as you can get off the couch and go somewhere when you'd rather stay home, or do something that scares you, you can choose to respond more effectively to your emotions than your first instinct might suggest.

To share or not to share?
Sometimes I'll ask my clients with burnout, "Have you told anyone how you feel about this?" only to discover that the answer is no. The difficult or painful emotions we carry with us can feel like a heavy load, especially if they are unexpressed and we are alone with them.

People with high emotional intelligence are usually good at appropriately expressing their emotions to others. They don't typically bottle them up and repress them. They also don't typically run around *overly* expressing their emotions, by screaming irately in public or loudly sobbing to draw attention to themselves. Instead, they have a sense of when it feels safe and appropriate to share their emotions. They can talk openly about how they feel, sharing even vulnerable emotions. They can sit with the discomfort of others and validate their emotions instead of dismissing them.

Depending on the situation, consider whether expressing your feelings would be helpful. Of course, if you're in an environment where that wouldn't be appropriate, or if a particular person would not be responsive and supportive of you, it might not be a good idea. But sometimes it can help tremendously to name your feelings and express them out loud to someone. If you aren't used to doing this, for instance if a stoic disposition is prized in your community, it can feel risky and scary. But what you might find is that once you share your feelings, others will respond in kind. And you might discover that you aren't the only one feeling the way you do!

From self-harshness to self-compassion

Here is something else that often strikes me as a therapist: I sit in my office and meet with clients with burnout who are incredibly smart, kind, hard-working people, who manage a great deal of responsibility and do their best to hold it all together. By any measure you use, they are successful and accomplished in many domains of life. They look as if they are thriving on the surface.

But as I talk with them, they reveal harsh self-criticism. They beat themselves up for not doing enough and they fixate on minor mistakes. They feel guilty and "not good enough," even if they are accomplishing a lot, running themselves ragged with work and other responsibilities. They have extremely high expectations of themselves, so that no matter how much they achieve, it never feels like enough. And they talk to themselves internally in a way they would never talk to a co-worker or close friend who was going through a similar hard time.

"Becky" is a tenure-track biology professor with a young child. Anyone looking at her life would agree that she's a high-functioning person, managing to have both a successful career and a satisfying home life. But what they can't see on the surface is that Becky is miserable. No matter how hard she works, publishing papers in her field, teaching classes, applying for grants, and mentoring graduate students, it never feels like enough. She compares herself both to younger colleagues, with seemingly boundless time and energy for work, and tenured professors in her department who are world famous in their research areas. And because her job is so demanding, she's unable to spend as much time with her child as some of the other parents. Her kindergarten-aged son is in after-school care most days, and only rarely is she able to pick him up from school or attend school events. Although she spends as much time as she can with her family, it never feels as if she's doing enough. Her son is behind most of his peers in school, and Becky blames herself for this. She wonders if she had worked less when he was in preschool, she could have helped him learn the basics. Sometimes she considers leaving the tenure track for a less demanding job, but when she thinks of that option, only one word comes to mind: "Failure."

Becky's story is one of self-harshness in all domains. Many of us will see ourselves in this story. The key to transforming self-harshness into a kinder and gentler stance is self-compassion.

What is self-compassion?

Like the "A word" (acceptance), sometimes people are a little resistant to the idea of the "C word" (compassion). They might have some misconceptions about what that means, thinking of self-compassion as a touchy-feely word that means weakness, self-pity, or self-indulgence. In reality, compassion is none of these. It has been defined simply as "that feeling in the heart that wants to help others and ourselves be free of suffering" (Goldstein 2013, pp.296–297). Self-compassion means non-judgmentally observing your pain, mistakes, and failure, understanding that these are an inherent part of being human, and practicing self-kindness.

Recent research supports the importance of self-compassion in protecting us against stress and burnout. In several research studies with mental health workers (Atkinson *et al.* 2017), nurses (Duarte, Pinto-Gouveia, and Cruz 2016; Durkin *et al.* 2016), midwives (Beaumont *et al.* 2016), pediatric medical residents (Kemper *et al.* 2019; Olson, Kemper, and Mahan 2015), healthcare professionals in general (Hashem and Zeinoun 2020), and clergy (Barnard and Curry 2012), higher self-compassion was associated with resilience against burnout. In other words, a lack of self-compassion seems to contribute to burnout, and higher self-compassion can protect against it.

Self-compassion can help us remain calmer in the face of stress. Kristen Neff writes that "people with higher levels of self-compassion had more perspective on their problems and were less likely to feel isolated by them," and that "self-compassionate people are able to deal with the challenges life throws their way with greater emotional equanimity" (Neff 2011, p.123).

Being higher in self-compassion, as opposed to self-criticism, is associated with lower biological markers of stress (Rockliff *et al.* 2008), and with—guess what...drumroll please—higher emotional intelligence (Neff 2003)! As Neff writes:

> Self-compassion gives us the calm courage needed to face our unwanted emotions head-on... Given that all experiences eventually come to an end, if we can allow ourselves to remain present with our pain, it can go through its natural bell-curve cycle—arising, peaking, and fading away. (Neff 2011, p.124)

How to be kinder toward yourself

If Becky's story above sounds at all familiar to you because you too tend toward self-harshness, you might benefit from practicing self-compassion. You can take active steps toward being kinder toward yourself. In her book *Self Compassion: The Proven Power of Being Kind to Yourself*, Kristen Neff (2011, p.42) describes three core components of cultivating self-compassion:

1. *Self-kindness,* or being gentle and understanding with ourselves rather than harshly critical and judgmental.
2. *Common humanity,* or feeling connected to others, rather than alone with our suffering.
3. *Mindfulness,* or holding our experience in balanced awareness, rather than ignoring our pain or exaggerating it.

CULTIVATE SELF-COMPASSION

Here are some tips you can try:

- When you notice that you are being harsh or critical toward yourself, try being gentle instead. Talk to yourself

---

the way you would talk to a good friend or child who was struggling with a similar problem.

- Let go of perfectionistic standards and forgive your mistakes and shortcomings. You're only human, after all.
- Observe your pain, mistakes, and struggles non-judgmentally.
- Provide yourself with comfort, whatever that means to you, the way you would to someone else who was suffering. Remind yourself that life is full of difficult experiences, and ask how you might better care for yourself in the midst of difficulty.
- Try saying a self-compassionate mantra to yourself, like "This is a hard situation for me. I'm doing the best I can right now and that's enough."
- Give yourself a soothing moment by placing your hands on your chest (one on top of the other), closing your eyes, and taking a few slow, even breaths.
- Remember to go easy on yourself for struggling; it's okay not to be okay sometimes.
- See your struggles in the context of your history. Ask yourself the question, "Given what you know about your history, how does it make sense that you might feel/think/act in that way?" (Kolts 2016, p.37).
- Tap into common humanity. Remember that you are not alone. See the shared nature of your pain and be more compassionate toward yourself for feeling what you feel. Remind yourself that these feelings are part of being human.

REFLECTION QUESTIONS

1. What burnout-related emotions tend to trip you up?
2. What wisdom can you glean from your emotions?
3. What emotions tend to lead you to ineffective automatic reactions? How can you "do the opposite" in those situations?
4. Would it be helpful to share how you feel with someone?
5. Do you tend to be harsh and critical toward yourself? How might you be kinder toward yourself?
6. What self-compassion practices above might be helpful to you?

CHAPTER 8

A New Point of View
Perspective-Taking on Burnout-Related Thoughts

magine yourself on a day in the past when your burnout was severe—a day when you were extremely exhausted and disconnected from your work. If I could somehow sneak into your mind that day and eavesdrop on your thoughts, what would I hear?

I may not know the specifics of what you were thinking that day, but I'm going to take a wild guess that you weren't in a very positive headspace. If you tend to be a busy bee type, it might have been something about how many things you need to do, and how behind you are on everything. If you're a perfectionist type, it might have been how you're falling short of your own high standards. If you're a people-pleaser, it might have been about how you're letting someone down, or perhaps having resentful thoughts about people who keep taking up your time. If you're a cynic, it might have been about how terrible everything is, or how incompetent the people around you are.

One of the official criteria of burnout is "increased mental distance from one's job, or feelings of negativism or cynicism related to one's job" (World Health Organization 2019). When I talk to people about burnout, I usually find that they're stuck in unhelpful thinking patterns. They often worry about what might go wrong, compare themselves to others, focus on mistakes and criticisms, and ignore any strengths or positive feedback. They tend to be preoccupied by their thoughts—which certainly doesn't help when it comes to feeling engaged with work—and have underlying self-stories and narratives that are driving their behavior in unhelpful directions. Usually, they don't even realize this is what's happening! Instead, they assume their cynical, self-critical thoughts accurately reflect reality.

To some degree, this is the nature of the human mind; it's constantly chatting away, trying to think its way out of life's problems. The human mind is very good at this, and often it's quite helpful to us. But when this happens to an extreme it can exacerbate burnout.

It's possible to take a new point of view about unhelpful thinking patterns. Instead of getting stuck in unhelpful thinking or locked in a control battle to rid yourself of certain thoughts, you can take a step back and observe your thoughts from a new perspective. ACT offers a way of practicing this skill, called cognitive defusion. We can learn to see our thoughts for what they are—thoughts, not facts—and get a little distance from them. When we do this, our thoughts become less powerful, and have less impact on our emotions and our behavior.

This chapter will be an exploration of burnout-related thoughts and internal narratives. I'll help you have a new point of view about your thoughts and pay less attention to the ones that aren't helping you. First, let's start with a brief tour of the human mind.

The human mind—a thinking machine

If humans are good at anything as a species, it's thinking. We have these big frontal lobes of our brain, which allow us to think abstractly. Compared to other animals, we have a unique ability to form words and other symbolic representations of objects that aren't right in front of us. We are also quite good at making comparisons and judgments, which can be a helpful short-cut (Hayes *et al.* 2016).

This ability is one of our greatest blessings as a species. It can be extremely helpful to create words to convey information to others via language—speaking, reading, and writing. You're doing this right now, as you're reading the words I've written to convey information about burnout to you! We can use our minds to help us solve problems, evaluate the past, and plan for a future we've constructed in our minds. We can create, imagine, and make meaning out of the world.

Unfortunately, the ability to think abstractly is also our curse. We predict future catastrophes and worry excessively about things that may never actually happen, and which are statistically quite unlikely. We ruminate about our mistakes and problems, get down on ourselves, compare ourselves to other people, to expectations and ideals. We form judgments and evaluations—about ourselves, the world, other people— that can be inaccurate. And, worse, that can lead to problems like prejudicial treatment of others, or self-doubt that holds us back.

The problem occurs when we confuse these judgments and evaluations for facts. We start to take our thoughts as the literal truth, responding to mental constructs we create in our minds as if they really exist in the world. We live in our heads, losing sight of what's right in front of us.

We have a running inner monologue that plays constantly throughout the day as we go about our lives. Sometimes these thoughts are helpful to us, and sometimes not so much. Sometimes our mind is calm, but sometimes our thoughts ricochet around in our mind, like bumper cars ramming into each other at full speed.

And, like the fish that is unaware of the existence of water, we are so surrounded by our thoughts, constantly, that we don't even notice we are thinking most of the time. Being aware of our thoughts can be a big first step.

Burnout-related thoughts

When it comes to burnout, all kinds of unhelpful thoughts might arise, and the content of one person's thinking will be different from someone else's. As I've worked with clients over the years, I have noticed some common thinking patterns that come up again and again. See if any of the examples of burnout-related thoughts in this table seem familiar to you.

Table: Examples of burnout-related thoughts

Types of burnout-related thoughts	Examples
Self-pressure	"I have to work harder and achieve more." "I'm too busy to take a break. If I do, things will fall apart." "I can't say no. I'm indispensable." "I'm more valuable if I'm productive."
Self-criticism	"I'm not good at this." "I'm too lazy." "I'm an imposter, everyone can tell I don't belong here."
Catastrophizing	"I might get fired." "Something terrible might happen (to me, someone else, or the world)."
Worry	"I have so much to do tomorrow, how will I get it all done?" "Everything is going to be terrible." "Something bad is going to happen."
Blame (self or others)	"It's all my fault. I should be able to handle this." "I'm burned out because my coworkers don't pull their weight." "If they ran this place better, I wouldn't be so unhappy here."
Escape fantasies and unrealistic mental time travel	"If only I could quit my job or go on a long vacation." "I'll be less busy next week, then I'll relax." "I wish I could have a minor injury and relax in the hospital for a few days." "Maybe I should retire early and move to Sweden."
"Shoulds"	"I should be doing more." "My boss/co-workers/workplace should…" "My spouse should…"
Guilty thoughts	"A better parent would have…" "I messed up. I feel terrible about it." "I'm burdening my co-workers."
Comparisons (to others or to an ideal self)	"Other people have their life together better than I do." "I'm not as good as (so-and-so)." "I should be more productive."

Our mental filters: Self-stories and cultural narratives

If you look closely at your mind's running commentary, you'll start to notice some themes. Our minds love to tell us stories about ourselves and the world around us, to try to make sense of everything.

Our experience is filtered and limited through these narratives. When we get consumed by these stories, and take them too seriously, our point of view is limited and we are unable to see the whole picture. We can latch onto those labels and be confined by them. Two examples of this are self-stories—the narratives we have about ourselves—and internalized cultural narratives that have consistently been told by the world around us.

Self-stories

We all have self-related stories—the narratives, labels, and identities—that we hold about ourselves. These stories come from our personal history, rooted in a desire to understand where we fit into the world. It can feel comforting to have a story about ourselves, because that gives us a sense of coherence.

When people identify strongly with a work role, as people who experience burnout often do, they might hold a particular type of self-story. They might over-identify with that role, as if it consumes them. For instance, I am a psychologist. This is a fact about me, because I have a PhD in psychology and a psychologist license in the state of Colorado, which grants me that title. But what if I over-identify with "I am a psychologist," and that role becomes an overly important way of thinking about myself? My work role could cause me to lose sight of other parts of myself, or other important roles I hold. I might confine my behavior to match the way I think "a psychologist" should act, even if it isn't authentic to myself or consistent with my values. Or, if I retired early or lost my license, I might feel lost.

We might also strongly identify with labels about ourselves, like "I'm a hard worker," to the point where that narrow definition of ourselves takes over and confines us by limiting our behavior to whatever is consistent with that label. What if we desire time to rest for a while, to recharge and get some balance, but feel that we must stay true to that "hard worker" label? Or if we become a workaholic who feels guilty any time we aren't working hard?

Even seemingly positive self-stories, like "I am special," or "My work is important" can be confining. We might have trouble letting go of those narratives, getting consumed by our career instead of treating it as just one part of our lives.

Cultural narratives

Narratives that are predominant in the world around us have a way of working themselves into our consciousness. When you hear a message enough times, it can become internalized—a narrative that shapes and filters how you see the world. This can be so implicit and subtle that we often aren't aware of it. But these cultural narratives are there, and sometimes they can be problematic.

An example of a seemingly positive narrative that can be internalized, with unintentionally harmful consequences, occurs in healthcare. There are cultural narratives about physicians, nurses, and other healthcare professionals being superheroes. During the early phases of the Covid-19 pandemic we saw many public expressions of gratitude and support for these people doing essential life-saving and dangerous work, and depictions of healthcare professionals in superhero costumes in artwork. While these narratives were a touching and well-intentioned form of support and gratitude, they fed into the belief that medical providers should work tirelessly and be invincible; that they should be untouchable stoics, willing to wade into stressful and dangerous situations regardless of the personal risk and impact. Some people have spoken about the negative impact of the superhero narrative on their already stressful lives (Stokes-Parish *et al.* 2020; Yerramilli 2020).

There are many different types of cultural narratives out there that can seep in. Throughout this book, we've seen examples of some cultural narratives related to our emotions, such as "emotions don't belong in the workplace," and burnout-related cultural narratives about work and productivity. We may have been exposed to narratives about how busyness and achievements are good and worthy, and slacking off or being "lazy" is morally inferior. Or narratives about how we must hustle and grind, or must always sacrifice ourselves to give and please others.

Cognitive defusion

How can we get ourselves out of these types of unhelpful thinking patterns? Allow me to start by telling you what typically *doesn't* work—trying to control our thoughts, by emptying our minds of a particular thought, or trying to think more positively. Plenty of research has shown us that attempting to suppress our thoughts is an ineffective strategy (Wegner 1994). Have you tried this before? If not, take a moment to stop reading, and try a very brief exercise.

THOUGHT SUPPRESSION EXPERIMENT
Grab your phone, and time yourself for 30 seconds. You only have to do one thing: Do NOT think about hippopotamuses at all, not even a little bit, no matter what. Go!

How did that experiment go? Could you do it? For most people, it's harder than it sounds. By trying not to think about hippos, hippos pop to mind. But why? If you could control your thoughts, as we sometimes think we should, you would be able to do this easily.

The reason is that, much like in the burnout cycle we learned about in Chapter 4, attempts to control or suppress our thoughts often backfire, resulting in an argument in our minds. We get trapped in a struggle with our thoughts, feeling we must change them for things to be better. But we can't.

Not only that, we often make harsh self-judgments about our own inner experience—we might view certain thoughts as "bad." For instance, if someone is highly self-critical, they might think, "I'm incompetent." They might then evaluate that thought as "too negative" and think they must think positively in order to feel better about themselves and have more confidence. This locks them in to a struggle with their thoughts and, worse, they might believe they must wait to feel more confident before they can take a desired action.

A different approach, which has been found to be more effective, is called cognitive defusion (Hayes *et al.* 2016). In ACT, when we are "fused" with unhelpful thoughts, we are hooked into them, seeing them as the literal truth, and they take over our point of view. Defusion is when we step back from our thoughts and see them for what they are—words and symbolic constructions happening in our minds—and then choose to respond to them in a way that is more effective.

Seeing thoughts for what they are

A solid first step toward defusing from our thoughts is to be aware of our thoughts and understand what our minds are doing. Again, like fish in water, often we don't notice our thoughts or that we are thinking, and awareness can help. To play around with this idea, let's try another little exercise.

THOUGHTS ARE JUST THOUGHTS

Get out your journal or a piece of paper, and follow these steps:

1. Choose an unhelpful burnout-related thought you've struggled with. Pick a real "doozy" of a thought if you can—one that you really experience that feels upsetting to you, like a harsh self-criticism. (You can look at the table of burnout-related thoughts above if you need an example.)
2. In your journal or on a piece of paper, write down that thought, as a verbatim quote, exactly as your mind said it to you.
3. Sit back and look at that thought. How seriously have you been taking it?
4. Rewrite it as, "I'm having the thought that..."
5. Take another look at the thought. How is it different when it's phrased in this way?

The difference between facts and evaluations

Now you can zoom out and see them for what they really are: just thoughts! Thoughts are not the same as reality. And sometimes we might confuse judgments, opinions, and evaluations with facts. Our thoughts are not always the literal "truth" about the world, just constructions that occur in our minds, but sometimes we act as if they are the truth.

FACT OR EVALUATION?

Take another look at that "doozy" of an unhelpful thought from the previous exercise (or you can pick a different one if you'd like). What do you notice about this thought? Was your mind trying to help or protect you in some way? Is this thought an indisputable fact of the universe, or merely a subjective opinion or evaluation? Are you doing any judging or comparing (for example, comparing yourself to an unrealistic, "ideal" version of yourself or to other people)? Are you getting caught up in being right, "shoulds," all-or-nothing thinking, assuming the worst, or catastrophizing? Does that thought tell the whole story?

Observing thoughts with awareness

It can also help to observe thoughts by stepping back from them and watching them from a distance as they go by. Awareness of thinking reminds us that our thoughts are just one fleeting part of our experience. We forget this sometimes, especially when the inner monologue takes over! You know what this is like if you've ever been so preoccupied with your thoughts that you've been distracted—for instance, if you've read the same thing repeatedly because you are too lost in thought to focus.

OBSERVE YOUR THOUGHTS

To practice awareness, you can be more mindful of your thinking. You'll learn more about mindfulness and burnout in the next chapter. For now, give this a try:

- First, read through these directions so you know what to do.
- Set a timer on your phone for two minutes.
- Close your eyes, take a breath, and focus on your thoughts.
- For two minutes, pay attention to your mind. Observe it like an animal in the wild, to see what you can learn about it. Is it relatively quiet, or busy today? Is it distractable, or focused? What is it thinking about?
- Now, notice that you can get some distance from the content of your thoughts when you observe your mind in this way. Notice how this is different from how you typically experience thinking.
- When the two minutes are up, make a note of anything you noticed in your journal.

Don't let unhelpful thoughts run your life

Sometimes it feels as if our thoughts dictate our behavior, and we must follow along with what they tell us, whether we want to or not. For instance, if your mind says, "I have to finish this tonight," you stay up late. If your mind says, "I can do this later and check Instagram for a few minutes," you check Instagram. Or if your mind says, "I don't have time for a lunch break today," there you are, eating lunch in front of your computer, dropping crumbs on your keyboard.

The problem lies with giving our thoughts too much power over us. It is possible to evaluate whether a thought is helpful, in terms of responding in an effective and values-consistent way to situations. If it is, fine, go ahead and follow that thought. But if your thought is unhelpful to you, you can do the opposite (like "opposite action" in Chapter 7). I'm sure you have done this many times before. For example, you've probably gone to work even when your mind said, "I don't feel like it today," exercised when your mind said, "that sounds terrible, I'd rather sit on the couch," or done something hard and courageous even though you had self-doubt.

WHO IS IN CHARGE? YOU OR YOUR THOUGHTS?

To practice the skill of not letting unhelpful thoughts run your life, let's try another little exercise.

- In your journal or on a piece of paper, write down an unhelpful thought that interferes with something you want to do either more or less of. (Two of my own examples of this are "I'm too busy to go for a walk today," and "I have to squeeze in one more meeting on Friday, even if that means working later.") Write it down verbatim.
- How much power does that thought have over your behavior? How do you typically respond to that thought? How often do you let that thought dictate your behavior?
- Who's really in charge here—you, or that thought?
- How else might you respond to that thought? What would happen if you were to do the opposite? (I can choose to go out the door and go for a walk, even if I have the thought that I don't have time.)

Perspective-taking: A more expansive view of yourself

When our mental filters—those self-stories and internalized cultural messages through which we see the world—consume us, we can end up with a limited view of ourselves and the world around us. It's as if we're looking at the world through a dirty window that's partially blocked by a curtain, and we can only see an unclear and limited view. We all have self-stories, and they aren't always a problem. But at their extreme, they can make us ego-centric, filtering the world through a particular view of ourselves, and causing us to lose sight of the bigger picture, or other perspectives. They can limit how we view our experience.

It is possible to remove the filter—to take down the curtain and fling the window open—and see a broader perspective. You can do this by transcending those self-stories, stepping back from thoughts and narratives, and tapping into a larger sense of yourself. You are here now, experiencing this moment—able to observe the narratives and thoughts that arise, without getting consumed by them. Much like the weather passing through the sky, your thoughts come and go, and you can step back and observe them from a new point of view. You can see what it's like to remove the filter and contact your experience more directly.

There's more to you than your thoughts or the stories your mind creates about yourself and the world. If you can let go of ego and strong attachment to self-stories and identity labels, you can free yourself from getting tangled up in unhelpful thoughts, by zooming out and seeing them for what they are—something your mind is doing. You are the one experiencing your thoughts, but you are not defined by them. When you let go of focusing on your own performance and inner self-evaluation, you can have a more expansive view of yourself, and can more easily turn toward others. You can step outside yourself and be more effective and engaged with the world.

TRANSCEND SELF-STORIES

To go a bit deeper with this concept, try this exercise in your journal, or on a piece of paper, to help you transcend the self-stories and internalized cultural narratives that limit you.

- First, identify a self-story. Pick a label or narrative you ascribe to yourself, using some of the examples in this chapter if you get stuck. You can also try filling out these sentences:

    "I am a (enter a role)."

    "I'm the kind of person who..."

    "I am (enter a label or adjective about yourself)."

    "Something special about me is that I..."

    "A problem with me is that I..."

- Write the story or narrative down, as a verbatim sentence you would say to yourself.

- Now, ask yourself a few questions. Are you always? Do does this story completely define you? Is there more to you? Are there aspects of yourself that don't fit with this story?

By taking a different perspective on unhelpful thoughts and self-narratives that arise during periods of burnout, you can see your burnout experience in a new way. Imagine how free you would be if you were able to take a step back from those self-narratives and zoom out to a broader, more flexible point of view about yourself. If a particular identity was somehow taken away from you, you would still be you. You are a complex person; one identity or label does not define you. To paraphrase the poet Walt Whitman, you contain multitudes.

REFLECTION QUESTIONS

1. Do you have a busy mind? Do you tend to get preoccupied by thoughts?
2. What are some types of unhelpful thoughts you tend to have related to burnout?
3. How might these thoughts contribute to your experience of burnout?
4. What self-stories, labels, and identities do you tend to latch onto about yourself? How do these stories filter your experience of the world?
5. What cultural narratives have you been exposed to and/or internalized related to work and burnout?
6. What is it like to step back and observe your thoughts?
7. Are your thoughts influencing your behaviors in ways that are helpful? How about in ways that are not-so-helpful?
8. What was it like to zoom out and take a new perspective on your self-stories? How might a perspective shift toward a more expansive view of yourself free you up and be less limiting?

CHAPTER 9

Mindfulness for Burnout

It's Complicated

You're likely familiar with the term "mindfulness": the experience and practice of awareness of the present moment. I have a complicated relationship with mindfulness. For one thing, I'm naturally a rather "un-mindful" person. I live up in my head, overthinking everything, so busy with my thoughts that I can be self-focused and oblivious to the world around me. I have trouble resting and sitting still. I'm someone who has been known to bring my computer and a huge pile of books on a "relaxing" vacation and start getting antsy for lunch five minutes after I arrive at a beach or a rustic mountain cabin. At home, I get consumed by tasks, caught up in the swirling stress of my busy life, hurrying from one thing to the next. I get impatient. I miss my exit on the highway and can't remember if I've already shampooed in the shower. In other words, I struggle.

Sometimes I roll my eyes at how mindfulness is used within Western wellness culture these days. I can see a lot of problems with the way it's often presented as a quick-fix wellness intervention, more focused on self-improvement and attaining a blissful feeling state than on doing good in the external world. I'm drawn to books and articles (e.g. Kelly 2022; Purser 2019; Raphael 2022) that offer a cultural criticism of the wellness industry and the capitalistic use of mindfulness. I end up being a voice of skepticism, a little too quick to point out why individualistic mindfulness practices, on their own, won't provide a lasting solution to the world's major problems (like burnout).

And yet...I do practice mindfulness sometimes—irregularly and imperfectly—and it has helped me tremendously. I've experienced how mindfulness practices, both formal (sitting down, closing my eyes, and meditating for a period of time) and informal (checking in with myself periodically as I go about my day), can be beneficial. When I'm practicing mindfulness, I'm less distracted and better able to focus. It helps me slow down and be more present. I'm more aware of my thoughts and emotions, less reactive, and able to handle difficult moments more effectively. I am more accepting of everything I experience; instead of trying to run away or avoid discomfort, I can zoom out and get "out of the weeds" of stressors and grievances. It seeps into my daily life, allowing me to step back, slow down, observe, and be more present in my life. Perhaps more importantly, it gives me the capacity to face the problems of the world directly, even though it can be discouraging and uncomfortable to do so.

In this chapter, we will explore mindfulness. I will not present mindfulness as wellness practices that are meant to be a "quick-fix" solution to burnout. Nor will I encourage its use as a tool to tolerate bad circumstances. Rather, mindfulness will be presented as a potentially helpful practice in support of lasting social change, that can promote meaningful engagement and give us greater capacity to recharge from burnout. With mindfulness, we can be kinder to ourselves and others, and transcend our struggles to connect with greater humanity—the shared human experiences that unite us all.

For some readers who are stressed to the max right now, already too busy with the many pressures of life, practicing mindfulness might sound slow and difficult and unappealing. I get that. Some of you might be skeptics (like I can be sometimes). That's okay. For others, this may be old news, as you've already discovered and practiced mindfulness, perhaps much more than I have. Some of you may wonder why your mindfulness practice hasn't already solved your burnout problem. Wherever you're coming from, I encourage you to stay with me and play around with the relationship between mindfulness and burnout in your life, and see what happens.

Mindfulness 101

In Chapter 8, we learned about some of the many gifts of the ceaselessly thinking human mind, and some of the downsides. One major downside of the human mind is that its incessant thinking can cause us to lose contact with what's happening here and now. We end up living our lives up in our heads, acting on autopilot, and missing out on important experiences as they happen.

Mindful awareness is one of the core processes of ACT. Mindfulness is about bringing our attention fully to the present moment. Various forms of mindfulness meditation have been practiced for thousands of years. Originally associated with Eastern religious and spiritual practices, it has made its way west in recent decades. Many experts have written extensively on the complex intricacies of mindfulness. But for those who are new to the concept, here's what you need to know for our purposes.

Mindfulness includes paying attention in a certain way, by tuning in to what's happening now and taking a non-judgmental stance toward all aspects of our experience—the comfortable and uneasy or painful experiences alike. At its origins, mindfulness is rooted in the belief that struggling against the inherent pain of living is the true source of suffering. Sound familiar? (See Chapter 6 on acceptance.)

When we are mindful of the present moment, we can observe our thoughts, emotions, and bodily sensations from a new perspective. We can respond more flexibly to life's ups and downs, and be more responsive to events as they unfold. We don't have to run away from our experience or be hard on ourselves for feeling what we feel. Instead of reacting on autopilot, we can fully experience our lives, and make more deliberate and intentional choices that serve us well.

For myself, the naturally "un-mindful" one, I've seen this shift in my own life (sometimes—as I said before, I'm quite imperfect at this). As just one of about a million personal examples, I have seen a shift in my work as a podcaster. Even though I've been doing podcast interviews and professional speaking engagements for years, I feel nervous every time. Historically, I can get preoccupied with my own performance, attending more to what my inner running commentary is saying about my performance (read: it's usually not positive!) than about what we're talking about or what my podcast guest is saying. No surprise, that's not helpful. When I do that, I tune out what my guest is saying, and clutch on too tightly to my pre-written questions. When I listen to myself later, I sound stilted and overly formulaic. When I am more mindful, I am in the moment, my full attention focused on listening, rather than anticipating what I will say next or preoccupied by my inner monologue. I occasionally notice my feelings of nervousness and my self-critical thoughts and can shift my full attention back to the conversation at hand. I can have a real, genuine connection with my interview guest. The pressure is still there, but I don't focus on getting rid of it. I can just be fully in the moment. And, I might add, that moment while recording a podcast episode is full of vitality for me; I wouldn't want to miss it!

Mindfulness for burnout: Controversy and benefits

In August 2020, there was a set of cartoons published in *The New Yorker* called "This is what your unsolicited advice sounds like" by artist and writer Natalya Lobanova (2020). In the first cartoon, a woman is being burned at the stake, her neck, arms, and torso tied firmly to a pole as flames engulf her. Another woman standing nearby unhelpfully asks, "Have you considered taking up yoga?"

The cartoon reflects a rightful critique on the use of mindfulness and other "wellness" interventions in response to burnout. There is a rising backlash against managers and organizations that offer their employees mindfulness and other self-care wellness programs without addressing the systemic problems that are at the root of burnout. In response to a rise in burnout, leaders will recommend, sometimes require, mindfulness interventions while changing nothing about workplace culture, busy schedules, understaffing, inadequate leave time, pay, and benefits, and so on. Rather than resolving the cultural and systemic problems driving burnout, these efforts miss the mark, sometimes angering employees who are tired of superficial approaches that put the onus of change on the employees themselves.

As an example, this type of intervention happens frequently in overburdened healthcare systems. Wendy Dean and Simon Talbot, two important critical voices in the world of physician wellbeing, write, "Mindfulness programs have been implemented by many facilities as a low-cost, easily implemented solution to clinician distress. However, it shifts responsibility for resolving the distress from the organization to the individual, and it fails to address the underlying causes" (Dean and Talbot 2020). They state, "Mindfulness is a useful technique to optimize performance in high stress, hard-charging environments, but on its own, the practice is insufficient to address moral injury or burnout" (Dean and Talbot 2020).

Ronald Purser, the author of *McMindfulness: How Mindfulness Became the New Capitalist Spirituality* (2019), has been quoted as saying, "The problem isn't that using mindfulness for stress-reduction doesn't work—the problem is that it does work!" (Gilmore 2020). He points out that when mindfulness works, however, sometimes it ultimately serves most the interest of someone who is making a buck—perhaps an employer looking for recharged employees, or someone profiting in the mindfulness/wellness industry.

When mindfulness interventions target the level of individual wellness, without acknowledging or addressing systemic issues, it can be a temporary band-aid at best, and harmful at worst. It can perpetuate the harmful implicit narrative that real stressors (and culturally created problems) are an individual "you problem" that we must each fix within ourselves. Financial stress, lack of childcare, an overly taxed schedule... these are not just in our heads; they are real problems that we can't mindfully breathe away.

Sure, many individuals enjoy practicing mindfulness, like I do. But can wellness interventions be another form of avoidance, in which turning inward allows us to ignore the deeper problem in our lives, and the ones in the world around us? Yes, sometimes they can. (As wellness warrior types know well from personal experience!)

For many in demanding caregiver roles, self-care wellness interventions can feel like one more stressful item to add to an already busy life, one more task to fail at. At the doctor's office one day, an oncologist asked writer Kate Washington, author of the book *Already Toast: Caregiving and Burnout in America* (2021), who was simultaneously caring for her young children and her husband with cancer, how she could take care of her husband if she didn't take care of herself:

> Fragile and overextended, I heard in that question an implication that the only point of me, as a human and not coincidentally as a woman, was to care for another person... The so-called self-care that the oncologist had prescribed felt like yet another task I resented, yet another obligation I had to fill. What I wanted was for somebody else to volunteer to care for me. (Washington 2021, p.2)

Individuals experiencing burnout, like the woman who is offered the suggestion of yoga as she is being burned at the stake in the cartoon, will usually benefit more from a change in circumstance than from any given wellness intervention. But can mindfulness help us cope with burnout at all? In a nutshell, according to a great deal of research, the answer to that question for many people is yes. In recent years, much research has supported the effectiveness of mindfulness interventions for burnout and managing stress (e.g. Baer, Carmody, and Hunsinger 2012; Green and Kinchen 2021; Khoury *et al.* 2013; Krasner *et al.* 2009; Spinelli, Wisener, and Khoury 2019). And by fully engaging in the present, we experience events in our lives in a richer, fuller way. Mindfulness can help bring us out of a state of burnout-driven disconnection, to help us engage more fully in the experience we are having as it unfolds. For those who are experiencing the "increased mental distance from one's job" criterion of burnout, this aspect of mindfulness can be extremely helpful. Mindfulness can help us to be present with our work, and with the people we interact with, to cope with stress, and to respond effectively to emotional discomfort.

How to be more mindful

Mindfulness practice is not a relaxation exercise, meant to change your feeling state. Rather, it's an attitude of living more consciously. In fact, there's a paradox here: the minute you use mindfulness or meditation to avoid or get rid of an unpleasant experience, you are no longer practicing true acceptance-based mindfulness. Rather than simply noticing and being attuned to your experience as it is, you are attempting to change your experience, and this perpetuates the cycle of suffering.

You might picture formal mindfulness exercises, where you are on a cushion in a beautiful room, with relaxing sounds in the background. While these kinds of experiences can be lovely, they aren't the only way to deliberately practice mindfulness. You can simply take a little bit of time each day to sit quietly and pay attention to your experience.

I know, I know. Sometimes busy people like you don't have the time or energy to make that happen. It's okay! Informal mindfulness practices, which are embedded in your daily life as you are living it, can also promote mindful awareness. And, ultimately, we really want to be mindful in our real lives, not just reserve it for sitting in a quiet room or going on a two-week meditation retreat, outside the fray of our real lives. It needs to trickle into our real, daily lives to be beneficial. Fortunately, every moment, no matter what you might be doing, is an opportunity to be more mindful. Here are some tips for practicing mindfulness both formally and informally.

Formal mindfulness practice
You might want to try a guided mindfulness exercise, using an app or other recording. But you don't need that, as you can practice mindfulness on your own. Here's how.

MINI-MINDFULNESS PRACTICES

Start small: Pause what you are doing right now (reading this book), close your eyes, and take one breath. See what you notice about this moment, right here and now.

Sit and practice: Sit somewhere comfortable and quiet with minimal distractions. If you will be distracted by the time, set a timer for five or ten minutes. Each time you practice, try one of the following:

- **Tune in to your body's sensations:** Scan through from

---

head to toe. Notice what you feel—your body touching your chair, any aches and pains, places where you feel tension. Just notice. If you get distracted, it's okay—this is the practice—just notice that your mind has wandered, and tune back in. Mindfulness is not about never being distracted (that would be impossible); it's about noticing each time your mind has strayed, and gently redirecting your attention back to the present.

- **Use mindfulness of your senses:** Choose one of your senses, like the sense of hearing. Just pay attention to the sensation of listening. Whether there's a sledgehammer drilling outside your window or birds chirping pleasantly, tune in to the sound. When you get distracted, tune back in to your sensory experience.

- **Go for a mindful walk:** See if you can engage fully in the sensation of walking for a few minutes at a time. Notice your feet as they contact the ground. Notice the sensations in your leg muscles and how those change as you lift and lower your feet. Notice the air around you. Notice the thoughts and feelings that arise as you walk.

- **Pay attention to your breath:** It sounds simple, but it's a powerful tool and it can be a challenge. Notice the air as it enters and exits your body. Feel the sensations on your upper lip or in your nostrils. Notice the parts of your body that move as you breathe, and how each inhale and exhale is synchronized with the gentle rise and fall of your chest or belly. If you get distracted (and you will), simply return your attention to your breath.

- **Label breath and "not breath":** If you get stuck with mindful breathing, one of my favorite techniques, based on the advice of author and meditation teacher Sharon Salzberg (2011), is to say to yourself, "breath" when you notice breathing, and label everything else as "not breath." Whether you are experiencing a blissful feeling or a highly disturbing thought, simply label it in your mind as "not breath" while you do this practice. And then any time you notice anything that is "not breath," simply return your attention back to your breath yet again.

- **Watch your thoughts:** Close your eyes to turn your attention inward and minimize distractions, sit back, and observe your mind. Imagine that your thoughts are flowing by you, like cars passing you on the road. Each time a new thought crosses your mind, observe it until it is out of sight. There's no need to evaluate or try to change any of your thoughts, just watch each one as it passes by. Maybe you're having thoughts about the exercise itself, like "this is boring" or "I'm too busy to sit here like this." Whatever it is, just observe. Notice what it's like to watch your thoughts from a slight distance.

- **Notice your current emotions:** Close your eyes to turn your attention inward and minimize distractions, sit back, and observe your emotions. Tune in to how you feel. Notice whatever emotions happen to be here in this moment. Mindfully observe where you feel those emotions in your body. Notice the sensations associated with your emotions. Notice how your emotions fluctuate over time. See if you have any feelings of discomfort that arise during the exercise. Don't try to change how you feel, just notice.

Formal mindfulness practice does not need a big time commitment. Some people find it difficult to be still for very long, or simply struggle to find much time to commit to a practice. See what happens when you do a brief mindfulness practice, even just for a few minutes, three or four times per week, for a couple of weeks. Or, try attending to your breath or sounds when you have a few minutes to spare. Instead of grabbing your phone, mindfully breathe while you are waiting in line, sitting still in a traffic jam, or going to bed at night.

Mindful living

Whether or not you choose to try a formal mindfulness practice, mindful awareness can enhance your life. It can help you be more focused and present when you are doing things that matter to you. You can also use regular, everyday activities you are already engaging in as an opportunity to practice mindfulness informally. One way to do this is to practice the "Pause, Notice, Choose" exercise from Chapter 7 from time to time as you go about your life.

Here's another way. Try this exercise.

MINDFULNESS IN DAILY LIFE

- Choose an activity you engage in. This could be one that you do regularly, and that you tend to do on autopilot, like taking a shower, eating, making tea, cleaning dishes, or grocery shopping.
- As you do that activity, really tune in to what's happening. Instead of doing it on autopilot, bring your full attention to what you are doing.
- Pay attention to the sensation of movement as you do the activity.
- Notice any sensory experiences that arise, like the smell of your shampoo, the warmth of your tea, the sound of the dishes clinking, or the color of the lemons in the produce aisle.
- Notice your thoughts and emotions. Tune in to what it feels like to be doing this activity right now. Be aware of the state of your mind.
- If you get distracted, that's okay. Bring your focus back to the activity.

My hope is that some of the simple practices above will help you to transform the experience of burnout by reconnecting with the present moment. I hope you try these practices, and find some that work for you. If you find it hard, don't get discouraged. Practicing mindfulness can be difficult at first. But if you keep it up, you might start to notice a shift. You can start with these types of simple practices, build on them, and work toward being mindfully present in your difficult work, and in the face of chronic stress.

Mindfulness to promote social change

Mindfulness practices aren't just helpful for managing personal stress. Perhaps more importantly, when used to their full potential, they can give us more capacity to see the problems of the world clearly, face them head on, and work toward changing them. Historically, mindfulness practices are rooted in Buddhism, one of the tenets of which, sometimes referred to in English as "right action" or "wise action," is about living ethically. Instead of associating mindfulness with buying the latest trendy yoga clothing every two months, or with being cloistered away in a temple or retreat center for weeks or longer, we can channel these practices into "right action" in our real lives and use it to work toward important changes in our lives and in the world.

Mindfulness should not be used in an avoidant way, to turn away from reality, but rather as a tool to turn toward it. As Steven Hayes, co-founder of Acceptance and Commitment Therapy, has written, "contemplative practice is NOT about getting rid of your experiences. It's about anchoring yourself so that you won't be swept away, and remain steady and present even in the presence of rain, thunder, and crashing waves" (Hayes 2022).

Wendy Dean and Simon Talbot, the critical voices I mentioned above, while concerned about the way mindfulness is currently being used in medical settings, have stated that they both use mindfulness personally, and see it as a helpful and necessary technique in "high-tempo, high-stress settings for self-management, and emotion regulation" (Dean and Talbot 2020). They note that mindfulness can be used to accept our experience without judgment, without tolerating broken systems and accepting bad situations as unchangeable. It can help us sharpen our awareness of challenges, better recognize the drivers of distress, and advocate for change. As Dean and Talbot suggest, "Let's approach mindfulness like Picasso: 'Learn the rules like a pro, so you can break them like an artist'" (Dean and Talbot 2020).

Indeed, some psychology research supports the idea that contemplative practices like meditation have the potential to increase prosocial responses, like increased compassion for others (Kemeny *et al.* 2012).

"Deep acceptance is not inertness," writes Buddhist teacher Sharon Salzberg in her book *Real Change: Mindfulness to Heal Ourselves and the World*, and "Meditation can provide tools to help courage grow out of rage and resilience out of grief" (Salzberg 2020, p.3).

When mindfulness is used for both personal self-care and in the service of prosocial change, you get the best of both worlds - individual benefits and a bigger impact. Here are some tips for how to use mindfulness for social change:

- *See things clearly:* Mindfulness can help you open your eyes and be more present with the difficult realities around you. Use it to tune in to what's going on and see things clearly.
- *Use mindfulness of emotions as a guide:* As we saw back in Chapter 7, our emotions can contain wisdom, if we pay attention to them in a particular way. Sometimes anger can indicate a sense of injustice, or our despair and exhaustion can point to a systemic or social problem. Use awareness of your emotions as a source of important information about your values.
- *Pause for prosocial action:* When you act on autopilot, you can easily react impulsively, in ways that aren't consistent with your values. You can use mindfulness skills to help you pause and intentionally act in a way that feels morally and ethically right.
- *Use mindfulness for reflection:* Your actions have an effect, and we all make mistakes. When we are left feeling a sense that we did something incongruent with our values, we can learn something. Mindfulness can help you be aware of the impact of your actions on the world.
- *Increase your capacity:* We've seen how a mindfulness practice has

personal benefits to help you with stress, burnout, and self-compassion. Sometimes taking ethical action, or working toward social change, can feel hard and draining. Caring for yourself with mindfulness practices can help to sustain you as you take action in the world.

REFLECTION QUESTIONS

1. What is your experience with mindfulness? What are your assumptions about it? If you've practiced it, have you found it beneficial in any way?
2. When and how do you get distracted or "in your head"? Do you have trouble staying in the present moment?
3. As you tried the mindfulness exercises in this chapter, what did you notice about your present-moment experience? Be specific here.
4. What challenges arise when you practice mindfulness, formally and informally? What benefits do you notice?
5. How might you use mindfulness practices to support change—in your life and/or the world—if that's important to you?

CHAPTER 10

Values

Reconnecting to Meaning and Vitality

When people are burned out, they are missing a spark of vitality. Where once there was passion, motivation, and purpose, there is now a disengaged, "meh" feeling. People who experience burnout are usually working in roles that are an important part of their lives, but their sense of purpose and fulfillment has eroded due to chronic, prolonged stress. To me, this is the biggest tragedy of burnout. As the clock of life ticks by, the cost of feeling unfulfilled for long periods of time is high.

According to the Value Fulfillment Theory of Wellbeing, pursuing a good life means working toward fulfillment of our most important and meaningful goals and values (Tiberius 2023). To live a good life might mean having supportive relationships, meaningful work, a spiritual or religious practice, and/or enjoyable leisure activities, and fitting those together in your life in a way that works for you over time.

Similarly, the ultimate goal of acceptance and commitment therapy is engagement in a meaningful, values-directed life (Hayes *et al.* 2016; LeJeune and Luoma 2019). Feelings of happiness and contentment may come and go over time, but a deeper sense of satisfaction comes from engaging in life in a values-consistent and meaningful way.

But how do you get there when you're feeling burned out and disconnected from meaning? In this chapter, I will introduce you to the concept of values, and we will discuss the relationship between values and pain. I will guide you in exploring your personal values in important domains of your life, and the meaning behind the work that is causing you burnout. We'll explore some important questions. In the time you have left in your life, what really matters to you? What are your most important, deeply held values, and how can you reconnect with meaning and purpose in the face of burnout? And I will help you to re-engage with your work role with a greater sense of meaning, and to consider values-based actions you might take.

What are values?

In ACT, we define values as qualities of meaningful action that are tied to what deeply matters to us. Values offer us guidance about the kind of person we would like to be, and the kind of life we want to live. Unlike goals, which we can accomplish and check off our list, values are ongoing; they are a direction we can always head, rather than a destination we will ever reach. You can't check them off a list as "done" (Hayes *et al.* 2016; LeJeune and Luoma 2019).

Values are not the same as pleasure or happiness. As we'll see below, when we are doing the most important and meaningful things in life, we won't always feel a sense of comfort or pleasure. Values also aren't "shoulds." When we connect with what's important to us deep inside, we feel a sense that we truly and deeply care about something, whether or not it is in line with society's expectations of us.

Values aren't just an intellectual concept of what's "right" that lives only in your mind. Rather, values are meant to be put into action. We express our values in how we live. The magic happens through taking meaningful and values-based action.

Meaningful roles—a paradox

Like many American adults, I own a car. I like my car and am grateful to have one! But cars aren't very important to me personally. As long as it's reliable, safe, fuel efficient, and comfortable enough, I don't mind driving an old junker around town for years. While I might occasionally worry about an auto repair bill or an overdue oil change, my role as a car owner doesn't typically cause me much distress. In fact, on a typical day I don't think about car ownership at all.

I'm also a psychologist, a mother, and a spouse. These areas of my life are far more important to me. They are also far more emotionally demanding; unlike car ownership, I feel deeply upset when I face problems in these areas. If I find myself plagued by self-doubt, or awake in the middle of the night worrying, it likely has something to do with my work or my family. If these areas are so meaningful to me, why do they tend to cause me so much more discomfort than car ownership? If I love my work and care deeply about my children and husband, shouldn't I mostly feel joy and contentment in these roles?

Our most meaningful roles in life, the ones we truly care most deeply about, are usually the very same ones in which we are most prone to stress, discomfort, and, yes, burnout. On the surface, this may seem counterintuitive. But it's *because* you care that you are prone to experiencing difficult emotions when you are engaged in meaningful roles. When we engage in our values, we often feel discomfort; it's because we care that we feel pain. As Steven Hayes says, "you hurt where you care, and you care where you hurt" (Hayes 2019, p.24).

Engaging in any meaningful role necessarily requires experiencing some stress—it's inevitable. Doing something hard but important to you will be more difficult than doing something easy or unimportant, or doing nothing. And when you care about something, you face the possibility that things will go wrong or that you will lose what you care about. If it didn't matter to you in some way, you wouldn't feel much of anything if that happened.

There can be a slippery slope in areas of life we care deeply about. Sometimes we can care so much about something, that over-engaging can become a problem. We've seen this earlier in the book, with do-gooder and people-pleaser types. Their hearts are in the right place, and we certainly wouldn't want them to stop caring. But they can go too far with their values of caring about people and doing good. For instance, valuing high-quality work can slip into workaholic behavior or feeling upset when things aren't done up to our standards. We can over-identify with a job role that's a "calling." Caring about others can lead to neglecting ourselves, and caring about doing morally good deeds can lead us to distress when faced with injustice or setbacks.

Buddhist teacher and anthropologist Joan Halifax (2018) writes about "edge states." The very qualities that we want to have, qualities we deem important to leading a compassionate and courageous life like altruism, empathy, integrity, respect, and engagement, can slide into extremes. Although these ideals are important, they can be harmful when we lose our footing with them. Altruism can become pathological, empathy can lead to empathic distress, and engagement can lead to overwork and burnout. Fortunately, Halifax argues, we can recognize when we are getting close to the edge, or have gone over it, and learn how to make it back to the "high edge" of the qualities we like most about ourselves. We can always seek that sweet spot where our values are kept from slipping into extremes.

Identifying your values

An important first step in reconnecting with values is to be clear about what is most important to you. You might already have a pretty good sense of your values, or this might be a new concept to you. Maybe you've never fully explored your values, or perhaps life has changed in unexpected ways and it's time for a re-evaluation. Or perhaps you have a good sense of your values, but you've just lost sight of them lately.

Almost anyone can benefit from exploring their values, at any time. I invite you now to do a little soul-searching about what's important to you.

Qualities of living

Think of your values as indicators of the kind of person you most want to be and how you want to live your life. Getting a clear sense of this can guide you about how to act, and you can always return to these qualities, even when things feel hard.

WHAT KIND OF PERSON DO YOU WANT TO BE?

Think about yourself when you are acting in a way that you feel proud of, or at a time when you've felt a sense of vitality and meaning. What words would you use to describe yourself in a moment like that? If you think of the people you admire, how would you describe what you admire about them? What are the qualities you most want to embody in how you live?

Next, paint a picture of what a meaningful life looks like for you. To you, what does "a life well lived" look like? What words would you use to describe the life you would most want to live?

Values in important areas of life

Our values show up in many domains of our lives, but in this model, life domains themselves are not values. For instance, work itself is not considered to be a value. Neither are marriage, parenting, or health. Values are more about *how* we show up in these domains. You can think of the kind of person you want to be, in the various domains that are important to you. Perhaps it's being reliable at work, or being respectful as a teammate. Or, maybe you care about being caring and connected in your personal relationships, or generous with your community.

VALUES WRITING EXERCISE

Try the following writing exercise (adapted from Hayes 2019). Select domains below that matter to you. Circle the domains in which you would like to explore your values, and answer the questions below. Try not to worry about what other people would think, but write freely from your heart.

- Romantic partner-
  ship
- Parenting
- Caregiving
- Friendships

- Work/Productive
  activities
- Education/Learning
- Religion/Faith/Spirit-
  uality

- Creative expression
- Personal growth
- Recreation
- Health/Physical self-care
- Home

- Nature
- Earth/Environment/ Animals
- Citizenship
- Community
- Other..........................

Start by choosing *one* area you want to write about. Answer the following questions in your notebook or journal:

1. Why is this area of life important to you?
2. What words would you use to describe your "ideal self" in this area?
3. Who do you admire in this area? Who do you *not* admire in this area? And why?
4. When have you acted consistently with your values in this area? What was that like?
5. When have you strayed from your values in this area? What was that like?
6. What challenges get in your way in this area?
7. What changes would you need to make for your actions to be more in line with this value?

If you want, you can repeat this exercise with other life areas you circled above.

When it's all said and done, what matters most?

Psychologist Erik Erikson (Erikson and Erikson 1997) called his seventh stage of psychosocial development, which roughly spans the productive years of middle adulthood, "Generativity vs. Stagnation." During this stage, the focus is on contributing to society in some way, perhaps through caring for children, work productivity, or community involvement. According to Erikson, people who successfully navigate this stage of adulthood end up with a feeling that their life was meaningful and productive. Rather than feeling stagnant or unfulfilled, they feel a sense of having participated in something bigger than themselves that will outlast them. (No pressure, right?) The result, for those who do navigate this stage successfully, is a sense of caring, connection, and involvement with the world.

As I revisited Erikson's stage theory model for the first time since I learned about it in graduate school, it put things into perspective for me. I thought, wow, this is right where I am in my life. No wonder I feel tapped out! I'm in a high-responsibility stage of life, where I'm trying to be productive—raising my kids and doing my work. The load I'm carrying sounds both important and exhausting at once. It makes me wonder... when I'm done with this stage, what *will* I leave behind? And what will I remember most about this period of my life? Will I remember the small things, or the things that really mattered to me? Will I remember how hard it was, or how meaningful it was? Or both?

When it is all said and done, what kind of mark do *you* want to leave on the world? What would leave you with the feeling that your life was meaningful in some way, small or big? How do you want to be remembered? What relationships will have mattered most to you? Your answers to these questions might reveal your most deeply held, big-picture values.

THE BIG PICTURE

Choose a role in which you are currently experiencing burnout—such as work, caregiving, parenting, and so on. Close your eyes, take a few breaths, and imagine that it is a day in the future—your last day in this role. After this day, you will be finished with this role forever. Maybe you are retiring, making a change, or about to die. What would you want to feel when you look back on the time you spent in this role? Now get out your journal or notebook. Imagine that someone is going to give a speech about your work in this role, at a party held in your honor on this, your last day. Write down the speech you would want them to deliver. What words would you want them to say about your engagement in this role, and the contribution you made? What would you want them to say about the kind of person you were in this role?

On the lookout for values

If you're on the lookout, you can find out about your values by paying careful attention as you go about your life. Psychologist and author Jenna LeJeune uses the metaphor of sniffing out your values the way a truffle dog finds truffles buried deep under the ground (LeJeune and Luoma 2019). When you catch a whiff of vitality or deep caring, you might be on the scent of something. You might sniff out your values in moments of longing, regret, envy, social comparison, or the pain of missing out on something. You can ask yourself what those kinds of feelings tell you about what matters to you. Be attuned to those moments when you feel fulfillment, or proud of how you've handled something—whether those moments happen frequently or are a rare occurrence. The scent of our values is often there, perhaps buried, and we can find these values if only we use our noses to sniff them out.

Values in action

Values only take hold in our lives when we take steps toward them; if we don't act on them in some way, they are just an idea without substance. Now that you've clarified some of your values, it's time to think about how to take steps to put them into action.

In ACT, we think about values as the big-picture qualities that matter to you, whereas goals are the steps you can take in the direction of those values. There can be big, long-term goals, and those can be broken down into smaller goals. Big or small, goals are the behavioral steps we can take to get a bit closer to the life we want. We can always start with the smallest action we can think of related to that value. What can we do *today* that's a step in the direction of our values?

Sometimes, we might experience some barriers and challenges that get in the way of reaching our goals. These can be very real and sometimes we don't have control over them! When that happens, it can help to return to the big-picture value. We can ask what *really* matters in regard to this particular goal and be flexible in how we translate that value into actions. For instance, if I want to devote my life to volunteering for a cause, but I need a full-time paycheck to make ends meet, I might be able to find a smaller action I can take to contribute to that cause. By finding ways, big or small, to bring our values to life in a realistic, sustainable manner, we can create a meaningful, values-driven life.

As you put values into action, notice what shows up for you. If difficult thoughts and emotions arise, notice them. Again, values sometimes inherently involve discomfort! Remind yourself that this is an indicator that you care.

Have you drifted?

Newer cars sometimes come with lane departure alert systems. These are designed to help you avoid crashing when you've drifted out of your lane. The alarm reminds you to gently steer your car back in the direction you are meant to be heading. Even if the road ahead is winding rather than straight, you can use this system to stay on track.

In a sense, we humans have a built-in system that gives us a little "beep beep" when we've drifted away from our values. Sometimes our emotions can remind us that we've gone off track from what we care about, as we saw in the section in Chapter 7 on the wisdom of emotions. But we might miss the sound of our "beep beep" warning when we are too busy to pay attention, or when we've been on living on cruise control. Fortunately, we can tune back in by checking in once in a while on how closely our lives are lined up with our values, and whether or not we're still heading the right direction. Sometimes, especially when we are busy and stressed, we can lose sight of our values and stray so far out of our lane it's as if we are driving the *opposite* direction down the highway, at full speed. We may need a big change to get back to the direction we want to head in. At other times, we've just drifted a bit but are still generally heading in the right direction, and a slight readjustment is enough.

When we're off track, readjusting can take intentional effort. For instance, if I care about deep connection with my clients, but notice that we're always focusing on minutiae in session, I'm probably off track. If I value quality time with my family but I'm working too much and ignoring them, I've drifted. Or if I care about taking care of my health but

I've been neglecting myself, beep beep. It's time to steer myself gently back in the right direction.

Big P, little p: Reconnecting with purpose

When feeling burned out, it can be helpful to reconnect with purpose—the sense that we are part of something that matters, something that's bigger than ourselves in our work roles. We can do this both by connecting with the "big picture" importance of the work we are doing and by finding small day-to-day ways to build purpose into our work lives.

"Big P" purpose

There's a story that when US President John F. Kennedy toured NASA headquarters in 1961, he ran into a custodian. He asked him what he was doing, and the custodian responded, "Mr. President, I'm helping put a man on the moon." I don't know if this story is really true or if it's just a tale. If it did happen, this janitor was able to see custodial work as part of an important, bigger mission.

I call this type of connection to a larger mission "Big P" purpose. Big P purpose is all about remembering the big-picture "why" behind the work you do. It's about realizing that your work, regardless of what kind of work you do, has an impact on the world.

Amy Wrzesniewski, currently at the Yale School of Management, and her colleagues have researched how people make meaning of their work in different contexts. In one study, people who cleaned hospitals told stories about their work. Some of the participants in the study viewed their work as critical to the hospital's functioning and to patient care. Feeling important to others in the hospital mattered to them. Interactions in which they felt appreciated and acknowledged gave their work a sense of meaning. Times they felt devalued, however, were associated with painful emotions, such as anger, hurt, and frustration (Dutton, Debebe, and Wrzesniewski 2016).

Similarly, Adam Grant and colleagues (Grant *et al.* 2007) studied people who work in a call center, soliciting alumni donations. This can be a rather demoralizing job, which requires facing a great deal of rejection.

Some of the call center workers talked to the beneficiaries—recipients of scholarships funded by alumni donations—about the personal impact of the scholarships that resulted from their calls. The callers who talked to the scholarship recipients were more motivated and productive than the callers who didn't. Reminding the callers of the purpose of the hard work they were doing helped them to know that their sometimes demoralizing work mattered.

Regardless of the kind of work you do, you can assign some kind of meaning to it, and doing so can help you feel more satisfied with your work. Meaning does not inherently exist in anything, really. It's there because *we ascribe meaning* to the things we care about, the things that matter *to us*. Sometimes we might be able to identify some really obvious intrinsic meaning in work, for example if we pursued a calling. Sometimes we just want a paycheck. Either way, many of us have a fundamental desire to engage in work in a meaningful way, or at least find pockets of meaning in our work. Remembering the impact and importance of our work can help us to be happier and more engaged. We spend so much time working, why not find a way for it to increase our general wellbeing and fulfillment?

Some people are engaged in obviously meaning-driven work—work they started doing because it felt important and meaningful, a calling to help people or make the world a better place. Examples of this might include teaching, social work, clergy, and nonprofit work. But over the years, when a job like that becomes stressful, and the "pebbles in your shoe" start to wear you down, you can start to lose touch with the important part of the work. It can help to reconnect with your Big P purpose.

As an example of this, my husband works in the field of renewable energy technology. He decided years ago to use his science education and programming skills in a field where he can help with the problem of climate change. His job can be demanding, with a high workload. During periods of time when his stress is high and he feels burned out, he sometimes loses sight of the importance of his work, focusing instead on the daily stressors. For my husband, remembering the big-picture "why" behind his decision to do this work, and the important impact it has on helping with energy efficiency, carbon emissions, and climate change, keeps him going. It helps him get through the times when he's feeling stressed, and it reduces his burnout.

Knowing that sometimes your work will be difficult or unpleasant, but that you are doing it for a reason that matters in some big-picture way, can help you tap into Big P purpose.

TAP INTO BIG P PURPOSE

To tap into Big P purpose in your work, take a moment to stop and reflect on the meaning you ascribe to your work. Why did you chose to do this particular type of work in the first place? It might be that you are in a meaning-driven field, or simply that you want to earn enough money to provide for your family or enjoy your life. Either way, be clear about the big-picture "why" behind your work. Think of a few words that resonate for you, and that remind you of your "why." Return to those words from time to time.

"Little p" purpose

Another way to bring more sense of purpose into your work is to take small, meaningful actions in your day-to-day life. I call this "little p" purpose. This kind of purpose comes about through those small, daily moments in life that may not seem like much, but that can add up to a meaningful day.

First, decide what little p purpose means to you. What are the small, daily things that give your life vitality? How do you want to show up for the small moments that matter in your life? For example, someone might enjoy taking a few minutes out of a busy day to water a plant in their office or to chat with the checker at the local grocery store, who they've seen in five-minute spurts for years. Someone else might take the time to put a little extra creative flair into an otherwise boring project, put down their phone for a couple of minutes to read a poem on the subway ride to work, or cuddle with their child for a few minutes in the morning. None of these examples seem like a very big deal on their own, but a life filled with meaningful moments like this, however small, can be a purposeful life too.

CULTIVATE LITTLE P PURPOSE

To cultivate little p purpose in your life, take a moment to make a list of small things you can do in your life that are meaningful to you; this could include everything from checking in on a friend or co-worker, to engaging in a daily activity that gives you a little spark of vitality. See if you can intentionally make room for these kinds of purposeful activities, and notice what happens to your life satisfaction when you do. And when you have those meaningful moments, try to slow down and savor them.

REFLECTION QUESTIONS

1. After doing the values exercises above, what qualities stand out to you as your most important values?
2. What does a meaningful life look like to you?
3. What domains of life are important to you? Are you on or off track with your values in those domains?
4. How do you know when you've drifted from your values? What can you do to get back on track?
5. What is the "Big P" purpose behind your work?
6. How might you increase "little p" purpose in your daily work life?

PART THREE

MAKING CHANGES

CHAPTER 11

From Burnout to Growth, Possibility, and Change

At this point in the book, you've learned about burnout and explored psychological flexibility skills to transform your burnout experience internally. While these types of psychological practices can help transform suffering, sometimes we need to make some external changes—changes in our lives, our behavior patterns, our relationships, or even the culture around us. In the section ahead, we'll look at changes—all the way from small, daily habits to big-scale cultural and systemic shifts—that might help you with burnout.

I don't wish burnout on anyone, but if there is one silver lining of a burnout experience, it's that sometimes it can spark growth and inspire positive change. Burnout might be an indication that we have lost our way, that we need to do some soul-searching to learn about ourselves or find a new direction. It can be a catalyst for change. Sometimes, this could be a small change, like a daily habit, a bigger one like reprioritizing or finding support, or even a huge one like a complete career change. Sometimes, burnout can be a great teacher, inspiring us to renew our lives in ways that ultimately improve our quality of life or lead to personal growth. And when we get support from others during times of adversity, burnout can lead to closer, more connected relationships.

People struggling with burnout are often grappling with "big picture" questions about their lives, such as:

- What do I need? What am I longing for?
- What possibilities are out there for me?
- Is my current work going to keep me satisfied in the years ahead? Should I make some kind of a change, or make the best of this situation as it is?
- Would a different career path be a better fit for me? Is it worth the effort of starting over? How do I decide what to do?

This chapter will help you consider some of these questions, explore possibilities, and think through decision-making about changes you might be considering, from a place of your values. I am not here to give you advice about what you "should" do—it's your life to live. But I can help you explore the possibility of change and guide you as you look for your own answers, based on your own personal values. My hope is to encourage some soul-searching that will lead you toward personal growth.

Change can be hard and scary. It inevitably involves adaptability, risk, and facing uncertainty. But when change is within reach and brings us closer to our values, it can be worth the discomfort.

Growth through adversity

Anyone who lives long enough will experience periods of adversity sometimes. Here are just a few:

- Loss
- Trauma
- Health problems (your own or people you care about)
- Financial stress
- Relationship problems and conflicts
- Emotional distress
- Extreme work stress
- Setbacks and unexpected changes
- Rejection
- Major world events like natural disasters, pandemics, war, political strife
- And more.

I have experienced some of these myself, of course. When I look back on the difficult periods of my life, times when life was hard for me, I can also see that each of these periods of my life changed me. They brought me into close contact with what matters most to me, taught me important lessons about myself, and strengthened my most important relationships. Given the choice, I would have preferred not to have experienced any of those events. But I can see that they helped me grow in some ways that I can now appreciate. Each helped me clarify what matters most to me and helped me to be more adaptable to unexpected challenges. I've learned that life can be unpredictable, and that I have the ability to make it through difficult times.

Richard Tedeschi and Lawrence Calhoun define post-traumatic growth as "positive psychological change experienced as a result of the struggle with highly challenging life circumstances" (Tedeschi and Calhoun 2004, p.1). The positive changes that can occur as the result of adversity include:

- *An increased sense of personal strength:* We discover psychological resources we didn't know we had.
- *Closer, more meaningful relationships:* We may find unexpected social support, connect deeply with someone we open up to, or become part of a community during times of struggle.
- *Increased appreciation for life:* Challenges can remind us that our time to be alive is relatively brief, bringing us into contact with our values and priorities.
- *Identification of new possibilities:* As our priorities change, we may open up to new ideas about what our lives could be. This sense of possibility can lead us down a new or unexpected life path.
- *Spiritual or existential growth:* Adversity can spark a re-evaluation of meaning, and a better understanding of what is truly important. Engagement with spiritual or existential questions can help us tap into self-transcendent wisdom.

Stephen Joseph (2013) uses a metaphor of a shattered vase to describe the process of growth through adversity. Instead of trying to put the broken pieces back together the same way they were before, we might pick up the pieces and use them to make something new and different, like a colorful mosaic. Resilience and growth do not mean that you haven't struggled emotionally; growth occurs *because* of the psychological reaction we have to stressful events. It is possible to experience both suffering and growth simultaneously.

Might the stress and burnout you're experiencing spark growth and positive change? Yes, it's possible. You can build a beautiful new mosaic out of your life, if you use this moment of burnout to do some soul-searching and reconnect with areas of life that are meaningful to you. As you read this chapter, I invite you to take a step back, consider what's important to you, and move a step closer to the life you want—whatever that looks like for you! Your life is happening every minute. What are you going to do with it?

Exploring possibility

On social media, I sometimes stumble on posts by families who have sold their homes and possessions and pulled their kids out of traditional school to live and travel in recreational vehicles. In their posts, you'll see how their kitchen table converts into a bed, the little nooks they use to work remotely and homeschool their kids, and how they bathe their infant *and* do the dishes in a tiny kitchen sink. And there they are, several kids in tow, at the Grand Canyon on a Tuesday morning in October!

I am intrigued by the decision they've made to leave behind expectations of a middle-class American family and live a nomadic life of close quarters and few possessions. While I might not choose that lifestyle for myself, part of me admires their bravery for going outside convention and being open to other possibilities for how to live.

If you've been living in a burnout rut for a while, you may have lost contact with your own needs and values. Often, people get a fixed idea of themselves—what they are capable of and what they are "allowed" to do. We can be creatures of habit, implicitly assuming that we must keep doing things the same way we always have, or the way everyone else does. To even begin to consider making a change, it can help to start by opening yourself up to a sense of what other possibilities are out there for you. You can go beyond what's right in front of you, to think more flexibly about what to do.

Some people with advanced degrees and professional careers choose their path early in life—perhaps in college or even high school they decided on a "med school or bust!" path, for example. Decades later, some of these people, burned out on a medical career, might consider for the first time ever the possibility of leaving medicine. And some even do it! When that seed of an idea comes to mind, it can seem outlandish to even consider such a thing. A highly specialized skill set, which is in high demand, and hundreds of thousands of dollars of student loan debt can feel like a cage that keeps you contained. But the truth is, we always have choices. Whether it's worth it or not is another issue, but even a surgeon can make a choice to continue or do something different. It's in the realm of possibility to make a change.

All too often, we hold ourselves back, limit ourselves. It can be helpful to start from a place of possibility, to free yourself up from expectations and routine, even if you don't make much of a change in the end. Once you've tapped into that sense of possibility, you can get more practical and translate that into realistic goals. But first, let go of expectations and constraints, and see what's there!

EXPLORE THE REALM OF POSSIBILITY

1. Get out some paper or a journal, or start a new doc in your computer.
2. Write a list of what you'd like to do if there were no limits. If you were totally free—from your current situation, from constraints, from self-doubt—what would you want to do? Without concerning yourself with real-world barriers (those are real, but we're putting them aside for now), what are some of the possibilities that have intrigued you? Would you move to northern Alaska? Learn to belly dance or speak French? Go back to school? Become a professional

ice skater? Hike the Inca Trail? Fly to the moon? Don't hold back here!

3. Ask yourself what appeals to you about these ideas. Write about what you learn.

4. Do some journaling about what's missing from your life. What are you longing for? What do you daydream about? Which "paths not taken" do you look back on with regret?

5. What calls to you? Do you feel that you have any particular "calling" in life that resonates strongly for you?

6. Pay attention to what interests you. If you notice that you're drawn to the history section of the bookstore or imagine getting a job decorating cakes at a bakery, jot it down.

7. Keep this exploration going over time—it will take more than one writing session to tap into possibility.

Again, the point of this exploration (for now) is not to set goals you will necessarily put into action. It's to free you up and tap into a sense of possibility. From there, you might simply have learned something new about yourself, even if you ultimately keep things the same. Or you might, just possibly, find a new direction to consider.

On acceptance and change

Philosophically, burnout-related life questions often involve tension between what to accept and what to change. Earlier chapters of this book focused mostly on the acceptance side of the equation —sometimes we must accept that uncomfortable thoughts and emotions will arise when we are doing difficult things. And many things in this world are most certainly outside of our direct control. But sometimes change is necessary and important. When it comes to burnout, it can be tricky decide what to accept as it is, and what to change.

Traditional interventions for burnout, especially those offered by employers, will typically focus on keeping burnout at bay so that people can keep working. In capitalistic societies, the goal is often to keep workers productive, no matter what. Sometimes, continuing in your current work role may be your only realistic option - there is privilege in having the ability to make a change. Or, if you care deeply about your work, staying right where you are might be the best way for you to go. After all, burnout can happen even when you do important and meaningful work that you genuinely care about. If so, when burnout passes, you will be glad you stayed. If this is the case, your best path is probably to settle into how things are now and find greater contentment with what you have.

But sometimes, making a change can be just as important as acceptance, if not more so. When maintaining the status quo isn't working, in terms of living the life you truly want to live, it might be time to consider what needs to change. This might happen if your work isn't satisfying, or your environment isn't congruent with your values and goals. It could be that you've been feeling undervalued and unappreciated, and your efforts to advocate for yourself haven't paid off. Or maybe you're just ready for an upward step (or downward step), or want to try something new and different.

When it comes to acceptance and change, the hard but important part is, in the wise words of the serenity prayer, having the wisdom to know the difference.

Choice and making hard decisions

When therapy clients come in to see me for burnout, sometimes they are grappling with big decisions. They might be considering whether to apply for a new job, relocate to a slower-paced community, leave a relationship, go back to school, or make a major career change into a new field. Decisions like that can be difficult to make, because there are always pros and cons on both sides, and uncertainty about what each path forward will bring. My job as a therapist isn't to tell my clients what they should do, but rather to help them explore the decision.

The challenges of choosing
Decision-making can be exhausting and carry a mental load. I get

decision-fatigue when I make decisions about minor things, like whether or not to go to a party or what to cook for dinner. When my old oven needed to be replaced, it took me years to decide what kind of new one to buy! Major life decisions, like whether to relocate into a new home or change jobs? Even longer.

Sometimes people go back and forth in their minds for long periods of time (like me), or continually tally pros and cons on both sides of the decision. Occasionally there might be a clear path forward that makes the most sense. But many times, there's not one "right" answer to a big life questions—because it's far more complex than that. If one direction was clearly the only superior path forward in all ways, it would be so easy—but that's rarely how it goes in real life.

Knowing when to quit and when to settle

I once held a part-time "side hustle" position that I enjoyed but didn't really have time for. As time went on, I found it harder to prioritize, and ended up constantly short-changing it. I didn't feel good about that because I struggled to give it the time it deserved. But I liked the people and the work itself, so I was reluctant to give it up and quit. So I didn't, for too long. I basically waited until short-changing it became a bit of a problem for me (and for the other people involved), and then the right decision became obvious. In hindsight, I should have quit the position long before it got to that point.

Many of us have been sold on the virtues of loyalty, perseverance, and grit. We hold those in higher regard than quitting, which can be deemed a sign of failure. You may have heard adages like "quitters never win, and winners never quit." And if you do quit something (a job, a career path, an extra project you are working on, a relationship), you may be left wondering if you couldn't hack it, or if people will judge you negatively for walking away.

But there are times when quitting is our best option. It can be helpful to look at quitting in a new light. Knowing when to quit, and doing it at the right time, can be very important. Decision-making expert, and former professional poker player, Annie Duke writes in her book *Quit: The Power of Knowing When to Walk Away*, "Success does not lie in sticking to things. It lies in picking the *right thing* to stick to and quitting the rest" (Duke 2022, p.xix). Duke argues that quitting is not the opposite of perseverance, but rather they go hand-in-hand. Deciding means choosing one thing over another, and sometimes quitting one thing is required to put our energy into something else.

Similarly, sometimes we need to settle. Much as Duke appreciates the importance of quitting, time-management expert Oliver Burkeman, author of *Four Thousand Weeks: Time Management for Mortals* (2021), extols the virtues of settling and describes it as one of life's inevitabilities. "You will settle—and this fact ought to please you" (Burkeman 2021, p.84). You need to settle on doing something (a relationship, a career path), otherwise you won't move forward but will be stuck in indecision or a pattern of striving for something better, and won't make forward progress on anything.

> When people finally *do* choose, in a relatively irreversible way, they're usually much happier as a result. We'll do almost anything to avoid burning our bridges, to keep alive the fantasy of a future unconstrained by limitation, yet having burned them, we're generally pleased that we did so. (Burkeman 2021, p.87)

How to make a hard decision

Because it can be challenging to make a decision based purely on tallying pros and cons, I find it helpful to look to other sources of information in decision-making, like values and emotions. As we learned earlier in Chapter 7, our emotions contain wisdom that can teach us something and might guide decision-making.

Start by accepting the reality that you have a choice to make, and that it's hard. By choosing one option, you are turning your back on another, and there's no way around that being difficult.

If you've been debating your decision for a while, it may feel as if you are waiting for something to happen to make your final decision. That may be so, but not deciding (yet) is also a choice—the choice of not choosing. Sometimes it can be wise to intentionally decide *not* to choose right now. For instance, I recommend that you don't make any big decisions impulsively when you are at a low point of burnout, anxiety, anger, or depression. It can be hard to see things clearly when you're upset. Instead, pause to sit with it, and notice how you feel about it over time. Check back in later, when your emotions have changed, and see if your thoughts about the situation have changed.

If you are facing a decision, here are some questions to consider, to help guide you in decision-making.

QUESTIONS FOR MAKING A DECISION

If you are making a big life decision, answer a few questions:

- Zoom out to consider your most deeply held values (remember back to Chapter 10 if you need help with this). In this domain of your life, what are your most important values and priorities?
- Is there a gap between your values and the situation you're in? Would your life be better if you left this situation? What would you give up? Would you be making any trade-offs by staying? What would your future look like if you stayed the course with your current situation? What are the upsides to staying? The downsides?
- If you imagine making a change or taking one of your potential paths forward, how do you imagine the new or different circumstance would fit with your values? What do you imagine your future would look like if you made that change?
- What kind of situation would help you to be the best version of yourself? Describe it.
- When you think about the finite period of time you'll be alive, what choices and missed opportunities do you think you might regret later?
- Tune in to your emotions and body sensations related to this decision. What do your gut instincts and inner wisdom have to say about this situation?

- What are you afraid of if you make a change? What are you afraid of if you don't? What information does your fear give you about your decision?
- What are some of the potential risks and benefits of making a change? Of not changing? How much risk are you willing to take for the potential benefits?
- Often, making a choice involves loss either way because we lose out on whatever opportunities we don't take. What feelings of loss would you experience if you made one choice rather than another? Does your grief tell you anything about what is important to you here?
- What gets in the way of deciding? Are you avoiding something? Do you worry about making the wrong decision? What's at stake? What would have to happen to make the choice easy for you?

After you make your decision, you might still question whether or not you made the "right" or "best" decision. It's very normal to feel this way. Often, making a choice is followed by psychological distress—such as dissatisfaction, regret, doubt, comparison, and disappointment. You might need to be willing to have that doubt, and unhook from the narrative that you chose badly, using your cognitive defusion skills (see Chapter 8). Instead of getting stuck in those emotions, you can focus on your values, learn something from the experience, and make the best of the decision you did make.

Change, uncertainty about the future, not knowing what the outcome will be—these can be scary! There's discomfort in not knowing where things are heading in the future. No matter what you end up deciding, expect that there will likely be mixed feelings, doubt, and uncertainty. Try to make room for all the feelings that arise, as you consider changes that might improve your burnout situation.

REFLECTION QUESTIONS

1. What adversity have you faced so far in your life?
2. How has burnout changed you? How have you grown, and what have you learned about yourself?
3. What has burnout taught you about what is most important to you?
4. If you were freed from all constraints, what would you want to do in your life? What possibilities are out there for you?
5. What major life changes are you considering (if any)? What is difficult about the decision? What do your values teach you about the decision?
6. Is there something you are thinking about quitting? Is there an area of your life in which you should settle, to make room for something important to you?
7. Describe the life you want. What changes would you have to make to have that life? What would you have to let go of?

CHAPTER 12

Recharging with Values-Based Daily Habits

Have you heard the term "revenge bedtime procrastination" (Liang 2020)? It's when you stay up too late for your own good, sacrificing sleep for a few hours of leisure time late at night, at the end of a busy and demanding day. When I read about this concept online, I immediately recognized my former (and occasionally my current) self in this habit. Sometimes the only free time I have arrives after my kids and dog are asleep, the essential household chores are done for the day, and I can finally put work aside. Even though I know I'll regret it in the morning, I stay up well past the time that is good for me.

At some point, I realized this habit wasn't working for me anymore. I needed more sleep than I was getting to feel rested, and chronic sleep deprivation was too costly for my wellbeing. I realized that I felt much, much better after nights when I went to bed early. I decided to change my habits.

My new habit is to get into bed with a book soon after my kids' lights go out and read until I feel sleepy. I don't do this every night—I still have my occasional revenge bedtime procrastination and choose to stay up late sometimes on purpose. But I've realized that when I am in the regular habit of getting to bed early and prioritizing a solid seven or eight hours of sleep, I feel much better in the long run. I'm fresh in the mornings and can get up early and use the time to read, write, or do a little work. The more I give myself the gift of sleep, the better I feel. I've started to love my new habit, because I give myself permission to unplug and rest in the evenings, instead of charging on past the point of feeling tired.

Many people with burnout would benefit from looking at their daily habits—those little daily things you do regularly, like brushing your teeth—and thinking about which are helpful and which are harmful. You can ask yourself which missing habits would be beneficial to help you recharge from burnout and take better care of yourself. Sometimes, small habit changes can make a big difference with burnout prevention.

Even when we know what habits would be helpful, behavior change can be hard, especially when we are busy and stressed. This chapter is here to come to the rescue! Now that you have a sense of your values and your burnout patterns, let's dive into your habits, highlight some areas of change that may help with burnout, and learn simple strategies for forming values-consistent daily habits to enrich your life.

Burnout prevention habits

When chronic stress leaves us feeling depleted and exhausted, it can help to find ways to recharge our batteries. Some habits and behaviors add more to our chronic stress and depletion, while others can help to energize us. It can be tricky because sometimes behaviors that seem to work in the short term don't work in the long term.

Granted, the last thing you need is me trying to burden you with a lot of self-care advice and things you "should" be doing on top of your already busy life! We all probably have some behavior changes we know we could make—the things we know are "good for us" but that have been neglected on the back burner, or the ones that we use for short-term comfort but don't serve us well in the long run. You know yourself better than I do, and a lecture on self-care could just add one more stress and contribute to more burnout. Shaming yourself about your habits can be unhelpful too. You aren't a better person if you exercise than if you don't, or if your house is clean than if your house is messy.

The key is figuring out how to reduce habits that deplete you, and adding more of those that replenish you. And this will be different for each person. If you're like me, you have some awareness, from your past experience, that certain behavior patterns do help you in the face of stress and others make things worse. Every time I exercise and feel a release of stress right away, I think to myself, "Wow, that was helpful, I should do that more!" And every time I short-change sleep, I think, "Wow, I feel worse, I should prioritize sleep more." (Easier said than done, though, am I right?)

Let me be crystal clear about something: I'm not recommending that you take better care of yourself so that you can be more productive. I'm recommending it so that in so doing you can save yourself, in this world that just won't stop being chronically stressful. It doesn't do anyone any good for you to sacrifice yourself and be an exhausted wreck. In the famous words of Audre Lorde, "Caring for myself is not self-indulgence, it is self-preservation, and that is an act of political warfare" (Lorde 1988, p.130).

In ACT, the core process known as committed action consists of the actions we take toward our values. We can commit to taking active steps toward a meaningful life, even when it's uncomfortable to do so. And habit changes often are uncomfortable—we've slipped into the habits we currently have because there's something about them that works for us, at least in the short term. Maybe our habits are based on taking the path of least resistance, or maybe they provide comfort or escape, or just feel good in the moment.

Practices from ACT can help us to take steps now, even when it's difficult, toward our values. Instead of focusing on the outcome, we can find a behavior, no matter how small, that we can take. And ideally, the steps we choose will be ones that are worth it to us, even if they are difficult, because they are tied to our values and enhance our lives in the long run.

Know your tells

In poker, a "tell" is a slight, usually automatic and unconscious, change in a player's behavior based on their reaction to their hand. A player might slightly raise their eyebrows or shift their posture. An astute observer will look for these cues in other players to get an advantage in the game.

Similarly, sometimes we can slip into patterns that aren't so helpful, without realizing it. We can use our behavioral "tells" to be aware of our behavioral reactions to stress. Similar to the "beep beep" warning signal that you've drifted away from your values—the emotional cues that you're off track (that we learned about in Chapter 10)—your "tells" are behaviors that indicate that something is off. What are the signs that you're under too much stress and might need to recharge? What would someone notice if they were watching your behavior when you were extremely stressed? For example, they might notice increased irritability or substance use, procrastination, worry and rumination, overwork, or a feeling of being unfocused. My "tells" include not exercising for weeks (because I tell myself I'm too busy and exhausted), waking up with racing thoughts in the middle of the night, and acting as if the world will crumble if I take a break. It can take me a surprisingly long time to notice that this is going on! But when I do notice it, I am more aware that my stress level is too high and I need to do something about it.

You might be fooling yourself into thinking that your poker face is so good, no one will notice your stress and burnout. Or thinking that you should be able to handle tremendous stress with ease, without letting anyone see you break a sweat. Consider asking people in your life to be on the lookout for whatever "tells" they notice in your behavior. For instance, a spouse or partner might be the first one to notice that you are being disengaged or irritable at home (a purely hypothetical example, of course; none of us would ever do that, right?) before you realize it yourself.

A tale of two substances—alcohol and caffeine

There are too many examples of unhelpful habits to cover them all, but I did want to offer two examples of habits that contribute to burnout: our dear old friends, alcohol and caffeine.

As the months and years of the Covid-19 pandemic went on, I noticed a trend. Many people I talked to, including clients, friends, and family (and, yes, me too), started to recognize the impact of alcohol use during the stressful periods of the pandemic. I'm not talking about people with a major alcohol problem (but sadly that has happened too for many people). I'm talking about occasional to moderate drinkers, for whom alcohol became a "slippery slope." Among adults in the US, and many other countries around the world, alcohol use in moderation is a generally acceptable way to socialize and relax. Many of us enjoy unwinding with drinks with friends or like to pour a cocktail or glass of wine at the end of a stressful workday. Often we use alcohol to cope with stress or "take the edge off" our painful emotions. From the minute that first sip hits your lips, you can feel your tension go down and your anxiety melt away (until it comes back in full force a few hours later). Many people started drinking more during the pandemic and kept drinking as a way to cope with all the stressors we'd been facing over the last few years. Over time, alcohol became a more regular, sometimes daily, habit, and having "a drink" easily turned into several at a time.

Alcohol use can play a role in burnout (Jackson *et al.* 2016). For many people, there's a cyclical pattern with burnout and alcohol use. High stress and burnout can drive us to drink, and drinking alcohol can contribute to burnout.

I'm not here to moralize about alcohol (I enjoy an occasional glass of wine or a cocktail myself, and it's your choice). But I know that alcohol use can make things worse in people's lives, and is often an ineffective stress management strategy. Alcohol is known to disrupt sleep quality, and people often feel significantly worse in the morning after drinking alcohol. Feeling tired, irritable, embarrassed, or anxious after drinking certainly doesn't help when it comes to burnout. Choosing to cut back or quit alcohol can be an effective and helpful change toward burnout prevention.

Similarly, caffeine (perhaps my personal favorite mind-altering substance) is the most popular psychoactive drug in the world (Pollan 2020). Productive people around the world use it daily to boost energy and get their brains firing. If you're looking for something to energize you, look no further than a cup of strong coffee! But I've seen a cycle that can happen with caffeine. Often caffeine is used to push us into productivity and mask the tiredness we are feeling. When our bodies naturally want to rest, we can use caffeine to keep us marching along. Caffeine can increase anxiety, and stay in our system for hours, impacting our sleep quality at night, which makes us wake up tired and needing more caffeine to keep ourselves going! And so on... Again, I'm not here to moralize about caffeine—a high-quality cup of morning coffee with steamed milk is one of my greatest pleasures in life, and I have no plans to give it up any time soon. But not keeping caffeine use in check can contribute to stress and burnout.

Check your habits

When it comes to burnout, recharging and depleting habits can vary person-to-person, but I do want to help you think about a few habits that might be contributing to the situation. Typically, we want to look at our overall quality of life and consider habits that recharge our energy and sustain us. Let's take a quick inventory of your current habits, and indicators that you might be responding to stress in unhelpful ways.

The thing about habits is that they are automatic and routine by nature, and sometimes we are doing them without even thinking twice about it. I recommend starting with an honest look at your current daily habits, and asking yourself some questions.

TAKE A HABIT INVENTORY

Grab your journal or notebook and a pen, and be honest with yourself:

1. Think about your daily routine. What regular habits do you have that are working well for you? Give yourself some credit for the helpful things you're already doing!
2. Are there habits that aren't working well? Do you have any habits that might be contributing to stress or burnout in the long run? Or causing problems in your life?
3. Are you caring for your physical body and emotional health?

4. Are you using any substances (caffeine, alcohol, marijuana, or others) in excess, or to cope with stress and burnout?

5. Are you engaging in any regular exercise and movement as a form of self-kindness? Would more movement recharge you?

6. Are you taking time to feed yourself consistently?

7. Are you eating food in a way that causes you not to feel good, like overeating or restricting food? Are you relying too much on emotional eating to cope with stress?

8. Are you sleeping enough on a regular basis? How are you doing with sleep hygiene behaviors?

9. Do you take breaks when you need them, for instance stopping to eat lunch away from your computer or taking a quick walk around the block? Or do you tend to "power through" the day?

10. Are you using behaviors like shopping, social media, TV, video games, eating comfort food, and so on, in a way that's negatively impacting your life?

11. How are your spending habits? Do you need to clear up any financial issues that are contributing to your stress?

12. How are your work habits? Are you keeping solid work boundaries in place, or does it spill over into the rest of your life? Do you get into problematic procrastination patterns? How are your work-related technology habits?

13. Are you taking time to enjoy rest, fun, leisure, hobbies, adventure, spiritual practice, nature?

14. Is your living environment comfortable enough for you? Is too much clutter piling up, and adding to your stress?

15. Are you taking care of basic hygiene and physical care of your body and clothing? Or are you spending more time than you really want to on hygiene and clothing?

16. Are you socializing enough? Too much?

17. Are any of your habits having a negative impact on your relationships? Are there any habits that you are minimizing or keeping secret?

18. Are there habits that would help you recharge, that you aren't doing? What new daily habits might help you to deal with stress and recharge from burnout? What gets in the way?

In some situations, it makes more sense to just go easy on yourself about your habits. You're not perfect, and you don't have to be! A few less-than-ideal habits are fine, and you might want to just make a conscious choice to keep some habits as they are, and let some potentially helpful habits go, at least for now. When I'm extra stressed, I'm notoriously bad at housekeeping. My home environment gets messy, and I can live with that—messiness doesn't bother me that much. But if some of your habits seem to be contributing to burnout, a change could be helpful to you.

Learn to pace

Every now and then, I have to schedule more therapy clients over a single day than I probably should. And when I'm struggling to schedule everyone, I occasionally give up my lunch hour to see a client, foregoing breaks and time to eat lunch. Every time I do this, I relearn a valuable life lesson: while I can survive a day like that, and do my best to still be present and attentive to all of those clients, at the end of the day I am guaranteed to be completely wiped out.

In this modern era, constant workload and back-to-back meetings are not rare occurrences, and we can feel that we don't have time to take breaks to recharge. We'll learn more about the importance of rest ahead in Chapter 13, on managing time. In the meantime, an important habit to consider is called "activity pacing." I learned about this important, yet underappreciated, concept when I worked with people with chronic pain and health conditions that cause fatigue. Pacing is where you alternate periods of work and rest, before you get to the point where you are maxed out and then crash and burn. Pacing allows us to sustain our activity level in the long run, because we take breaks before we overdo it.

Activity pacing sounds much easier than it is to execute. The challenge is getting yourself to take a break *before* you feel you need one. Some people schedule in breaks at a certain interval, like stopping for a stretch after 45 minutes of work, or allowing themselves some "cyberloafing" time during less productive times of the day. You could alternate deep mental work with less mentally demanding tasks, socializing, or a more physical task. For instance, today I took a break from writing to take a shower, and another break to do the dishes. Or it might be alternating activities that take a lot of mental or physical energy with more restful activities. For example, someone with chronic fatigue syndrome might take a few breaks while mowing the lawn to sit down and check their emails. Ideally, you want to find things that rejuvenate you, and prioritize mixing those in throughout the day.

Be aware of shiny objects

You might want to consider the habits, or "mini-addictions," that temporarily tempt you but ultimately get in the way of the life you want to live. Sometimes, people get distracted by certain web pages that they check constantly throughout the day, or get tempted by urges to use food, substances, or spending. These are the bright, shiny objects that distract us and take us away from the hard but meaningful things in our lives.

When we are faced with temptation, it can be all too easy to get swept away by urges and distractions. These types of behaviors can become a habit, without intention or sometimes even awareness. While some degree of distraction can be harmless, or even offer us an enjoyable break, when temptations become too much, they can lead us astray from our values.

Tips for making sustainable habit changes

As I've said before, behavior change can be difficult! Here are a few tips to consider, that might be helpful if you do want to work on any habits to help you recharge.

Keep your values in mind

Remember, we are recharging with *values-based* habits! It can be helpful to remember the "why" behind the change you want to make, especially when motivation wanes. These aren't random habits you choose for no reason, nor are they "shoulds." Tie them to something that matters to you. Do you want to make this change to take better care of yourself, to make your work more sustainable, or to improve your relationships? Can you think of it as an act of kindness to your future self? Whatever your reason, keeping your values in mind can make the changes you implement feel more satisfying and less like a "should." We all have plenty of those already! Remembering why you are making a change can help you remain committed to your new habits when it feels tough.

Consider the timing

If this is a highly stressful period of your life, it might be wise to hold off on bigger changes until you are in a more stable phase. It can be very hard to change your habits when you are busy and stressed. In fact, when people come to me for therapy hoping to change a habit, like curbing overeating or cutting back on alcohol, during extremely stressful periods of their lives, I sometimes suggest they wait. The last thing anyone needs is more pressure when they're just trying to survive a rough patch! So think about the timing, and whether you want to go ahead and make a change, or wait until later. Go easy on yourself, and try not to be overly ambitious about changing your habits.

Start small

Small, clear, realistic goals are more likely to stick. Try keeping your goals simple, so you can maintain them up even during moments of low motivation. I caution you against trying to change everything all at once; you'll just get discouraged if your goals are unrealistic. Instead, pick one small step you can take toward a new habit, and start there. Start with one walk around the block, going to bed 15 minutes earlier, one glass of water, five deep breaths, or one page of that book on your bedside table. As James Clear points out in the book *Atomic Habits: An Easy & Proven Way to Build Good Habits & Break Bad Ones*, those small habits can add up and make a big difference over time:

A slight change in your daily habits can guide your life to a very different destination. Making a choice that is 1 percent better or 1 percent worse seems insignificant in the moment, but over the span of moments that make up a lifetime these choices determine the difference between who you are and who you could be. Success is the product of daily habits—not once-in-a-lifetime transformations. (Clear 2018, pp.17–18)

Take a pause

The problem with some unhelpful habits is that they can be so automatic, we do them without thinking about it. You might find yourself scrolling on your phone for 45 minutes before you realize it, or reaching for a beer in the fridge you opened to grab an ingredient for dinner. Learning to pause in that moment and be more intentional makes all the difference. Try to find ways to build in a pause before acting automatically. Take a breath, and ask yourself whether you are sure you want to engage in this behavior, before you do it. This would be a great time to use the "Pause, Notice, Choose" exercise from Chapter 7!

Practice urge surfing

When faced with an urge, like an urge to smoke or drink, or even to reach for your phone or a bag of potato chips, it can be tempting to just follow the urge and do the behavior. This is because urges can be intense and uncomfortable, and the only way to end an urge immediately is to engage in the tempting behavior. This is where "urge surfing" (Bowen and Marlatt 2009) comes in handy. If you step back and watch an urge, you will notice that it rises and falls in intensity, like ocean waves that come and go. Urges will often pass quickly, often within minutes, and they rarely last more than half an hour. You can feel an urge in your body and watch what happens with your thoughts and emotions during the urge. Try urge surfing and you'll learn through experience that you don't have to follow an urge, especially if it is driving an unhelpful behavior. Urges may be uncomfortable, but they won't hurt you. Instead of engaging in the behavior that's driving the urge, you can ride the waves as the urge comes and goes.

Try stimulus control

"Stimulus control" means setting up your environment in ways that help you make sustainable behaviors easy for yourself. This can enable you to engage in helpful behaviors easily when motivation is low, and make unhelpful behaviors more difficult. For instance, I try to brush my teeth when my kids do. My kids brushing their teeth cues me to brush mine, and I'm usually nearby so it's easy to grab my toothbrush and just do it. And, as an extra benefit, I'm less likely to engage in revenge bedtime procrastination if my teeth are brushed and it's easier to put myself to bed on time! Other examples might include keeping your phone away from your bed, and keeping alcohol out of the house, or at least out of reach.

Bundle temptations

In her book *How to Change: The Science of Getting from Where You Are to Where You Want to Be*, Katy Milkman (2021) writes about what she calls "temptation bundling." It's when you bundle together a less enjoyable task with one you enjoy, like watching your favorite TV show while folding laundry, or listening to an audiobook while you go for a walk. In fact, at the very moment I write this sentence I'm bundling the painstaking task of editing my own writing with drinking a delicious latte at my favorite local café by my house! As long as you aren't pairing two cognitively demanding tasks or two physically demanding tasks, you can do both together, and you might find that bundling makes a less pleasant task more enjoyable, which helps to reinforce the habit.

Use rewards and substitutes

Think about how you might also promote behavior changes by rewarding yourself and using a less "harmful" substitute. You might drink a glass of sparkling water instead of a glass of wine, or reach for your favorite magazine instead of scrolling online. And when you do make a values-based habit change, think about how you can reinforce it with a little reward. Maybe let yourself spend a few minutes enjoying a pleasurable activity after you've taken one of those small steps you're trying for.

Use tracking (if it's helpful)

For some behaviors (and some people), tracking can be helpful. This can especially be the case for behaviors that we don't naturally pay much attention to. For instance, you can jot down how much alcohol you're drinking, or keep track of how often you are meditating or flossing. The act of tracking can build awareness, and later you can look back at your log and see what patterns you notice. Sometimes people get bogged down with tracking or find it unhelpful. If that's the case, there's no need to do it! It's not the tracking that matters, it's the awareness it brings, and ultimately the behavior change itself.

Accept your discomfort

As we've noted, we are usually engaging in certain habits because they feel pretty good in the short term. This can be especially true for comfort-seeker types, who often engage in habits that feel comforting. When we change these patterns, all the discomfort we've been trying to avoid shows up. If you are prepared for it to be uncomfortable, you can use your skills (like mindfulness, cognitive defusion, and acceptance skills) to help you cope.

Try a 30-day "dopamine detox"

Psychiatrist and author of *Dopamine Nation: Finding Balance in the Age of Indulgence* Anna Lembke (2021) recommends a 30-day "dopamine detox" for any addictive habit, because it takes that long for the pleasure-seeking parts of our brain to settle down and reset. You may have heard of "dry January" and "sober October" as common examples of this for cutting back on alcohol. You don't have to change your habits forever if you don't want to, but a longer period of behavior change can help you objectively consider the impact a certain behavior is having on your life. Think of it as a short-term experiment to learn something new about yourself.

Reach out for support

If you're struggling with a habit change, social support can make a huge difference (Greaney *et al.* 2018). Support could come from family, friends, co-workers, or even professional support from a therapist or other expert on the change you want to make. With friends and family, it can be helpful to directly ask them for support and encouragement.

Even speaking a goal out loud to someone might make your new goal more likely to happen. Once when I was leading a therapy group, each group member talked about a personal goal. I did too, and my goal was to try a tai chi class at my gym for the first time. The day before the next group, I realized I hadn't done tai chi yet! I looked it up on the gym's class schedule, and went that afternoon. I am 100% sure that if I hadn't told the group about my goal, I wouldn't have done it. I wanted to be able to share my success with the group. (And by the way, I loved doing tai chi.) No more secrecy, let the world know that you are working on this habit.

If you slip up, get back on track

Sometimes you may struggle and slip back into old patterns. No need to beat yourself up or feel as if you've failed. Slip-ups are part of the process, so go easy on yourself. Behavior change can be an up and down process. Self-compassion is more effective at helping people stay motivated to keep going than self-criticism (Breines and Chen 2012). Just forgive yourself, get back on track, and keep at it!

REFLECTION QUESTIONS

1. Based on the habit inventory above, what changes to your habits do you think would help you to recharge?
2. What are your "tells" that indicate you are under chronic stress?
3. What are some ways you can take better care of yourself, to recharge from burnout?
4. Which "tips" for behavior change do you think would be helpful to you?
5. What small step can you start with this week?

CHAPTER 13

Managing Time

As I am a middle-aged, straight/cisgender, white professional woman in America, social pressure tells me that to have a productive and successful life, I should do the following:

- Be highly productive at work, and put in the long hours it takes to get ahead and make a decent income.
- Be a team player by saying yes to projects and requests by colleagues.
- Keep up with my ceaseless email inbox and respond promptly to text messages.
- Maintain an active social life by staying in touch and spending time with family and friends.
- Care for the people in my life who need support and help.
- Give thoughtful gifts to my friends and family.
- Have a romantic partnership (or if I don't have one, go on the dating market to find one), with emotional and physical intimacy and regular date nights.
- Have a few kids, provide them with quality care and my full attention. Host their birthday parties, make their holidays special, and chauffer them around town to playdates and enriching activities. Make sure they turn into well-adjusted, decent human beings.
- Get a solid eight hours of sleep each night.

- Exercise frequently and practice daily self-care.
- Maintain an attractive physical appearance.
- Purchase the latest fashions, home décor, and car.
- Keep my home, yard, and car clean and organized.
- Cook healthy meals and grow my own organic food.
- Take vacations and make time to rest and have fun.
- Take some time for leisure, to be creative and engage in my hobbies.
- Engage in a spiritual or religious practice.
- Read books, learn new skills, and keep up with current events.
- Do some community service or volunteer work, and be politically active.
- And so on...

Do you see a problem here? I don't know about you, but reading this list makes me feel exhausted, stressed, and guilty about the many areas of my life I'm currently short-changing. There simply aren't enough hours in each day, week, month, and year to do all these things. At least I can't do them well, at the same time, without feeling constantly busy and overwhelmed. And eventually, burned out.

Time is, perhaps, our most valuable and limited resource, and one of the biggest struggles I've seen in my burnout work is how to manage time effectively in a busy life, with plenty of responsibility and not enough time to get everything done. Often, people experiencing burnout are engaged in productive roles that are so all-consuming, they lack the time it would take to recharge and enjoy other parts of their lives. There's simply too much work, and each day feels hectic if we do too much. Our work can suffer from the chronic stress of having less time than it takes to keep up with all of our tasks, and we can suffer personally if we don't spend enough outside our work roles. Time slips by, and we can never get it back.

A constant sense of time urgency increases our stress level, contributing to the problem underlying burnout. We tell ourselves that once we catch up, which always seems to be right around the corner, we'll have time to relax and do more of the things we love. But for most chronically stressed people, that isn't realistic. The emails will keep coming, the dirty laundry will keep piling up. There will always be too much to do in the amount of time we have. Unless we make a change with how we manage our time, this cycle will continue.

In this chapter, I will invite you to think about time management in some new ways that may help with burnout. Most time management advice out there teaches you strategies to be more efficient in using time. While sometimes a schedule shift or more efficient time management system can help lighten the load, often what's really needed is a philosophical shift in how you think about time.

Take an honest look at your priorities

As a chronically busy, overwhelmed person, I spent years looking for "life hacks" to help me with time management. I would read productivity books on organizing my schedule better and try out new systems to help me overcome my time management problems. Looking back, I can see clearly now that my real problem wasn't that I didn't have a good enough planner or scheduling system. My problem was that I wasn't prioritizing the most important things in my life and letting go of the rest.

In some work roles, there's little time freedom, and a schedule change is outside our control. But sometimes, we take on more than we realistically have time for. And we face tremendous social pressure to engage in too many areas at once. It's not your fault that you can't keep up with everything. It's simply not possible to do it all. Instead, we must all make some hard choices about how we choose to spend our time.

In his book *Four Thousand Weeks: Time Management for Mortals*, Oliver Burkeman writes:

> You'll do what you can, you won't do what you can't, and the tyrannical inner voice insisting that you must do everything is simply mistaken. We rarely stop to consider things so rationally, though, because that would mean confronting the painful truth of our limitations. We would be forced to acknowledge that there are hard choices to be made: which balls to let drop, which people to disappoint, which cherished ambitions to abandon, which roles to fail at. (Burkeman 2021, pp.38–39)

Recently, I went to a party with my husband's co-workers. I was talking to one of the hosts of the party, a woman whose children were about ten years older than mine. She had just remodeled her home, and it was beautiful. I confessed to her that mine was in a sorry state. My living room needs to be repainted, and I would like to replace some of my worn-out furniture. She asked me how old my children were. When I told her they were in elementary school, she firmly told me not to worry about fixing up my house right now. "This time will go by so quickly," she said. "Soon your kids will be independent. Focus on spending time with them, talking to them, and reading to them instead of decorating. You can fix your house up later, don't worry about that right now." She finally redecorated her own house when her children were off busy with their own lives in high school and college—and she didn't regret waiting so long. I immediately felt myself let go of guilt. To me, some neglected home projects are a small price to pay to be able to focus on my children and my work. She gave me the perspective shift I needed!

At the deepest level, managing time is about deciding how you spend it. When we decide to spend time on one thing, we are choosing not to spend time on countless other things we could be doing instead (Burkeman 2021). It can be difficult to prioritize what's important and to engage less in less important areas. To really prioritize, you need to zoom out and look at the big picture. You need to be truly realistic about how much you can and can't do, what makes the cut, and what can go.

To carve out the time to write this book, for example, I sacrificed leisure time and turned down some other professional activities I would have enjoyed. When we choose to spend our time on one activity rather than another, the cost of giving something up can be painful. The question is, are you willing to experience that pain, in order to have more time to do the things that matter most to you?

Sure, there are going to be some things we'd rather not do but must spend our time on in order to function effectively. If I could choose a superpower, it would be the Mary Poppins-style ability to magically clean my house with a snap of my fingers. Until then, unless I'm willing to live in absolute squalor, which I'm not, I must spend some of my precious time doing tasks I find boring, like cleaning the dishes. But I don't want to fritter too many precious hours away on the unimportant things every day. Instead, I can take a "good enough" approach to these kinds of lower-priority activities. I can put just enough effort into domestic chores to maintain my home in a way I can live with, but prioritize it lower than the things that matter more to me in the limited time I have available (until that Mary Poppins superpower kicks in, that is; I'm still waiting).

Trying to cram more into each day means perpetual stress and busyness, and there is a cost to that. We end up rushing around all the time, dissatisfied, and doing so leads to burnout. As painful and hard as it can be to let something go, consider the possibility that some of the less important tasks in your life may need to slip, to have the life you really want.

Use time intentionally

Here's a paradox that I bet you've experienced. You feel too busy and stressed to have enough time for the things that fulfill you, like vacations, reading for pleasure, hobbies, exercise, and fun with your friends. And yet, you spend hours each week mindlessly scrolling around online, playing video games, or watching TV shows you don't really care about.

Often, we can become a bit mindless in our use of time. When we are exhausted, we may feel that we don't have the energy to stop and choose meaningful activities, but rather let time slip away from us by automatically engaging in time-sucking activities we don't really enjoy. Author and time-management expert Laura Vanderkam writes, "A life is lived in hours, and living the good life requires being a proper steward of those hours. This stewardship often requires choices that come from being mindful of time" (Vanderkam 2018, p.3).

To be clear, I'm not suggesting that you should never relax or that procrastination is always bad. Sometimes we benefit from "cyberloafing" just to give ourselves a mental break! But I am suggesting that time can slip by quickly when we are spending too much time doing unimportant things and we can end up short-changing the things that are important.

And when we *intentionally choose* to relax or procrastinate, we might even enjoy it more!

When we are under stress, this can be particularly difficult because our reserves are low. It takes effort to prioritize what's important, and it can be difficult to engage in important things when we have stressful tasks lurking, unfinished, in the background. Often when I have a few hours available, perhaps in the evening or during a weekend, I don't feel as if I have enough time to relax and lounge around, but I also don't feel like getting anything productive done. I'm left in a limbo state of not allowing myself to rest or enjoy leisure time, but also not doing anything else that's productive. Important things are neglected, the chance to really relax is missed, and my time is frittered away.

In her book *Time Smart: How to Reclaim Your Time and Live a Happier Life*, Ashley Whillans (2020) writes about finding time and funding time. Whillans recommends finding time by paying attention to time spent doing meaningless things you don't enjoy and using that time in more enjoyable ways instead. And we can fund time by spending some of our discretionary money on not doing things ourselves that we don't enjoy. Instead of spending money on the latest technology device or that new pair of shoes you've been eying, you could use some of that money to free up time by paying for convenience. For example, you can pay a fee to have groceries delivered instead of shopping, and use that time to go to the park instead.

TIME-TRACKING EXERCISE

Vanderkam and Whillans both recommend starting with a time audit. You can track your time by jotting down what you are doing hour-by-hour for a couple of typical days. Then, take an honest look at where your time is going. Are there hours of time that feel mindlessly wasted? Ask yourself what important things you would rather be doing with your time, and look for areas on your schedule where you could potentially free some time up to do these things. It might help to block time out on your schedule and stick to it, to make the choice easier for yourself in the moment.

As I was thinking about the concept of finding time, I noticed an unexpected area of my own life where there was wasted time to be found: decision-making. As I shared in Chapter 11, I will hem-and-haw over the most minor of decisions. My husband and I can go back and forth for 45 minutes about what to eat for dinner, and even longer deciding what to do when we have a free Saturday and want to take our kids on an outing. If I have an hour available to catch up on work, I can spend most of that time mulling over which task to work on next. I'll be in an unproductive state that entire time as I fritter it away, unsure of what to do with myself. I don't find time spent making decisions to be enjoyable at all! I'm usually frustrated, as the conversation (in my mind, or with my husband) goes in circles and tangents, and I'm waiting to get started. Learning this has helped me recognize that pattern and try to streamline decision-making where I can. Now, when possible, I try to spend less time going back and forth with decision-making, and instead make a choice and jump into action, which feels like a better use of time to me. (For some tips on how to do this, go back to the section of Chapter 11 on decision-making.)

Redistribute your workload

I'm sure you've had the experience of filling a washing machine with too much bulky laundry. My machine, down in my basement, starts clunking when a load is unevenly distributed, or even comes to a complete stop when the load is too heavy to spin. When we are chronically stressed and burned out it can feel like that—when our schedules are overly full with too many heavy items, or when things are unevenly distributed, everything gets out of alignment and it's hard to keep everything spinning along. Burnout can be an indication that we need to lighten the load or redistribute the heavy stuff.

If you are currently highly stressed and burned out, it's likely that your use of time has shifted out of balance. You may be working long hours at the expense of having a social life, or you might be rushing from one meeting to the next without stopping to eat meals. You might be purposely short-changing sleep to get more done. Consider lightening your load. Let's look at some ways to do that.

Say no and subtract

I've noticed a trend among my therapy clients with burnout—they have a tendency to say yes to things, automatically. Many burnout-prone people suffer from "the curse of competence." They get a lot of requests for things that take time, because they are good at many things, and default to saying yes. Sometimes this comes from enthusiasm about opportunities being offered; there's a sense that they would genuinely love to do it all if they had more hours in the day. And sometimes it comes more from a sense of obligation or a desire to please others; it can feel as if they are letting someone down or dropping the ball when they say no. Either way, being more deliberate about saying yes, and exerting the right to say no sometimes, can be liberating in terms of demands on time. (We'll learn more about *how* to say no in Chapter 15.) Remember, just because you have a bird in the hand, doesn't mean it's the right bird for you!

Sometimes saying no to new time-consuming demands isn't enough. We may need to look at our schedule and decide to *remove* some activities or commitments. Removing obligations from our schedule can be difficult! Leidy Klotz, author of the book *Subtract: The Untapped Science of Less* (2021), points out that our brains are wired to pursue adding resources, and it can be more difficult to make decisions about what to subtract. "In our striving to improve our lives, our work, and our society, we overwhelmingly add" (Klotz 2021, p.11). According to Klotz, we tend to neglect the possibility of subtraction, often not even considering that as a solution to a problem we are facing. Similarly, Scott Sonenshein, author of the book *Stretch: Unlock Power of Less—and Achieve More Than You Ever Imagined* (2017), writes about how we often feel that we can never have enough achievements and resources, and must always strive to accumulate more, resulting in mindless accumulation and constant pursuit of more and bigger. Both authors point out the value of getting out of that trap, and instead making a conscious choice to slow down and pursue less instead of more.

When you think about the many stressors in your life, and your management of time, it's important to consider what can be subtracted from your workload. Are there useless meetings you habitually attend that you can convert to an email? Tasks that are no longer serving your goals? Social media accounts you'd be better off without?

Lower your standards

Believe it or not, I have occasionally recommended that one of my clients do a half-hearted job at something, on purpose. Slack off at work, eat French fries from the fast-food drive-through for dinner instead of cooking, shove some clutter in the closet and close the door, put the kids in front of the TV for a few hours. I think of this as exposure therapy for perfectionist types, who are used to doing everything well, all the time.

As you'll recall from Chapter 5, meeting your own high standards is highly reinforcing for perfectionist types. When you burn the midnight oil to do a great job at work, your boss will absolutely love it. You won't have to face the self-criticism that shows up when you don't do your best. But the pressure we feel to take time to do things very well adds to chronic stress. Having high standards in every domain is a reliable recipe for a time management problem, and lowering your standards can help!

Take a moment to consider some areas of your life where you have high standards, perhaps bordering on perfectionism. It could be related to your job or a personal domain, like parenting, housework, or personal care. Ask yourself what would happen if you eased up a little on your standards. Would the world keep on spinning? I can assure you, it would. Ask yourself whether doing a top-notch job on something is worth the time it would take. If not, maybe you can go easy on yourself by doing a "good enough" job on it.

Beware of low-hanging fruit

In Chapter 5, I shared that I tend to be a busy bee type who overworks and gets busy when I'm stressed. I will occasionally feel highly productive when I engage in what I call "low-hanging fruit tasks." These are tasks that I can accomplish quickly with little exertion or emotional energy, like catching up on a few emails, ordering something online, filling out a form, doing a household chore, or running a quick errand.

I get a burst of satisfaction from checking these kinds of tasks off my to-do list.

These kinds of tasks do need to get done sometimes, of course, but in excess they can be the enemy of time well spent. Sometimes I find that I can fill my day with them, eating up the time I had planned to spend doing something more important to me. Maybe I wanted to use a two-hour window to work on writing this book, and instead I responded to unimportant emails the whole time. Or maybe I planned to exercise in the morning and instead I puttered around the house organizing piles of papers.

Don't get seduced into feeling that you are being productive if you aren't doing the important things! The problem with low-hanging fruit tasks is that they can eat away your time, and keep you away from what matters more to you. Do you want your tombstone to say that you had inbox zero and ran all the errands you could? Or that you spent time with the people you cared about and left behind a creative legacy?

To be able to pursue your dreams, like your new boat-building hobby or that book you've been wanting to write for ten years, you can't let yourself be too consumed by these kinds of tasks. You'll have to pro-crastinate on the seemingly urgent tasks that constantly pile up and feel important, in order to do things that are actually much more important to you. I hereby officially grant you permission to neglect some of those never-ending low-hanging fruit tasks to free up some of your time for other things you truly want to be doing!

Renegotiate duties

In her book *Fair Play: A Game-Changing Solution for When You Have Too Much to Do (and More Life to Live)*, Eve Rodsky (2019) writes about how domestic work is largely undervalued, and tends to default to women in heterosexual partnerships. The women Rodsky talked to, and she herself (before making some changes in her marriage and writing the book), were doing the bulk of childcare and domestic work, "even in two-earner families in which both parents work full-time and sometimes even when the mother earns more than her partner" (Rodsky 2019, p.12).

Rodsky noticed that, in these relationships, men's time was treated like a precious resource, whereas the time women were spending on domestic tasks was treated as abundant. The mental and emotional load of holding responsibility for most of the work is exhausting and stressful.

In the case of redistributing the load of domestic tasks, Rodsky recommends that couples decide together which tasks are important to the family. Then each partner takes ownership over certain domestic tasks, from conception, to planning, to execution, in a way that meets at least the minimal standards of both partners. If your partner is taking on long-term responsibility for a task, Rodsky suggests making it clear that it is now their task to manage, thus freeing you up from the mental load of having to follow up and worry about who will get it done.

Redistributing your workload, domestic or otherwise, can be challenging. It requires flexible thinking to do things in a new way, instead of the way you've always done them. It may need some degree of letting go of control and perfectionism if you like things done a particular way, or it may require some assertive communication and boundary-setting skills (you'll learn more about those skills in Chapter 13). But the benefits might be such that it's worth it. Only then, when some of your heavy load has been redistributed, can the washing machine of your life start spinning again.

Carving out time for rest

In my early twenties, my friends and I would say the catchphrase, "You can sleep when you're dead!" This was usually when we had been busy all day with school and work, and wanted to stay out late, with full awareness that we would be tired the next day. Once I went dancing even though I had an early flight to catch for my grandparents' 60th wedding anniversary. I decided to stay up all night! Back then, my body could take such abuse, and I gleefully chose to sacrifice sleep to "work hard, play hard." A few hours of tiredness seemed like a small price to pay.

I long ago abandoned that youthful motto, but this mentality toward sleep reflects a cultural phenomenon here in the industrialized Western world. Sleep and rest are looked on as a waste of time. At Harvard, back when I was there for graduate school, sleep deprivation was almost seen as a badge of honor, a bragging right among high-achieving students and academics, who were so busy and important they had to pull all-nighters to work. Rest is often seen as something we must earn, and an indulgence to enjoy when our work is done.

In the book *Laziness Does Not Exist*, Devon Price (2021) points out the harmful cultural message that time spent in restful, non-productive activities is "lazy," a waste of time, and morally inferior to work. For busy people there are many barriers to rest and taking time off. There can be plenty of social pressure to work too much, and sometimes it doesn't feel worth it to stop. If I take a four-day weekend, will it be worth it for the pre- and post-vacation catch-up I'll have to do? No one else in my firm has had a three-week vacation this year; will I look less ambitious if I take one?

Sometimes, for the chronically stressed, it can even feel uncomfortable to take time off for rest. In the fall, when the weather gets chilly in Denver, my husband likes sometimes to sit outside by a little fire pit we have in our backyard. We just sit there, chatting a little, maybe drinking some tea or wine, and basically hanging out doing nothing for a couple of hours. Sounds delightful, right? Sometimes I enjoy doing this, of course, but I find that if I'm stressed about something I was planning to get done that night, I can feel very uncomfortable! I'm preoccupied by the work I was planning to do and feel guilty for just sitting there when I could be getting something accomplished. I start plotting my escape, to go back inside and be productive, which would feel better to me than relaxing in that moment. When I'm at my best, I catch myself doing this, and give myself permission to let go of guilt and spend this time with the people I love.

Recently, there has been greater appreciation for the benefits of sleep, and new points of view about our societal aversion to rest. In the book *Rest: Why You Get More Done When You Work Less*, Alex Soojung-Kim Pang (2016) points out the paradox that rest and work are not opposites; rather, taking time to deliberately and actively choose rest over work is essential. Rest boosts creativity, efficiency, deep focused work, and more sustainable long-term productivity—all the good stuff that's hard to access when we are in busy bee/grind mode. If we want to do our deepest, most creative work, rather than piling on more hours of work, we should intentionally choose to take some downtime to engage in restful activities, like sleep, a hiatus from parenting, a leisurely meal, a stroll, or just chilling out at home on the couch.

It would be a mistake to think of resting as a tool for being more productive in the long run. The goal is not to rest, just so you can come back a more productive and stronger person contributing to a capitalist system. Rooted in social justice movements, Tricia Hersey, Devon Price, and others advocate for reclaiming rest as a basic human right, and promote a cultural movement against the capitalistic pressure to work constantly. Hersey points out that our worth is not defined by how productive we are, especially when we live within systems that exploit workers and teach us the subtle message that we are not worthy of rest. "Our drive and obsession to always be in a state of 'productivity' leads us to the path of exhaustion, guilt, and shame" (Hersey 2022, p.62).

If you're thinking that rest sounds great, but you can't afford the time or lost productivity it would involve, think again. Take it from the Nap Bishop, Tricia Hersey herself, who writes that rest is not a luxury only for the privileged few with excess time and money, it is a necessity for all of us, to reclaim our humanity. We've been told by capitalistic "grind culture" that we must either work at machine level, to the point of exhaustion, or fear how we'll pay the bills and survive. But we don't have to buy into that. We can push back against dominant narratives and unravel from the culture of overwork. We don't have to wait for permission from the dominant culture. We can sleep, turn off our social media, meditate, lounge around and do nothing.

Time spent resting, while easily sacrificed among the chronically stressed and overworked, can be time well spent. In her book *Sacred Rest: Recover Your Life, Renew Your Energy, Restore Your Sanity*, physician Saundra Dalton-Smith tells her own story of busyness and burnout as a mom and physician, and asks the question, "What kind of tired are you?" (Dalton-Smith 2017, p.12). She describes seven types of rest we may be missing and can benefit from bringing into our daily lives: physical rest, mental rest, emotional rest, spiritual rest, social rest, sensory rest, and creative rest. How do you need to give your exhausted mind and body a rest? Do you need to unplug, lie down, write in your journal, or connect with nature? And how can you make that a regular practice in your too-busy life?

I'm writing the last paragraph of this chapter early on a Saturday morning. My kids spent the night at their grandma's house last night, so my husband and I could go out to dinner for our anniversary. I carved out a few hours of time to write this morning. I just got hungry for breakfast, and paused to make myself eggs, a piece of toast, and some tea. I almost brought my laptop to the table to keep writing, but instead I sat at the table and took a break to eat quietly and drink my tea. I'm about to close my laptop for the day, pick up my kids, and spend the rest of the day relaxing with my family. We might watch a movie or have a picnic at the park. I need a break from work, and to prioritize relaxing with my family today. If I can do it, so can you!

REFLECTION QUESTIONS

1. How are you spending time? Are you using your time wisely by spending it on the things that are most important to you? What changes might you need to make in managing your time?

2. If you had an opportunity to spend a whole day with nothing planned, how would you want to spend it?

3. What are your top priorities? Are there any that are being short-changed? What lower priorities would you have to give up to focus more on the most important things in your life?

4. Do you need to redistribute your workload? Cut back on work? Say no? Ask for help, or delegate some work? Renegotiate domestic duties?

5. How might you lower your standards and be less perfectionistic? What low-hanging fruit tasks do you need to look out for?

6. Is it possible to change anything about your schedule? If so, should you?

7. What would you like to say no to in your busy schedule? What would you like to subtract? What would you like to have more time to say yes to?

8. Do you need more time to rest? Do you need a break, or a vacation? How can you carve out more time for rest in your daily life?

CHAPTER 14

Creating Community and Connection

I f I could offer you my one most important bit of advice for coping with chronic stress and burnout, it would probably be this: to reach out for support and remind yourself that you are not alone. Allow me to offer you two snapshots from my own life, to demonstrate.

In the first snapshot, I was working in a hospital on a medical team, during a period when I wasn't feeling burned out. I spent a lot of time interacting with my team. I would go to the nurses' station when I had a few minutes to spare, to see who was there for a chat. I would confide in my colleagues about how I was doing, they would do the same, and we would ask each other for help with tough cases. We had potlucks, retirement parties, ugly sweater contests, and chili cook-offs. We used "gallows humor" when we were faced with challenging situations, struck by the absurdity of it all, and would enjoy a good laugh together when everything felt like too much. I felt connected and happy at work.

In the second, it was the lockdown phase of Covid-19 in the early summer of 2020. We were all living in a strange new world, anxious about what was to come, sad about important plans that were canceled, and stir-crazy from being at home so much. In the evenings, my neighbors in my urban neighborhood in Denver would gather, several feet apart, on our front porches while the kids ran up and down the block to let off steam. The neighbors would all chat, telling stories about what we were going through, sharing the latest pandemic news we had heard. These moments were a memorable bright spot during a dark time in history and in our lives.

One potential upside of adversity identified in the post-traumatic growth literature (which we explored in Chapter 11) is closer, more meaningful relationships. When times are tough, we can reach out to each other for support. We might bond with someone who is experiencing a similar situation, support someone (or get support) during times of struggle, or find community among a group of people, in a life-enhancing way. If your burnout leads you to turn toward others, this might be the case. And supportive relationships, whether with family, friends, co-workers, a spouse or partner, or neighbors, can help you to prevent and recover from burnout.

In this chapter, we will explore the importance of relationships in burnout prevention, and discuss some strategies for building connection and community.

Living and working in silos: Isolation and loneliness

Humans' lives, which were once organized around close-knit communities, have become increasingly disconnected, as we saw back in Chapter 3. Over time, at least in individualistic cultures, like where I live in the United States, many people have experienced increased isolation. People are spending more time alone—many people live by themselves, or with a roommate or a small family, away from their extended families, often with limited support. People's close social networks are generally getting smaller (McPherson, Smith-Lovin, and Brashears 2006), due at least in part to the modern-day fast pace of life and increase in technology use, which have resulted in less time spent focusing on relationships. In general, in today's world many of us have fewer opportunities for in-person interactions and relationships.

Loneliness is the subjective feeling of having inadequate social connection (Cacioppo and Patrick 2008; Murthy 2020). It's not the same as solitude; you can be in comfortable solitude and not feel loneliness, and you can be surrounded by people but feel disconnected and lonely.

In fact, sometimes our deepest feelings of loneliness can be when we are around people we feel we *should* be close to but aren't, as in a distant relationship. Mere proximity to people without a supportive bond does not fulfill our fundamental need for belonging (Baumeister and Leary 1995).

Even prior to the Covid-19 pandemic, the United States Surgeon General, Dr. Vivek Murthy, declared that the world is suffering from "an epidemic of loneliness" (Murthy 2017). In recent years, a majority of Americans have been reporting loneliness (Anderson, Thayer, and AARP Research 2018; Cigna 2020). And during and since the pandemic, isolation and loneliness have continued to increase.

In the workplace, too often these days we are working alone or in silos. In a recent survey of American workers, about a third reported feeling disconnected from others at work, and lonely workers thought about quitting twice as often as other workers (Cigna 2020). As you'll see below, the loneliness and isolation so many of us are experiencing recently has a negative impact on our physical health and emotional wellbeing (Holt-Lunstad 2021; Holt-Lunstad, Smith, and Layton 2010; Murthy 2020).

Social psychology researchers Geoffrey Cohen and Greg Walton coined the term "belonging uncertainty" to describe the state of mind in which we experience doubts about whether we are, or ever could be, fully accepted in a particular environment, like a workplace, school, or gathering of friends (Cohen 2022). This is an extremely common, perhaps universal, human experience. We've all felt belonging uncertainty at some point in our lives; I know I have many times, and I'm sure you have too. Even people who usually have a strong social support network can find themselves feeling unsure of whether they fit in, in some situations. You've likely felt belonging uncertainty when you started a new job, or went to a party where you didn't know anyone. Interestingly, we often think we are alone in feeling this way because we tend not to share the experience with others. If we did acknowledge this more openly, we might find that we aren't so alone after all. We might realize that this universal experience connects us all.

While belonging uncertainty is a universal human experience, it tends to be stressful. When we feel it, we can feel anxious and self-pro-tective, closing ourselves off from others, and from engagement. It can also lead us to extreme self-doubt—perhaps believing ourselves to be unlovable or incapable—and to being more sensitive to perceived failure. And when people have been given the explicit or implicit message that they don't fit within a particular culture or situation—for instance, when they are part of a marginalized or minority group within a workplace—belonging uncertainty can be chronic.

Isolation and lack of support can contribute to burnout. The rela-tionship between social isolation and burnout is likely bidirectional; sometimes burnout can lead to a tendency to isolate ourselves, or burn-out-related disconnection can make us feel that we must tough things out on our own.

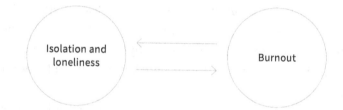

When burned out, we may feel reluctant to ask for help or seek support, assuming others will not respond favorably. Or, we may have been so stressed and busy that we've neglected to put enough time and energy into our relationships, opting instead to focus on work. As Jessica Grose put it in a *New York Times* essay, perhaps we are

> spending less time with friends because we're simply exhausted. At the end of a random Tuesday, I want to be in my soft pants watching old episodes of "Snapped." I don't want to get dressed, leave my house, sit upright or have an in-depth conversation. (Grose 2022)

Socializing takes more energy than we may feel we have to spare. But, as we will see, isolation and loneliness dig us in deeper with burnout.

Social support, health, and burnout

Having supportive relationships makes a positive difference in our health and wellbeing. Social connection, as opposed to isolation and loneliness, is associated with a number of health factors, including longevity (Holt-Lunstad 2021; Holt-Lunstad *et al.* 2010; Perissinotto, Stijacic Cenzer, and Covinsky 2012). It is a protective factor against depression, anxiety, schizophrenia, substance abuse, and suicide risk (Cacioppo, Hawkley, and Thisted 2010; Cacioppo and Patrick 2008). Social contact, even with strangers, can positively impact our health (Van Lange and Columbus 2021).

For over 80 years, researchers who conducted the Harvard Study of Adult Development followed a group of people, asking them questions every few years about their lives and measuring their physical health, mental health, and longevity outcomes. What was the one factor that stood out as most consistently tied to health and wellbeing? Good relationships. "Good relationships keep us healthier and happier. Period" (Waldinger and Schultz 2023, p.10).

Research has been conducted all around the world on the relationship between burnout and social support, including studies conducted with social workers in the UK (Sánchez-Moreno *et al.* 2015), university students in China (Ye, Huang, and Liu 2021), nurses in Oman (Al Sabei *et al.* 2022), human services workers in India (Brown, Prashantham, and Abbott 2003), healthcare professionals in Ecuador (Ruisoto *et al.* 2021) and China (Hou *et al.* 2020), medical students in Thailand (Puranitee *et al.* 2022), pediatricians in Austria (Leiss *et al.* 2021), and nurses around the world (Velando-Soriano *et al.* 2020). Unsurprisingly, the research supports the relationship between social support and reduced burnout. Honestly, I've been studying psychology for a very long time, and I don't think I've ever seen a single research study conducted anywhere in the world that didn't stress the importance of social support for all form of psychological wellbeing.

The research is crystal clear and pretty much indisputable on the importance of relationships. We humans are, after all, *highly* social creatures (Tomasello 2014) with a fundamental need for belonging (Baumeister and Leary 1995). We evolved to survive in groups, sharing resources and work. Our brains are wired to be highly attuned to social interactions, and many of our emotions are social in nature.

While social support may not eliminate a stressful situation, it can help with burnout by buffering us from the emotional impact. When we turn to people for support during times of stress and adversity, we can build close relationships. We are able to go beyond ourselves and our own personal problems, which can be great for perspective-taking; and engaging in prosocial actions can be a source of meaning and personal growth. Whatever stress we are experiencing feels more bearable if we have support—someone to talk to, a hand to hold, a shoulder to cry on. Relationships might not make the stress disappear, but they can lighten the emotional load and change how stress impacts us.

There are many forms of social support. It can involve being part of a cohesive team, like the medical team I described in my first snapshot. It can include getting practical help or useful feedback. It can be encouragement, comfort, humor, and a shared understanding that we are not alone with difficult experiences. And sometimes, it's just fun to hang out with people we like to be around.

Creating connection and community

We might need to take active steps to get the social support we want and need. It requires us to prioritize relationships, reach out, and take steps toward creating connections with individuals or groups. We can do this flexibly—support doesn't have to be all-or-nothing, and meaningful relationships don't have to be the perfect ones of your dreams (or as depicted in romantic comedies). But wherever you're starting from—whether you are feeling isolated and want to socialize more, or whether you have plenty of social interaction and want to deepen the relationships you have—you can take steps toward creating more connection and community.

If you feel that you could use more social support than you are currently getting, I encourage you to consider both small and large interactions that could bring you closer to the kinds of relationships and communities you want. Small interactions might include stopping to chat with a co-worker or neighbor for a few minutes, or texting an old friend you haven't talked to in a while. Bigger interactions might include inviting someone to lunch, joining a group, or hosting a gathering. Let's look at some more tips for creating connection and community.

Take a chance

Meeting new people, or getting past the superficial level with people you know, can be an act of courage. If you could do with more social interaction, take a chance and put yourself out there! Talk to people. Strike up conversations. Share a little something personal about yourself. Sometimes going out of our way to talk to people can lead to unexpected moments of connection, and even friendship. Who knows? It might feel scary and brave, but you can do it!

You can also take a chance by asking someone you see around for coffee, lunch, or a quick walk. You can say yes to offers to socialize. Even if you're busy, those small interactions add up. And don't forget small gestures of kindness. Drop off cookies for your new neighbor, or offer to return someone's cart in the grocery store parking lot for them. You never know when or how you might meet someone new.

You may not "feel like" socializing or meeting new people if you're burned out (review "Opposite action" from Chapter 7) or your mind might say that you are "too busy" (review "Cognitive defusion" in Chapter 8). You might be afraid of rejection or worry about what people will think of you. Instead of being swayed by unhelpful thoughts and feelings, keep your relationship values in mind (Chapter 10), and take action. You have to put effort into relationships and prioritize them to create meaningful ones. Like compound interest in a bank account, investment in relationships pays off over time.

Find your people

Like all kids (well, and most adults too, now that I think about it), my two elementary-school-aged daughters are trying to find their place in the social world. Sometimes they tell me about a social situation that's been upsetting them. I will often advise them to spend their time and energy with friends who are kind to them—the ones who help them feel good about themselves. I encourage them to be respectful toward people who aren't that way, but also to consider keeping some distance.

I offer the same advice to you. Find "your people"—the ones who give you energy, rather than suck it away. These are often people who support you, who you feel you can open up to, and who will open up to you in exchange. They're the people whose values you admire, or people who just make you laugh and are fun to be around.

In a TEDx Talk, psychologist Adam Dorsay (2021) recommends what he calls "the driveway test." After spending time with someone, perhaps as you're driving away, pause to reflect on how you feel. Do they leave you feeling supported and happy? Or deflated and exhausted? Does this friendship nourish you? Do you find time spent with this person to be meaningful and enjoyable? All relationships have potential to leave you feeling depleted sometimes, but if you find that negative feelings persist, you might choose to invest your time and energy in someone else.

Open up and ask questions

Sharing your experience and telling your story to people who respond with empathy and warmth is important. Establishing a close relationship is a reciprocal process. If you could use more emotional support, start by choosing (or seeking) someone you want to open up to, and then test the waters. Share one small struggle you are facing with someone and see how they respond. If they are receptive and respond with empathy, and especially if they open up a little bit in response, repeat. Over time, you can open up more. Meanwhile, ask them questions and show interest in their life. Asking people questions about themselves helps to build meaningful, and reciprocal, connections.

Never worry alone

The US Department of Veterans Affairs Medical Center located here in Denver offers a Suicide Risk Management Consultation service, which provides free consultation, support, and resources for mental health and healthcare professionals working with veterans at risk of suicide. The service offers a safe space to discuss the difficult work of helping people who are in a place of profound suffering. Promotional materials for the service included the tagline #NeverWorryAlone. I love that.

That concept of not worrying alone is profound. Often when we are faced with our most difficult challenges—everything from personal problems, to ethical dilemmas, to fear about someone's wellbeing, to feeling unsure if we can do our job adequately—we feel embarrassed or ashamed and think we should be able to resolve things on our own. But these are exactly the times when support is most crucial, and can help us navigate hard situations effectively.

In situations with potential for moral injury (the suffering that can occur in high-stakes situations that challenge our moral code) it is often recommended that ethically complicated and high-stakes decisions are made in teams (Borges *et al.* 2020). Support from teams trained in ethical decision-making around specific issues can help decision-makers to think through multiple angles of a difficult, high-stakes situation. That way, a consensus about the best choice is made as a group, and no one is left alone in feeling that they single-handedly made the wrong choice.

All of this is to say...to prevent burnout, when possible, seek support. Especially if you are grappling with a difficult or stressful situation. You don't have to worry alone!

Create supportive social groups

Being part of a social group or community, beyond one-on-one relationships, can be life enhancing. For me, a lesser-known perk of being a therapist is access to support from colleagues and friends who are also therapists. I belong to a few small groups of therapists, and these provide me with peer consultation, personal support, encouragement for professional development, and friendship. I'm also part of some professional organizations. When I attend a professional conference with colleagues I've known for years now, I feel fulfilled and recharged from reconnecting with people I care about. These relationships have been a source of tremendous meaning and growth for me over the years.

Supportive work teams are important (we'll talk more about how to create one in Chapter 16, on systemic and organizational changes), but of course not everyone will be interested in communities of people in their same professional field. (In fact, sometimes I find it refreshing to be around friends who aren't therapists, so we don't keep having psychology-related conversations!) For you, it might be a book club, a church or spiritual group, a group of dads from your kid's preschool, people who enjoy tai chi at the park, or watching basketball at a sports bar with other fans of your favorite team. You might join a group that already exists, or take the plunge and create a group you're looking for. You could consider joining a group of people who are experiencing a similar life situation to yours—like my therapist consultation groups, or a caregiver support group, or a group for early career professionals at your workplace. Groups that meet regularly are especially helpful because you will get to know each other and stay connected over the course of time. And regular contact is how relationships are made.

Regardless of who you enjoy being with, or what you do together, engagement in supportive communities of people with whom you have a connection is essential for wellbeing and burnout prevention. It can take some courage to join a new group or invite people to do something with you. I encourage you to face your fears and let values be your guide. You can do it!

Connect with co-workers

The workplace itself is a sometimes-overlooked source of social support. It can be "an arena in which a diverse array of interpersonal relationships are formed...and these relationships can have a strong influence on the meaning of work" (Rosso, Dekas, and Wrzesniewski 2010, p.100).

Relationships formed at work can play an important role in both personal and job satisfaction (Patel and Plowman 2022). So, if you haven't already, consider sparking conversations with your coworkers and getting to know them better. You spend so many hours at work, why not make some connections?

Beware of social comparison and competition

I will often ask clients with work burnout if they have any colleagues they can talk to about what they are going through. Sometimes my clients respond by saying they are the only ones struggling—everyone around them seems to be handling things just fine—and that they don't feel comfortable sharing their experience because they don't want to look bad in comparison.

As a clinical psychologist, I have the distinct privilege of being privy to people's internal experiences more than most people. And I can assure you that if you are finding your workplace stressful, and you work with a big enough group of people, it's very unlikely that you're the only one. Sometimes it seems as if everyone else has it more together than you, simply because no one is openly sharing what's really going on inside. This can be especially true in a culture of competition versus cooperation.

Sometimes, we can get so caught up in comparison and competition that we feel disconnected from, and "less than," other people around us. The tendency to compare ourselves to others is unavoidable; our minds are socially attuned, and extremely good at making comparisons. Social comparison often leads us to feeling lousy about ourselves, and it's a game we will never really win. A few years ago, I heard a radio interview with musician Paul McCartney, who was talking about how he compares himself with newer musicians who are creating interesting and cutting-edge music. If a member of The Beatles compares himself negatively to others, I'm sorry to tell you, we all will.

You can be aware of this tendency without buying into it. We're all human, we all struggle, and *none* of us are perfect. The change can start with you, by unhooking from comparison and competition, and getting real with people. And if you feel emotionally unsafe in a group of people who will rip you up and spit you out if you're a mere human, find others outside that group to lean on.

REFLECTION QUESTIONS

1. What relationships are important to you? How might you deepen your relationships, or build closer connections?
2. Are there people you would like to reconnect with? What steps can you take?
3. What communities do you have for support? What social groups would you like to be involved in? What steps can you take to be more engaged in communities? Are there groups you would like to create yourself? Who would you want to invite?
4. What are some of the important qualities you look for in friends and friendship?
5. What colleagues do you trust for support, help, and consultation?

CHAPTER 15

Speaking Up and Setting Boundaries

have long struggled with saying no to new projects, social events, and opportunities. I have a mix of a people-pleasing tendency and straight-up enthusiasm about so many things that life has to offer. An opportunity to give a talk? Sounds exciting, sign me up! Supervise a group of second graders on the museum field trip? Wouldn't want to miss that fun! Take on another project at work? If I don't do it, who will? Join another book club? They seem like good people, and I love to read, sure, why not?

This pattern went on for years. While I longed to relax more, there wasn't much room for that in my overly busy life. Still, I struggled to change this pattern in a substantial way.

I finally had to confront this tendency during the first year of the Covid-19 pandemic. As a mental health professional during a stressful historical time, I was busy and experiencing the world's stressors right alongside my clients. I was writing my first book, which I had agreed to do before the pandemic started. Like many people, I had kids at home, learning remotely most of that year. I was exhausted, and finally reached my breaking point.

Several professional opportunities came my way around that time, and it was painful for me, but I decided to turn them down. I also said no to almost everything "extra" that came my way; I cut out unnecessary errands, kids' activities, social gatherings, and so on. I started speaking up more for myself in interpersonal situations that were draining me. As the world eventually re-opened and in-person events were scheduled again, I was more deliberate about saying yes only to things I had room for. Things that felt important and life enhancing. I had finally learned how to assert myself better and set limits with people. Doing so has helped me tremendously with burnout. I find I am less drained when I can choose when to say no, express my needs, ask for help, and respond to conflict directly.

Being more intentional about saying yes, and more effective at saying no, felt like freedom to me. Freedom to do less and focus more on the important things, like time with my family. Freedom to choose the work I do, instead of just doing anything that came my way. I stopped feeling that other people were controlling me and instead felt more as if I was making my own choices.

Like me, many people who experience burnout have trouble setting limits, standing up for themselves, asking for help, and saying no. They (especially people-pleaser and do-gooder types) often tend to be empathic, absorbing the weight of others' emotions in addition to their own. They try to keep others comfortable and avoid conflict. They often feel they must do everything for everyone and do all things well. They worry about disappointing or letting others down. Because they are often afflicted with "the curse of competence," work, including domestic chores and caregiving tasks, often defaults to them automatically, without discussion or agreement.

If you are burned out, you may feel that you can't set limits with your work or confront a problem you are facing with someone, even if it's depleting you. You may be asking yourself questions such as:

- Should I speak up to my boss, or accept the situation as it is?
- How do I deal with that co-worker who is draining my energy?
- Should I say no to a project I'd like to do but don't have the time for?
- Should I ask if I can go part-time, or change roles?
- Could I use some help? How do I ask for it?

- Should I confront relationship issues with my spouse, partner, or roommate? Should we redistribute domestic tasks?
- How do I speak up for myself? If I want to say no to a request, how can I do so effectively?

If this sounds familiar, you might be tired of doing things for other people and feel ready to say "enough!" but feel unsure about what to say or how to say it.

Fortunately, effective communication skills can be learned. In this chapter, I will teach you about some communication skills that can help you to reduce burnout and interpersonal stress by speaking up for yourself, especially when you're stressed or under pressure. And I'll teach you how to say no and set boundaries. With practice, these skills can help you to express yourself more effectively and find the sweet spot between making your own needs known and being respectful of others.

The goal here isn't to be overly aggressive or demanding, but rather to create more balanced relationships, in which you can express your needs directly or perhaps set an internal boundary to create a shift in how you relate to others. The burnout you are experiencing might be the incentive to learn how to speak up for yourself more effectively and set boundaries. If I can do it, you can too. In the words of Nedra Tawwab, author of the book *Set Boundaries, Find Peace: A Guide to Reclaiming Yourself* (2021), "Burnout is overwhelming, and boundaries are the cure" (Tawwab 2021, p.29).

The importance of speaking up

People can't read your mind; if you want to say no, get some help, advocate for yourself, or express a preference, you're going to need to speak up. This creates more open and balanced relationships in which everyone, including you, can speak up and set limits. When we face problems head on, and deal with them directly, a weight lifts. This gives us a sense of freedom, a sense that we, not other people, are in control of our lives.

Years ago, when I worked in a hospital setting, we were short-staffed. Someone had left a half-time psychologist position on my team, and the position had not been backfilled yet. I was trying to do my own job, in addition to helping with that position. I was swamped! One day, my former boss casually mentioned that it seemed as if I was doing fine with both jobs and suggested that he might reallocate the funds for the open position. Wait, what?!? "No," I told him, "I am not doing fine!" I said I had just been barely keeping up, waiting anxiously for the new person to fill the role so I could be relieved of the extra work. I realized that my boss, a genuinely caring manager who always looked out for my best interests, had no idea how busy I was because I wasn't speaking up about it. Wheels that don't squeak don't get any grease! I spoke up clearly about the multiple demands and stress I was dealing with. He heard me—a new person was soon hired, and my workload went back to normal.

My friend who is a physician wanted to cut her work schedule down from five days a week to four. She was willing to sacrifice some of her income to have less stress and more time with her kids. She told me how much she wanted this change, but said that she wasn't planning to ask. She assumed she would be told no, because no one else in her hospital department had a schedule like that. I encouraged her to ask anyway. I reminded her that the worst they could do was say no, and that they were probably going to be highly motivated to keep her in her job. A few weeks later, I got a text from her out of the blue. She had asked, and the answer was yes. She loves her new schedule.

Communicating in this way makes our relationships better. This, in turn, fosters the social support that we know helps to protect us from burnout. Speaking up can also help to protect us from the chronic stress of overwork, because we can set limits and express our own needs.

Assertive communication skills

When my clients are struggling with speaking up for themselves, I teach them about assertive communication skills. Assertive communication skills can give us a framework for how to navigate tough situations, by speaking up in a direct, open, and respectful way. These are skills that can be learned and practiced. But they are not easy, and putting them into practice is an ongoing process. I still work on these skills, and regularly lapse into less helpful communication patterns. I recommend starting small, by asserting yourself with something minor, and continuing to practice over time.

What is assertive communication?

Think of assertive communication as the Goldilocks and the Three Bears of communication. Like Baby Bear's bed, which is not too soft or too hard, assertive communication is "just right!"

- *Passive communication is too soft.* The goal of passive communication is to avoid conflict. When passive, you don't speak up about your own needs or feelings. Although avoiding conflict can feel like a relief in the short term, the problems can linger and build up in the long term. If they build up, they can sometimes "explode" into aggressive communication. Passive communication often leads to emotional distance and feelings of resentment. People can't read your mind. If you don't speak up, they won't know what you want or need. It's hard to reach a solution to a problem if you are too passive.
- *Aggressive communication is too hard.* The goal of aggressive communication is to get control. You express your needs or feelings, but it's done in a harsh way. This can include verbal attacks, blaming, or criticism, and at the extreme can escalate into yelling, threats, or even violence. One problem with aggressive communication is that it will often evoke defensiveness, fear, or anger from the other person. They might shut down, disengage, or escalate the situation. Even if you get what you want in the moment, it can damage the relationship in the long term.
- *Assertive communication is just right!* The goal of assertive communication is to resolve the issue and increase understanding. You express your needs directly *and* care for the relationship by being respectful. Communication focuses on sharing your feelings, perspectives, preferences, and needs. Communication is direct and clear. This may include "I statements" (see below), making a request, setting limits or boundaries, negotiating, or

compromise. You listen to the other person and take responsibility for your own actions, rather than controlling others or letting yourself be controlled.

How to be assertive

To speak assertively, you'll want to be direct, polite, and honest, and keep it simple and to the point. Instead of making global statements ("You never...," "You always...," or "You're such a..."), stay focused on the specific issue at hand ("I noticed that earlier today you..." or "Next time, could you please..."). The more specific you can be about what you need, the better.

One way to do this is to focus on your own experience by making an "I statement." "I statements" are a way to express your feelings, perspectives, and needs, but without criticizing or blaming the other person. They get your point across in a way that does not evoke argument or defensiveness—you are simply sharing how you feel about something. An "I statement" might be something like this:

- "When you (state specific behavior), I feel (state feeling) because (state need). I would prefer you to (state request)."
- "I could use help with... Would you be willing to do me a favor and..."
- "I would love to help you with...if I had more time, but I can't right now. I have too much on my plate."
- "I know that we usually... But this time I would prefer to..."
- "I think that..."
- "I will need (state resources or support) and (state realistic amount of time) to get that done."
- "If you want me to do..., I can but I'll need to spend less time on..."

While asserting yourself can be difficult, especially if you aren't used to it, with practice you can improve. It's a skill, and like any other you can learn and get better at. As you start to speak up for yourself, you'll gain the benefit of prioritizing your own needs.

Why is it hard to speak up?

Communicating your own needs can be difficult, especially if you're not used to doing so. Many of us have been conditioned to be "good" and well behaved. Saying yes and pleasing others is highly reinforced; it feels good to be helpful and productive, and other people respond favorably when you fall in line with what they want. Those qualities are usually prized culturally. You may have learned in your family of origin that it's better to be quiet and agreeable. This may be especially true for girls and women, who are often socialized to be likeable and giving.

We also face potential pushback, fear of how we will be perceived, or disappointment from other people if we say no. And there is some truth to our fears. I'll be honest with you, my better boundary-setting hasn't always been greeted with a friendly response! I learned that people, especially those who were used to mostly hearing yes from me, didn't always appreciate this change in me. I think it's worth it to me to speak up more, but it certainly isn't always easy to do so.

Having direct and assertive conversations takes a lot of courage! Saying no often requires us to face uncomfortable emotions, like anger if the person pushes back or is being unfair, fear that the conversation will turn into a conflict, or worry that we will disappoint someone by asserting our needs. Difficult conversations can get our hearts pumping! If you choose to speak up, it is quite normal to feel some discomfort; and you can speak up anyway, if it's values-aligned and important to you to do so.

Many of us have developed unhelpful beliefs about speaking up (Paterson 2022). We might, for instance, think that it's impolite or selfish to speak up for ourselves, or that other people won't be able to handle it if we say no or disagree with them. We may worry that we will anger someone or hurt their feelings. Or, we may think that we'll lose control and blow up if we release the pressure valve by speaking our minds. We may have narrow self-stories, like "I'm the one who is always there for people." It can help to be aware of your beliefs about speaking up, and practice some defusion skills (see Chapter 8) to keep those thoughts from holding you back. Remind yourself that those kinds of thoughts and self-stories don't need to run your life; if it's more consistent with your values, you can speak up anyway.

There are some situations in which you don't have control, or you aren't able to safely speak up. For instance, if you might lose your job or be verbally, emotionally, or physically harmed by someone if you do speak up. There can be complex race, gender, and power issues around this. In some situations, the cost might be too high, or you might need to placate the person for whatever reason. If you are in a situation like that, I recommend prioritizing your own safety, getting support where you can, and trying to find small ways to speak up/set boundaries in order to protect yourself.

Asking for help

Sometimes my therapy clients are maxed out at work and feel that they have more on their plate than they can possibly manage. If I ask, "Have you asked anyone to help you?" they usually look at me as if I have two heads. That possibility never even occurred to them! Often their assumption is that they would look incapable or weak if they admitted they were struggling and could use help. But if they put that assumption aside and ask for support, the situation is often drastically improved.

Sharing the load with others can make a big difference in the face of chronic stress. You might need practical assistance with a task that needs to be completed, like someone to drive you home from the mechanic, or help in the form of emotional support, like someone to talk to when you're feeling down. Whether it's something small, like asking a neighbor to feed your cat, or something bigger, like delegating a work project, asking for help can be challenging. Sometimes, it can feel so uncomfortable that we would rather just do everything ourselves. We might feel embarrassed about asking, or afraid of rejection. Or we might have beliefs that get in the way, like overestimating the likelihood of rejection, concerns about how we will be perceived, or feelings that independence is better than seeking help (Sorensen 2022).

To get help, try a simple/not-so-simple strategy: just ask! A body of psychology research has shown that we tend to underestimate how likely someone is to say yes to a request for help (Flynn and Lake 2008). And although you might worry that someone will be upset with you, people actually seem to like someone more when they've done them a favor (Jecker and Landy 1969). Opening up to someone enough to acknowledge that you need help can lead to a deeper connection with them.

Be direct, clear, and as specific as you can about what you are asking. Cajoling, apologizing, or offering to reciprocate are not necessary. In fact, such strategies might backfire on you, making the recipient less comfortable, and less enthusiastic about helping you. In the book *Influence Is Your Superpower*, Zoe Chance writes that if someone you ask for help feels coerced, "they'll resist—either in the moment or later—by looking for a way out" (Chance 2022, p.133).

Keep in mind that you can make a request, but you can't control the outcome. It is okay for the other person to say no if they want to. If they say yes and help you, express thanks. If they say no, don't take it personally. You can always ask someone else, do it yourself, or try asking them again next time!

When relationships deplete us

Nothing wears me out as much as interpersonal problems and conflict. I lose sleep if I'm anticipating a difficult conversation, or worried that someone is upset with me. I feel resentful if I've said yes to something I don't want to do, and dread if I have to say no to someone. I feel as if I'm on eggshells around people with mood swings, and stew in hurt and anger if someone treats me with disrespect, "gaslights" me, or is harshly critical of me. I get preoccupied by how to handle a conflict, unable to focus on other things until it's smoothed over. I feel stress rising in my body when I'm dealing with a difficult interaction, or when I am in the role of diplomat between people who are having a conflict. Whatever the situation, relationships are important to me, and I find that complex interpersonal interactions can be draining, sucking away every extra ounce of my energy.

There's a funny thing about relationships. Although supportive and satisfying relationships are core to our humanity and essential to our wellbeing (as we saw in Chapter 14), at times they can be one of our biggest sources of misery! When relationships go sideways, the social threat we experience can be highly stressful. We must find a way to navigate relationships effectively, or the emotional toll will be extremely high.

I am not alone in finding interpersonal challenges draining. As an example, my hair stylist of over ten years, Christen Gill, is a small business owner, a mom of three, and someone who interacts with people all day at work. She has had periods of burnout. One day as she cut my hair, she told me about her most severe period of burnout. After her business reopened during the Covid-19 pandemic, many people she interacted with were grouchy and irritable toward her, because they were so stressed and exhausted. In her line of work, she is no stranger to talking with people all day, but during that period she experienced more rude behavior from more people than ever before. This kind of disrespect was happening to people in all kinds of customer-oriented jobs at the time.

Being the target of people's irritability took an emotional toll on Christen, who normally loves her work. She noticed that when people eventually went back to their normal level of stress, and became less irritable with her, her burnout lifted. After that experience, she made a conscious effort to consider which clients were exhausting her and tried (as much as possible) to keep her client load limited to people who didn't drain too much of her energy. While she may not have been able to completely control that, limiting her exposure to people who depleted her energy helped her manage her burnout.

There are many ways relationships might deplete us and contribute to our exhaustion. I've heard stories of people whose burnout was driven by a demanding or unfair boss, or by overly competitive co-workers. Indeed, "toxic workplace behaviors" (interpersonal behaviors like unfair treatment, non-inclusive behavior, belittling, and abusive management practices) are among the biggest predictors of burnout (McKinsey Health Institute 2022). Sometimes people feel the demands of being "always on" in their role and don't have enough breaks from social interactions to recharge. In environments of "toxic positivity," people might feel that they need to put on a happy face even when they aren't feeling happy—and being disingenuous can be draining. Collaborative overload caused by too much teamwork can exhaust us (Cross, Rebele, and Grant 2016). An emotionally distant or high-conflict partnership can add to chronic stress, as can a relationship with someone who is self-absorbed or emotionally immature (Gibson 2015) and treating you with disrespect.

THE RELATIONSHIPS THAT DRAIN YOU

Take a look at your own relationships. What relationship situations, or people, tend to drain your energy? Do you ever feel walked over, as if you can't express what you want or need? Do you face social pressure or social obligations you aren't interested in? Do your relationships feel fair, or are they one-sided? Are there people who expect you to say yes? Are there tasks that default to you, without question? Are there people in your life who don't react well when you say no, or who don't listen when you speak up with your own opinions? Are there people who treat you with disrespect? Are there people with whom you have a lot of conflict, or with whom you avoid conflict and then feel resentful? What is the cost of that?

As you answer the above questions, are there any signs that some of your relationships might be depleting you and contributing to burnout?

Setting boundaries

When you think of boundaries, you might initially think of firmly walling people off—or even (at the most extreme) cutting them out of your life. But there are many types and degrees of boundary-setting. While sometimes boundary-setting can come in those more extreme forms, it can also be a more subtle, internal shift or taking a slightly different stance toward people or situations. An internal boundary might look like taking less responsibility for things, or not taking things other people do so personally. It might also mean not taking on other people's problems or their emotions. Or, it might look like not seeking approval from others, or bending over backward to try to please them.

Sometimes, boundary setting can mean giving people (like for instance your children, spouse, co-workers, or clients) the message that they are capable of doing things themselves, instead of defaulting to you being the main person in charge of everything. This can help unload some stress from you, and can also be good for your relationship, and for the other person. As an example, according to my colleague Emily Edlynn, author of the book *Autonomy-Supportive Parenting*, parents who promote more autonomy and independence for their children "report less stress, greater needs fulfillment, and a stronger sense of well-being" (Edlynn 2023, p.26). She goes on to say, "Studies repeatedly show that children raised in autonomy-supportive homes experience greater well-being in general, including higher self-esteem, better life satisfaction, and fewer psychological problems...these children also demonstrate better academic achievement and overall social and emotional functioning" (Edlynn 2023, p.26). Consider the possibility that taking on less for others will not only help you with burnout, but is good for everyone.

There are a lot of domains of life in which boundary-setting skills come in handy for preventing burnout. Relationships are an obvious area, especially with people who frequently ask you to solve their problems, or who drain your energy. In the book *Laziness Does Not Exist*, Devon Price writes:

> Unfortunately, we can't actually fix another person's problems. So, we end up frustrated and run-down, realizing we've been pouring energy into helping someone who can't (or won't) meet us halfway... Before we get wrapped up in yet another dramatic, ill-fated attempt to "save" someone, we ought to ask ourselves if another person's problems truly warrant our involvement, and if so, which kinds of involvement. From there, we can begin breaking out of the insecure, approval-seeking patterns that make us throw away hours of effort trying to help a person who isn't receptive to that help. (Price 2021, pp.177–178)

You can also set boundaries with your time by, for instance, not working past a certain hour of the day, or limiting how many plans you make in a given week. My podcast cohost Jill Stoddard sent a podcast-related email to members of an organization we had recently started working with that said she sets a strict boundary around not working on weekends. She asked our other cohost, Yael Schonbrun, and me if we thought her email to them was too harsh. "No way!" I replied. From a burnout perspective, we should all be saying something like that, regularly!

We can also set boundaries around our emotional limits. Examples of this could be choosing to limit news consumption, or choosing a comedy over a depressing, heavy movie during a stressful period.

A good friend and colleague of mine who cares deeply about politics noticed that she was getting drained after major political events, like major elections and Supreme Court decisions. The day of one particularly personal and intense event, she found herself feeling down and concerned about the state of the world. My friend told me, "I remember feeling devastated that morning and telling myself that I needed to dig deep into my self-soothing skills in order to face a day of taking care of other people's needs."

After meeting with one of her therapy clients, who was ranting about politics that day (and who had very different political opinions from her), she noticed that she was becoming increasingly drained. "On any other day, hearing this would have landed differently with me. But on that particular day, it was too much." She went home sick after that session, canceling the rest of her clients for the day. "I decided to take the rest of the day off because I could no longer pretend I was well enough to perform my job. It was a mental health day that was very much needed. I do not see it any differently than a debilitating headache that comes on in the middle of a workday, preventing you from doing your job."

My friend now sets a boundary. She takes time off work around major elections and other political events. I asked her about this, and she said, "I do this to protect my mind, body, and soul. It is a boundary that has become sacred, but I can also see that boundary becoming more flexible in the future. It is important to me to exercise the right to put a lid, metaphorically speaking, on the container of my life. It does not matter if my container is the size of a thimble or a ten-gallon bucket. I see self-care as akin to boundaries, and the older I get, the more I want to look back on overwhelming times and think about how I did not abandon my needs when all I required was a break." Now that is some serious boundary-setting self-care!

When to say no

Although you will always have the option, at least to some degree, of setting a boundary by saying no, it doesn't always make sense to do so. For instance, if a task is a requirement of a job you want to keep, or if saying no will create a bigger problem for you, you might not. And sometimes you don't *want* to say no, even if you can, to an exciting opportunity that's worth it to you. On the other hand, sometimes we need to say no to keep ourselves from being overwhelmed. It can be hard to decide. How do you decide?

First, you need to accept the reality that your time is limited. It's important to ask yourself where you want to invest your time and energy, given that this is the case. Ask yourself what activities drain your energy or feel unfulfilling to you. Physician Tammie Chang (2022) writes about energy "zappers," energy "mehs," and energy givers. Consider any given activity, tune in, and ask yourself which of these categories it falls into. You can also do a values check, to decide if something is important to you (see Chapter 10 to guide you). Those questions can help you be more intentional about when to say no.

If you are crunched for time, and have a habit of impulsively saying yes to everything, start by building in a pause before answering. Instead of automatically saying yes, say, "Let me think about that. I'll get back to you." Randy Paterson, a psychologist and the author of *The Assertiveness Workbook: How to Express Your Ideas and Stand Up for Yourself in Work and in Relationships* (2022), gets many requests for his time. Knowing his tendency to overcommit, he has made a rule for himself of not saying yes to any time-consuming requests without first thinking about it for a full day. That eliminates the pressure to impulsively decide, which often results in saying yes even if he doesn't really want to. You can build (and practice!) a habit like his by, for example, waiting 24 hours before responding to email requests.

Sometimes you might be in a situation where you are being told to do something and don't have much choice in the matter; for instance, if your boss delegates an important project to you, and it makes sense for you to be the one to do it. Even if you are already busy, you may not be able to just say no and end the discussion without serious consequences at work. In that situation, you can remind the person (for instance, your boss) of the multiple other projects you are working on, and ask which they would like you to prioritize. This will bring them face-to-face with how overextended you are, and you can negotiate with them to spend less time on the other projects you're working on. Similarly, you can do this at home with domestic work. "I was planning to cook dinner tonight. If I have to swing by the grocery store because you're running late, I won't have time to cook. Let's decide which is more important for me to do today."

How to say no

Saying no is similar to the assertive communication strategies we discussed above. Ideally, you want to be direct and to the point, while still being respectful and polite. There's no need to punt the ball ("maybe later"), apologize for your decision to say no, or make excuses that can be argued against. Instead, just say it directly: such as "No, I won't be able to do that," or "Thank you for offering, but I am not interested." The clearer you can be with your no answer, the less pushback you will get.

And if you do get pushback (which will happen sometimes, especially with people who are used to hearing "yes" from you!), simply restate your no again. Use the "broken record technique" (Linehan 2015; Paterson 2022) in which you just keep repeating the same message until they hear it. You don't need to think of something different to say each time you respond, just maintain your position. The person who's asking may not like it, but it's okay for them to feel that way. You can still choose to say no.

REFLECTION QUESTIONS

1. What relationships drain you? What relationships energize you?
2. How might speaking up help you with chronic stress and burnout?
3. Do you tend toward passive, aggressive, or assertive communication? What needs and limits do you want to express?
4. What is challenging to you about speaking up? What are your fears?
5. What gets in the way of asking for help? What help might you ask for?
6. What do you want to say no to?
7. Do you have trouble setting boundaries or saying no? If so, what would help you?

CHAPTER 16

Working Toward Cultural and Systemic Change

A Vision of a Better Future

To really address burnout on a bigger scale, we must consider the cultural and systemic factors that contribute to burnout, some of which we explored back in Chapter 3. It's important for individuals to heal from burnout and make necessary changes in their own lives, but that's not enough to address the root of the problem. To have the most impact and prevent burnout to the degree it's been happening around the world, we must also work toward changing the problematic systems that contribute to it.

I must admit, I feel overwhelmed by this prospect. What can I do to change a large systemic problem? I'm just one person, I don't know what actions I can personally take that will make a lasting difference. And with all the problems in the world, where should I focus my efforts?

When the world feels hard, and you are in a place of feeling cynical and disillusioned, real change might seem elusive to you, as it does to me sometimes. It can be hard to move the needle on the big problems of the world. You might wonder if there's any point in trying when these problems are so big. I hear you. Sometimes the world feels beyond repair. Sometimes I'm left feeling overwhelmed by it all, and unsure where to begin. It feels hopeless.

When I'm feeling that way, I like to frame the idea of "hope" in a different way. Hope can be thought of as *taking action* in a hopeful direction, even as the *feeling* of hope comes and goes. Sometimes we feel hopeful that things will get better, and sometimes we just don't. But we can still choose hopeful action, by taking the steps we can, big or small, in line with the kinds of changes we would like to see in the world.

In this chapter, I will offer my vision, based on the research and social commentary I've been reading about. I am aiming to leave you feeling hopeful and empowered, and give you some concrete ideas if you want to join me in doing what we can to work toward high-level change, whether you are an executive or business owner, manager or team leader, or an individual with burnout.

This is not to say that the burden of fixing these big problems falls to you alone as an individual. You may or may not have the desire, resources, or emotional bandwidth to tackle systemic change. You might want to read this book just to help with your burnout, and then go about your life. Or systemic change might feel too big to confront yourself—too much for you to take on right now. That's okay! It's not your fault, and the responsibility doesn't fall on you to fix the world's burnout problem. In fact, you might give yourself permission to skip this chapter entirely as a form of self-care.

But we can't expect things to change on their own, or for the "powers that be"—the ones that benefit the most from the status quo—to change things for us. Some individuals must speak up, and we must come together. You might have a leadership position with some power to implement changes that would help. Or, like me, you might simply have a desire to speak up and take action when you can.

Ideas for executives, business owners, and leaders with power

If you happen to be in a position of power or influence within an organization, there are some specific changes that can help improve workplace culture (Maslach 2003; Maslach and Leiter 2022; Swensen and Shanafelt 2020). Organizational-level changes in the direction of a positive, supportive, and empowered work environment are important for employee engagement and satisfaction. And while some organizations give lip-service to worker mental health, really prioritizing employee wellbeing means creating humane and supportive policies (not just offering employees a free mindfulness workshop!). Executives should ask themselves, "How can this be a great place to work that employees will choose?" People will want to go to work when they enjoy the culture and feel a sense of belonging and a shared purpose at their workplace.

Of course, there are constraints: budget constraints and other work-related priorities that seem more urgent. I know this. But in the long term, an engaged and satisfied workforce is valuable. When employees are exhausted and stressed, they are less engaged, creative, and productive, and you are more likely to have staff turnover, ultimately costing the organization financially (Waytz 2023).

Prioritize a humane workplace environment

Remember the idea from Chapter 3 of the "pebble in your shoe" that wears you out? A helpful starting place for leaders and organizations can be to remove as many of those pebbles—the microstressors that grind people down—from the workplace as possible. To do so, look at workflow to reduce inefficiencies. Reduce pointless meetings, and as much of the unnecessary administrative work that bogs people down as possible. Leaders, ask your employees about their regular stressors and listen carefully. See which you can eliminate for them.

As a leader, it's important for you to keep an eye on workload and time pressure. Where possible, increase resources and reduce demands on employees. Workers don't have to be superheroes, and they shouldn't have to sacrifice their health and happiness for the organization. Don't base your performance metrics entirely on how much they work and how busy they are; doing so can not only create pressure to overwork and contribute to burnout, but also cause people to be less creative and productive (Waytz 2023). Prioritize hiring and staffing so that the employees you have aren't too overloaded. Build slack into the system; expect that employees will go on parental leave, take vacations, and get sick, and plan for that so you aren't short-staffed. Offer workplace support for parents and caregivers, and for employees with health issues, disabilities, and so on. Encourage people to take time off when needed, use their vacation time, and call in sick if they are sick. And it's important for you to role-model healthy work–life balance yourself.

Provide your employees with flexibility and autonomy when possible. Try to find more opportunities for employees to weigh in on decisions related to their jobs, or try implementing "job crafting," which allows employees to redesign their jobs in ways that can increase satisfaction, engagement, and performance (Wrzesniewski, Berg, and Dutton 2010; Wrzesniewski and Dutton 2001). You can use consensus decision-making instead of a more hierarchical approach, to allow employees to feel included in decisions that impact their work. If arrangements like scheduling flexibility, shorter workweeks, or working from home appeals to people, and is possible for the type of work they do, perhaps you should allow it. These types of arrangements can improve employee satisfaction and actually make employees more productive in the long-run (Pang 2020). Instead of micromanaging, tracking, or requiring frequent status updates, let people do their work, and provide support as needed.

Identify areas of interpersonal stress, and give people a break from being "on," especially if they do intense customer-facing or interpersonal work. Provide break rooms, downtime, and other "safe havens"—spaces that allow workday refuge (McLaren 2021). Some people might want a chance to share their experiences with co-workers and get support. Others might just want a few quiet minutes to scroll on their phones or do a crossword puzzle. While offering people a chance to recharge might seem as if it would be costly in terms of productivity, it will help sustain them in the long run.

People like feeling appreciated for their work. Provide employees and co-workers with adequate rewards for their work. Pay them enough. Review and optimize your employee evaluation, compensation, advancement, and recognition systems. Establish fair and just accountability processes. Don't expect employees to stay motivated if you give them unrealistic goals and deadlines; while some aspirational goals can motivate people, too many can backfire and leave people feeling stressed. Show appreciation, and try to build internal motivation by helping people to have a sense of purpose around their work. Above all, treat employees fairly and with respect. Don't exploit them to try to squeeze every ounce of labor out of them. It won't work in the long run, as they'll burnout or you'll lose them.

Create an organization that is trustworthy, values-oriented, and people-oriented. People will feel more satisfied with their work if it feels in line with their values. Communicate clearly and directly. Allow people to be human—emotions, mistakes, and all. Be aware that what you do matters in terms of setting expectations for how people are treated and setting workplace culture.

Finally, and perhaps most importantly, you can support team leaders in promoting a culture of belonging for *all* employees, and address aspects of your workplace that undermine that for certain groups. Work toward creating an inclusive environment in which people of all identities feel welcomed, respected, and valued. Understand how recruitment, promotion, retention, and evaluation processes may contribute to systemic oppression against certain groups of people. Encourage good relationships with peers and supervisors as a form of support. Prioritize relationships, create camaraderie within your organization, and foster collaboration.

Hire compassionate leaders

In a recent UKG Workforce Institute report called *Mental Health at Work: Managers and Money* (2023), 69 percent of respondents to the survey said that their managers had an impact on their mental health—more so than their doctor or therapist, and about on par with their spouse.

If you are involved in hiring decisions, consider hiring humble and emotionally attuned leaders above all else. These are the people who aren't in leadership positions for self-centered reasons, like career advancement, power, or money. Instead, they lead (sometimes reluctantly) because they care about people, and about the mission of the work. They are emotionally intelligent, and attuned to the emotions and wellbeing of their staff.

Not only do these qualities improve workplace culture, but compassionate and emotionally attuned leaders are more effective (McGowan and Shipley 2023; Trzeciak, Mazzarelli, and Seppälä 2023).

Ideas for managers and team leaders

Being in a management position can be difficult and stressful. Managers and team leads are often in the middle, the person in between the executives and the employees. Your hands might be tied when it comes to introducing policies and implementing high-level changes within your organization that are set by executives, board members, and shareholders. You are trying to protect the workers on your team, and help them be productive toward the organization's mission, but are constrained by policies and mandates. You yourself are at risk of burnout because of the high stress of your role.

There are things you can do to support burnout prevention, and in fact your role is an important one; the team level matters a great deal for employee wellbeing and work satisfaction (Davis 2021; Maslach 2003). The people we collaborate and interact with day after day have a direct impact on our wellbeing. As we've seen in previous chapters, a dysfunctional team can be extremely stressful and depleting. A team that works well together can lead to connection and enhance work satisfaction. High-quality teams are associated with individual wellbeing, and better perceptions of team culture are associated with less exhaustion. Team-based interventions seem to reduce burnout.

What makes a good team? A clear, unified vision and shared purpose. A culture of trust and emotional support. A place where people can find help, support, encouragement, and humor, and where cohesion is more important than competition.

Effective teams are psychologically safe. Psychological safety means a climate in which people are comfortable being genuine and expressing themselves, and can share concerns and mistakes without fear of embarrassment or retribution (Edmondson 2019). On psychologically safe teams, people can speak up and ask questions. They can trust their colleagues. They have a culture of helping, support, and openness.

There are steps that leaders can take to foster psychological safety. Leaders can speak openly and have a learning mindset, which means having curiosity and humility about mistakes and potential improvements. They can invite participation from the team by asking questions and listening. They can express appreciation and be clear with employees about expectations (Edmondson 2019).

In your role as a manager or leader, you can work to foster clear and open communication, and look out for struggles employees are having. These struggles can be useful information for improving the workplace culture. It helps to create a workplace culture in which employees feel that they are able to speak up without fear of repercussion. As Marc Brackett states, "Part of avoiding burnout is encouraging workers to speak up when feeling pressured or unfairly burdened. But that doesn't happen in isolation—the freedom to express yourself, positive or negative, has to be part of the everyday experience" (Brackett 2019, p.228).

Things we can all do—ideas for individuals

If you are an employee without direct authority to make changes in an organization, you might not be sure what you can do. I know it can feel as if we as individuals don't have much power in the face of these big problems. But there are things you can do in your own work and life that matter. Can you speak up? Talk to your co-workers and managers? Say no to that extra work project your boss is asking to add to your already full plate? Leave at 5pm even if everyone else is still at work? Make suggestions in employee satisfaction surveys? I recommend that you only do so if you trust that you can do so safely, without personal repercussions. (And if you can't, maybe it's time to consider getting out of there.)

Sometimes we might need to use our psychological flexibility skills to take courageous action toward our values. We may need to accept the uncomfortable emotions, like fear we'll get fired if we set a boundary with our workload, or guilt if we stop to take a rest break. Or, we might need to practice cognitive defusion if we worry how we will be perceived if we speak up about an injustice at work. It's possible for all of us to challenge the status quo, in small or big ways, instead of going along with it. And if enough of us do that, perhaps we can move the needle.

Set and support boundaries that prevent overwork

In 2022, the term "quiet quitting" swept social media and the news. Quiet quitting was the unspoken decision to stop over-engaging in work. Instead of going above and beyond, people started doing the necessary parts of their job but no more. For some it meant no longer staying late or bringing work home. While some people in power found this trend concerning, others (e.g. Kilpatrick 2022) were quick to point out that this isn't exactly "quitting"—it's setting appropriate work boundaries. People are doing this in response to toxic workplace environments, in order to preserve their own mental health and prevent further burnout.

I've worked with clients in work environments, like law firms, that expect and promote overwork, who felt they couldn't take days off or even stop working in the evenings to decompress, spend time with their families, or get a good night's sleep. I've seen people in healthcare and other industries who would lose vacation time they didn't use at the end of the year, because they felt they couldn't afford to stop working and take time off.

One thing we can all do to help with burnout is to stop pretending that this is okay. Setting boundaries with work is necessary to help people recharge and have a satisfying life. There might be consequences to taking time away from work, but there are also big consequences if we don't. We aren't built to work 20 hours a day, seven days a week, year round.

People at all levels of organizations—from chief executive officers (CEOs) down to entry-level workers—can set boundaries with overwork, and encourage others to do the same. You might do this by using your allotted vacation time. All of it. Or leaving work on time, even if you aren't finished with it. You can encourage others to do the same. This is especially important if you are in a leadership position. Role-model it. Remember from the previous chapter how my colleague Jill set a boundary about not working on weekends? Let's all do that!

One trend I love is seeing people, especially people in power positions, who stop sending work emails after hours. If you're choosing to work late, keep it to yourself! Sending a work email at 11pm should not be a badge of honor. Even if you compose an email at that hour, you can wait to send it at a reasonable time in the morning, like 8 or 9am. Some people include email signatures to reflect this. For instance, "I have a flexible work schedule and may send emails outside normal office hours. I do not expect you to read or reply to this email outside your working hours." This sends a message that you are not supposed to be monitoring your emails every hour of the day and night.

Let's all stop feeling that we must make excuses for taking reasonable time off. No need to apologize. Repeat after me: "I won't be available. I'll be taking the day off."

Value caregiving roles and domestic work

Throughout this book, we've seen how caregiving roles are often undervalued and unappreciated. We rely on the unpaid labor of people who are already maxed out. We have structural problems that make caring for one another under-resourced and extremely difficult. We saw in Chapter 3 how caregiving and domestic roles tend to default to women and historically marginalized groups. It's time to make invisible work visible, and to acknowledge that the time spent doing these things is valuable.

We need laws and policies that provide support (including financial support) for people in these roles (Washington 2021), like paid parental and sick leave, subsidized childcare, universal family leave, and living wages for caregiving professions. We need care networks to provide caregivers with both emotional and practical support. We must acknowledge the need for caregivers, and how difficult it is.

What can you do? We can all be aware of this and shift toward valuing caregiving as worthwhile and important. We can use our votes to support policies that support caregiving. Even if you yourself are not currently in a caregiving role, you can be aware of how a more humane culture will prioritize caregiving roles, and create a better world for us all. And if you are not one of the people to whom that type of work tends to default, you can reduce the stress on others by contributing more. When couples share the domestic and caregiving burdens equally, for instance, it frees up more space and bandwidth for paid work.

It's important for *all* people to speak up about the importance of caregiving roles, not only parents and women. For instance, if a white, heterosexual male CEO shares with co-workers that he is leaving work early to take his child to the pediatrician, perhaps others will feel more comfortable doing the same.

Burn it down: Support the dismantling of oppressive systems

We can work toward eliminating burnout by speaking up against systems that don't serve us—systems of power and oppression like unrestrained "maximize profits and rapid growth at all costs" capitalism, patriarchy, systemic racism, white supremacy, and authoritarianism.

I know that ending oppression in favor of liberation and justice is a very, very tall order. But we can all do our part to contribute, starting with ourselves. There are many resources out there—books, podcasts, groups, and so on—on social justice and antiracism. I recommend that all of us, especially people in positions of power and privilege, use those resources to look at our own, perhaps unintentional, participation in (or silence about) systems of oppression. How do we benefit from privileges, and can we acknowledge this? Can we look our own biases squarely in the eye? Can we "unlearn" unhelpful narratives that we were taught as a child? Can we speak up and work toward the liberation of all people?

In the often-quoted words attributed to Lilla Watson, an Aboriginal elder, activist, and educator from Queensland, Australia, "If you have come here to help me, you are wasting your time. But if you have come because your liberation is bound up with mine, then let us work together." Working toward liberation—any kind of liberation—helps to free us all.

Join together with others: Take collective action

By now, this chapter might be starting to feel daunting. And it is, if you are trying to make these changes happen on your own, or overnight. But what if you could work together with other people toward social change?

On my podcast *Psychologists Off the Clock*, I had the honor of interviewing Dr. Tina Opie and Dr. Beth Livingston about their book *Shared Sisterhood: How to Take Collective Action for Racial and Gender Equity at Work* (2022). In the book, they share how they, a Black woman (Tina) and a white woman (Beth), bridged the racial divide between them by forming a trusting relationship, which turned into a collaboration toward racial and gender equity. Tina and Beth are living examples of "collective action," which is when historically marginalized and dominant group members come together with the goal of liberation and collective advancement in the workplace (Opie and Livingston 2022). If we can't make substantial changes alone, perhaps we can make some by banding together in supportive groups with a shared goal.

Change the narrative: Let's get vocal!

Remember those unhelpful cultural narratives we talked about in Chapter 8? If we want to reduce burnout on a global scale, the narrative about work needs to change. We all have a role in this and can move the needle by speaking up (you can go back to Chapter 15 if you want help with speaking up).

We can do this in multiple ways. First of all, we can start by openly acknowledging our all-too-human struggles. Instead of keeping them quiet, shout them from the rooftops. Or at least whisper them to someone you trust.

We can give our kids a new message. Instead of pushing them to achieve or praising them for hard work, we can teach them a more balanced approach.

We can, of course, speak out against "toxic" workplace environments, systemic inequities, pressure, and narratives that prize productivity but benefit few. We can stop perpetrating the myth that a person's worth as a human is dependent on their productivity. We can stop falling for the idea that everything is urgent, that we must work toward rapid and endless growth, and earn profits at all costs. We must question greed on the part of executives and shareholders, and step off the treadmill of consumerism.

I've seen some shifts in social commentary around work over the last few years, which I think are in the right direction. Do I think change will be fast or easy? No. But I am feeling more hopeful that the narrative is shifting. One hopeful action I'm taking is trying to change the narrative as much as I can by speaking up when I have the opportunity. Will it matter? Maybe a little bit. I hope so!

Join me—let's get vocal!

REFLECTION QUESTIONS

1. What changes would you like to see in your workplace? What (if anything) can you say or do that might help?

2. What team dynamics might contribute to, or help with, burnout? And how might your team improve in terms of psychological safety, communication, and so on?

3. What oppressive systems of power would you like to see dismantled? What might you do, on your own or in collective action with others, that could help?

4. What cultural narratives do you want to speak up about? What opportunities might you have to do so?

References

AARP and National Alliance for Caregiving (2020) *Caregiving in the U.S.* www.aarp. org/content/dam/aarp/ppi/2020/05/full-report-caregiving-in-the-united-states. doi.10.26419-2Fppi.00103.001.pdf.

Al Sabei, S.D., Labrague, L.J., Al-Rawajfah, O., AbuAlRub, R., Burney, I.A., and Jayapal, S.K. (2022) "Relationship between interprofessional teamwork and nurses' intent to leave work: The mediating role of job satisfaction and burnout." *Nursing Forum, 57,* 4, 568–576.

American Psychological Association (2022) Division 12 (Society of Clinical Psychology). https://div12.org/treatments.

Anderson, G.O., Thayer, C., and AARP Research (2018) *Loneliness and Social Connections: A National Survey of Adults 45 and Older.* Washington DC: AARP.

Atkinson, D.M., Rodman, J.L., Thuras, P.D., Shiroma, P.R., and Lim, K.O. (2017) "Examining burnout, depression, and self-compassion in Veterans Affairs mental health staff." *The Journal of Alternative and Complementary Medicine, 23,* 7, 551–557.

Baer, R.A., Carmody, J., and Hunsinger, M. (2012) "Weekly change in mindfulness and perceived stress in a mindfulness-based stress reduction program." *Journal of Clinical Psychology, 68,* 7, 755–765.

Baker, K., Warren, R., Abelson, J.L., and Sen, S. (2017) "Physician Mental Health: Depression and Anxiety." In K.J. Brower, and M.B. Riba (eds), *Physician Mental Health and Well-Being: Research and Practice* (pp.131–150). New York, NY: Springer.

Barnard, L.K. and Curry, J.F. (2012) "The relationship of clergy burnout to self-compassion and other personality dimensions." *Pastoral Psychology, 61,* 149–163.

Baumeister, R. and Leary, M. (1995) "The need to belong: Desire for interpersonal attachment as a fundamental human motivation." *Psychological Bulletin, 117,* 3, 497–529.

Beaumont, E., Durkin, M., Hollins Martin, C.J., and Carson, J. (2016) "Compassion for others, self-compassion, quality of life and mental well-being measures and their association with compassion fatigue and burnout in student midwives: A quantitative survey." *Midwifery, 34*, 239–244.

Bianchi, R. (2015) "What is 'severe burnout' and can its prevalence be assessed?" *Intensive Care Medicine, 41*, 1, 166.

Borges, L.M., Barnes, S.M., Farnsworth, J.K., Bahraini, N.H., and Brenner, L.A. (2020) "A commentary on moral injury among health care providers during the COVID-19 pandemic." *Psychological Trauma: Theory, Research, Practice, and Policy, 12*, S1, S138–S140.

Bowen, S. and Marlatt, A. (2009) "Surfing the urge: Brief mindfulness-based intervention for college student smokers." *Psychology of Addictive Behaviors, 23*, 4, 666–671.

Brackett, M. (2019) *Permission to Feel: Unlocking the Power of Emotions to Help Our Kids, Ourselves, and Our Society Thrive.* New York, NY: Celadon Books.

Breines, J.G. and Chen, S. (2012) "Self-compassion increases self-improvement motivation." *Personality and Social Psychology Bulletin, 38*, 9, 1133–1143.

Brown, N.C., Prashantham, B.J., and Abbott, M. (2003) "Personality, social support and burnout among human service professionals in India." *Community and Applied Social Psychology, 13*, 4, 320–324.

Bryant-Genevier J., Rao, C.Y., Lopes-Cardozo, B., Kone, A. *et al.* (2021) "Symptoms of depression, anxiety, post-traumatic stress disorder, and suicidal ideation among state, tribal, local, and territorial public health workers during the COVID-19 pandemic—United States, March–April 2021." *Morbidity and Mortality Weekly Report, Center for Disease Control and Prevention, 70*, 26, 947–952.

Burkeman, O. (2021) *Four Thousand Weeks: Time Management for Mortals.* New York, NY: Farrar, Straus and Giroux.

Cacioppo, J.T., Hawkley, L.C., and Thisted, R.A. (2010) "Perceived social isolation makes me sad: Five year cross-lagged analyses of loneliness and depressive symptomology in the Chicago Health, Aging, and Social Relations Study." *Psychology of Aging, 25*, 2, 453–463.

Cacioppo, J.T. and Patrick, W. (2008) *Loneliness: Human Nature and the Need for Social Connection.* New York, NY: W.W. Norton & Company.

Chan, D.W. (2006) "Emotional intelligence and components of burnout among Chinese secondary school teachers in Hong Kong." *Teaching and Teacher Education, 22*, 8, 1042–1054.

Chance, Z. (2022) *Influence Is Your Superpower: The Science of Winning Hearts, Sparking Change, and Making Good Things Happen.* New York, NY: Random House.

Chang, T. (2022) *Boundaries for Women Physicians: Love Your Life and Career in Medicine.* Visionary Women Publishing.

Chen, C.W. and Gorski, P.C. (2015) "Burnout in social justice and human rights activists: Symptoms, causes and implications." *Journal of Human Rights Practice, 7*, 3, 366–390.

Cigna (2020) "Loneliness and the Workplace Survey." Cigna. www.cigna.com/static/www-cigna-com/docs/about-us/newsroom/studies-and-reports/combatting-loneliness/cigna-2020-loneliness-factsheet.pdf.

Clear, J. (2018) *Atomic Habits: An Easy & Proven Way to Build Good Habits & Break Bad Ones*. New York, NY: Avery.

Cleveland Clinic (2019) "Caregiver burnout." https://my.clevelandclinic.org/health/diseases/9225-caregiver-burnout. Last reviewed on 01/13/2019.

Cohen, G.L. (2022) *Belonging: The Science of Creating Connection and Bridging Divides*. New York, NY: W.W. Norton & Company.

Cross, R. and Dillon, K. (2023a) "The hidden toll of microstress." *Harvard Business Review*. February 7, 2023.

Cross, R. and Dillon, K. (2023b) "How small stresses snowball." *Harvard Business Review*. February 7, 2023.

Cross, R., Rebele, R., and Grant, A. (2016) "Collaborative overload." *Harvard Business Review*. January - February 2016.

d'Ettorre, G., Ceccarelli, G., Santinelli, L., Vassalini, P. *et al.* (2021) "Post-traumatic stress symptoms in healthcare workers dealing with the COVID-19 pandemic: A systematic review." *International Journal of Environmental Research and Public Health*, 18, 2, 601.

Dalton-Smith, S. (2017) *Sacred Rest: Recover Your Life, Renew Your Energy, Restore Your Sanity*. New York, NY: Faith Words.

Daniels, A.K. (1987) "Invisible work." *Social Problems, 34*, 5, 403–415.

Davies, J. (2022) *Sedated: How Modern Capitalism Created Our Mental Health Crisis*. London: Atlantic Books.

Davis, P. (2021) *Beating Burnout at Work: Why Teams Hold the Secret to Wellbeing and Resilience*. Philadelphia, PA: Wharton School Press.

Dean, W. and Talbot, S.G. (2020) "Mindfulness as a diagnostic tool, not a treatment." KevinMD.com. Accessed on 24/03/23 www.kevinmd.com/2020/07/mindfulness-as-a-diagnostic-tool-not-a-treatment.html.

Deligkaris, P., Panagopoulou, E., Montgomery, A.J., and Masoura, E. (2014) "Job burnout and cognitive functioning: A systematic review." *Work & Stress, 28*, 2, 107–123.

Dolan, E.D., Mohr, D., Lempa, M., Joos, S. *et al.* (2015) "Using a single item to measure burnout in primary care staff: A psychometric evaluation." *Journal of General Internal Medicine, 30*, 5, 582–587.

Dormann, C. and Zapf, D. (2004) "Customer-related social stressors and burnout." *Journal of Occupational Health Psychology, 9*, 1, 61–82.

Dorsay, A. (2021) "Friendship in adulthood: 5 things to know." TEDx Talk. www.youtube.com/watch?v=GhpM_V_arUY.

Duarte, J., Pinto-Gouveia, J., and Cruz, B. (2016) "Relationships between nurses' empathy, self-compassion and dimensions of professional quality of life: A cross-sectional study." *International Journal of Nursing Studies, 60*, 1–11.

Duke, A. (2022) *Quit: The Power of Knowing When to Walk Away*. New York, NY: Portfolio.

Durkheim, É. (1951) *Suicide, a Study in Sociology*. (J.A. Spaulding and G. Simpton, trans.) New York, NY: Free Press.

Durkheim, É. (2014) *The Division of Labor in Society*. (W.D. Halls, trans.) New York, NY: Free Press.

Durkin, M., Beaumont, E., Hollins Martin, C.J., and Carson, J. (2016) "A pilot study exploring the relationship between self-compassion, self-judgement, self-kindness, compassion, professional quality of life and wellbeing among UK community nurses." *Nurse Education Today, 46,* 109–114.

Dutton, J.E., Debebe, G., and Wrzesniewski, A. (2016) "Being valued and devalued at work: A social valuing perspective." In B.A. Bechky and K.D. Elsbach (eds), *Qualitative Organizational Research: Best Papers from the Davis Conference on Qualitative Research, 3,* 9–51.

Eckleberry-Hunt, J., Kirkpatrick, H., and Hunt, R.B. (2017) "Physician Burnout and Wellness." In K.J. Brower and M.B. Riba (eds), *Physician Mental Health and Well-Being: Research and Practice* (pp.3–32). New York, NY: Springer.

Edlynn, E. (2023) *Autonomy-Supportive Parenting.* Reedley, CA: Familius LLC.

Edmondson, A.C. (2019) *The Fearless Organization: Creating Psychological Safety in the Workplace for Learning, Innovation, and Growth.* Hoboken, NJ: John Wiley & Sons.

Erikson, E.H. and Erikson, J.M. (1997) *The Lifecycle Completed.* New York, NY: W.W. Norton & Company.

Erickson, R. (2005) "Why emotion work matters: Sex, gender, and the division of household labor." *Journal of Marriage and Family, 67,* 2, 337–351.

Flynn, F.J. and Lake, V.K.B. (2008) "If you need help, just ask: Underestimating compliance with direct requests for help." *Journal of Personality and Social Psychology, 95,* 1, 128–143.

Ford, B.Q., Lam, P., John, O.P., and Mauss, I.B. (2018) "The psychological health benefits of accepting negative emotions and thoughts: Laboratory, diary, and longitudinal evidence." *Journal of Personality and Social Psychology, 115,* 6, 1075–1092.

Freudenberger, H.J. (1982) "Counseling and Dynamics: Treating the End-Stage Person. The Burnout Syndrome." In J.W. Jones (ed.), *Park Ridge, III.* London: House Press.

Frögéli, E., Djordjevic, A., Rudman, A., Livheim, F., and Gustavsson, P. (2016) "A randomized controlled pilot trial of acceptance and commitment training (ACT) for preventing stress-related ill health among future nurses." *Anxiety, Stress, and Coping, 29,* 2, 202–218.

Gallup (2021) *State of the Global Workforce Report.* www.gallup.com/workplace/349484/state-of-the-global-workplace.aspx.

Galvin, G. (2021) "Nearly 1 in 5 health care workers have quit their jobs during the pandemic." *Morning Consult,* October 4, 2021.

Gibson, L. (2015) *Adult Children of Emotionally Immature Parents: How to Heal from Distant, Rejecting, or Self-Involved Parents.* Oakland, CA: New Harbinger Publications.

Gilmore, N. (2020) "The problem with the mindfulness movement." *The Saturday Evening Post,* January 9, 2020.

Goldstein, J. (2013) *Mindfulness: A Practical Guide to Awakening.* Boulder, CO: Sounds True.

Gorski, P. (2019) "Fighting racism, battling burnout: Causes of activist burnout in US racial justice activists." *Ethnic and Racial Studies, 42,* 5, 667–687.

Grant, A.M., and Campbell, E.M. (2007). "Doing good, doing harm, being well and burnout out: The interactions of perceived prosocial and antisocial impact in service work." *Journal of Occupational and Organizational Psychology*, 80, 665-691.

Grant, A.M., Campbell, E.M., Chen, G., Cottone, K., Lapedis, D., and Lee, K. (2007) "Impact and the art of motivation maintenance: The effects of contact with beneficiaries on persistence behavior." *Organizational Behavior and Human Decision Processes, 103,* 53–67.

Greaney, M.L., Puelo, E., Prunck-Harrild, K., Haines, J., and Emmons, K.M. (2018) "Social support for changing multiple behaviors: Factors associated with seeking support and the impact of offered support." *Health Education and Behavior, 45,* 2, 198–206.

Green, A.A. and Kinchen, E.V. (2021) "The effects of mindfulness meditation on stress and burnout in nurses." *Journal of Holistic Nursing, 39,* 4, 356–368.

Grose, J. (2021) "America's mothers are in crisis: Is anyone listening to them?" *New York Times*, February 4, 2021.

Grose, J. (2022) "We're spending more time alone. Maybe it's because we're exhausted." *New York Times*, December 3, 2022.

Gupta, P., Moore, R., and Neto, G.F. (2015) "Occupational wellbeing in anesthesiologists: It's relationship with educational methodology." *Brazilian Journal of Anesthesiology, 65,* 4, 237–239.

Guthier, C., Dormann, C., and Voelkle, M.C. (2020) "Reciprocal effects between job stressors and burnout: A continuous time meta-analysis of longitudinal studies." *Psychological Bulletin, 146,* 12, 1146–1173.

Halifax, J. (2018) *Standing at the Edge: Finding Freedom Where Fear and Courage Meet.* New York, NY: Flatiron Books.

Hansen, V. and Pit, S. (2016) "The Single Item Burnout measure is a psychometrically sound screening tool for occupational burnout." *Health Scope,* 5(2):e32164.

Harvard Business Review (2021) *HBR Guide to Beating Burnout: Recognize the Signs, Make Sustainable Changes, Reengage at Work.* Brighton, MA: Harvard Business Review Press.

Hashem, Z. and Zeinoun, P. (2020) "Self-compassion explains less burnout among healthcare professionals." *Mindfulness, 11,* 11, 2542–2551.

Hayes, S. (2019) *A Liberated Mind: How to Pivot Toward What Matters.* New York, NY: Avery.

Hayes, S.C. (2022) "Why meditation doesn't work for you." *Medium*, February 8, 2022. https://medium.com/@stevenchayes/why-meditation-doesnt-work-for-you-839a6d2cd2c4.

Hayes, S.C., Bissett, R., Roget, N., Padilla, M. *et al.* (2004) "The impact of acceptance and commitment training and multicultural training on the stigmatizing attitudes and professional burnout of substance abuse counselors." *Behavior Therapy, 35,* 4, 821–835.

Hayes, S.C., Strosahl, K., and Wilson, K. (2016) *Acceptance and Commitment Therapy: The Process and Practice of Mindful Change* (second edition). New York, NY: Guilford Press.

Hersey, T. (2022) *Rest Is Resistance: A Manifesto*. New York, NY: Little, Brown Spark.

Hill, A.P. and Curran, T. (2016) "Multidimensional perfectionism and burnout: A meta-analysis." *Personality and Social Psychology Review, 20*, 3, 269–288.

Hill, D. and Sorensen, D. (2021) *ACT Daily Journal: Get Unstuck and Live Fully with Acceptance and Commitment Therapy*. Oakland, CA: New Harbinger Publications.

Hochschild, A.R. (2012) *The Second Shift: Working Families and the Revolution at Home*. New York, NY: Penguin Books. (Original work published 1989.)

Holt-Lunstad, J. (2021) "The major health implications of social connection." *Current Directions in Psychological Science, 30*, 3, 251–259.

Holt-Lunstad, J., Smith, T.B., and Layton, J.B. (2010) "Social relationships and mortality risk: A meta-analytic review." *PLoS Medicine, 7*, 7, e1000316.

Hou, T., Zhang, T., Cai, W., Song, X. *et al.* (2020) "Social support and mental health among health care workers during coronavirus disease 2019 outbreak: A moderated mediation model." *PLoS One 15*, 5, e0233831.

Jackson, E.R., Shanafelt, T.D., Hasan, O., Satele, D.V. and Dyrbye, L.N. (2016) "Burnout and alcohol abuse/dependence among U.S. medical students." *Academic Medicine, 91*, 9, 1251–1256.

Jecker, J. and Landy, D. (1969) "Liking a person as a function of doing him a favour." *Human Relations, 22*, 4, 371–378.

Joseph, S. (2013) *What Doesn't Kill Us: The New Psychology of Posttraumatic Growth*. New York, NY: Basic Books.

Kaschka, W.P., Korczak, D., and Broich, K. (2011) "Burnout: A fashionable diagnosis." *Deutsches Ärzteblatt International, 108*, 46, 781–787.

Kelly, K. (2022) *American Detox: The Myth of Wellness and How We Can Truly Heal*. Berkeley, CA: North Atlantic Books.

Kemeny, M.E., Foltz, C., Cavanagh, J.F., Cullen, M. *et al.* (2012) "Contemplative/emotion training reduces negative emotional behavior and promotes prosocial responses." *Emotion, 12*, 2, 338–350.

Kemp, J. (2021) *The ACT Workbook for Perfectionism: Build Your Best (Imperfect) Life Using Powerful Acceptance and Commitment Therapy and Self-Compassion Skills*. Oakland, CA: New Harbinger Publications.

Kemper, K.J., McClafferty, H., Wilson, P.M., Serwint, J.R. *et al.* (2019) "Do mindfulness and self-compassion predict burnout in pediatric residents?" *Academic Medicine, 94*, 6, 876–884.

Kendi, I.X. (2019) *How to Be an Antiracist*. New York, NY: One World.

Khoury, B., Lecomte, T., Fortin, G., Masse, M. *et al.* (2013) "Mindfulness-based therapy: A comprehensive meta-analysis." *Clinical Psychology Review, 33*, 6, 763–771.

Kilpatrick, A. (2022) "What is 'quiet quitting,' and how it may be a misnomer for setting boundaries at work." *National Public Radio*, August 19, 2022. www.npr.org/2022/08/19/1117753535/quiet-quitting-work-tiktok.

Klotz, L. (2021) *Subtract: The Untapped Science of Less*. New York, NY: Flatiron Books.

Kolts, R. (2016) *CFT Made Simple: A Clinician's Guide to Practicing Compassion-Focused Therapy*. Oakland, CA: New Harbinger Publications.

Koutsimani, P., Montgomery, A., and Georganta, K. (2019) "The relationship between burnout, depression, and anxiety: A systematic review and meta-analysis." *Frontiers in Psychology, 10,* 284.

Krasner, M.S., Epstein, R.M., Beckman, H., Suchman, A.L. *et al.* (2009) "Association of an educational program in mindful communication with burnout, empathy, and attitudes among primary care physicians." *Journal of the American Medical Association, 302,* 12, 1284–1293.

Leiss, U., Schiller, A., Fries, J., Voitl, P., and Peyrl, A. (2021) "Self-care strategies and job satisfaction in pediatricians: What we can do to prevent burnout-results of a nationwide survey." *Frontiers in Pediatrics, 9.*

LeJeune, J. and Luoma, J. (2019) *Values in Therapy: A Clinician's Guide to Helping Clients Explore Values, Increase Psychological Flexibility, and Live a More Meaningful Life.* Oakland, CA: Context Press.

Lembke, A. (2021) *Dopamine Nation: Finding Balance in the Age of Indulgence.* New York, NY: Dutton.

Leo, C.G., Sabina, S., Tumolo, M.R., Bodini, A. *et al.* (2021) "Burnout among healthcare workers in the COVID 19 era: A review of the existing literature." *Frontiers in Public Health, 9.*

Liang, L. (2020) "The psychology behind 'revenge bedtime procrastination.'" BBC, November 25, 2020.

Linehan, M. (2015) *DBT Skills Training Manual* (second edition). New York, NY: Guilford Press.

Lorde, A. (1988) *A Burst of Light.* New York, NY: Firebrand Books.

Lobanova, N. (2020) "This is what your unsolicited advice sounds like." *The New Yorker,* August 25, 2020.

Manne, K. (2017) *Down Girl: The Logic of Misogyny.* New York, NY: Oxford University Press.

Maslach, C. (2003) *Burnout: The Cost of Caring.* Los Altos, CA: Malor Books.

Maslach, C. and Jackson, S.E. (1981) "The measurement of experienced burnout." *Journal of Organizational Behavior, 2,* 99–113.

Maslach, C., Jackson, S.E., Leiter, M.P., Schaufeli, W.B., and Schwab, R.L. (2017) *Maslach Burnout Inventory Manual: Fourth Edition.* Menlo Park, CA: Mind Garden.

Maslach, C. and Leiter, M.P. (1997) *The Truth About Burnout: How Organizations Cause Personal Stress and What to Do About It.* San Francisco, CA: Jossey-Bass.

Maslach, C. and Leiter, M.P. (2022) *The Burnout Challenge: Managing People's Relationships with Their Jobs.* Cambridge, MA: Harvard University Press.

Maslach, C., Schaufeli, W.B., and Leiter, M.P. (2001) "Job burnout." *Annual Review of Psychology, 52,* 397–422.

Mayer, J.D., Roberts, R.D., and Barsade, S.G. (2008) "Human abilities: Emotional intelligence." *Annual Review of Psychology, 59,* 507–536.

McCluney, C.L., Robotham, K., Lee, S., Smith, R., and Durkee, M. (2019) "The costs of code-switching." *Harvard Business Review,* November 15, 2019.

McGonigal, K. (2015) *The Upside of Stress: Why Stress Is Good for You, and How to Get Good at It.* New York, NY: Avery.

McGowan, H.E. and Shipley, C. (2023) *The Empathy Advantage: Leading the Empowered Workforce.* Hoboken, NJ: John Wiley & Sons.

McKinsey Health Institute (2022) "Addressing employee burnout: Are you solving the right problem?" May 27, 2022. www.mckinsey.com/mhi/our-insights/addressing-employee-burnout-are-you-solving-the-right-problem.

McLaren, K. (2021) *The Power of Emotions at Work: Accessing the Vital Intelligence in Your Workplace.* Boulder, CO: Sounds True.

McPherson, M., Smith-Lovin, L., and Brashears, M.E. (2006) "Social isolation in America: Changes in core discussion networks over two decades." *American Sociological Review, 71,* 3, 353–375.

Melnick, E.R., Dyrbye, L.N., Sinsky, C.A., Trockel, M. *et al.* (2020) "The association between perceived electronic health record usability and professional burnout among US physicians." *Mayo Clinic Proceedings, 93,* 3, 476–487.

Mental Health America (2021) *Mind the Workplace Report.* https://mhanational.org/research-reports/2021-mind-workplace-report.

Mikolajczak, M., Gross, J.J., and Roskam, I. (2019) "Parental burnout: What is it, and why does it matter?" *Clinical Psychological Science, 7,* 6, 1319–1329.

Milkman, K. (2021) *How to Change: The Science of Getting from Where You Are to Where You Want to Be.* New York, NY: Portfolio/Penguin.

Mishel, M. (2021) "Growing inequalities, reflecting growing employer power, have generated a productivity-pay gap since 1979." Economic Policy Institute, September 2, 2021. www.epi.org/blog/growing-inequalities-reflecting-growing-employer-power-have-generated-a-productivity-pay-gap-since-1979-productivity-has-grown-3-5-times-as-much-as-pay-for-the-typical-worker.

Moen, F., Myhre, K., Klöckner, C.A., Gausen, K, and Sandbakk, Ø. (2017) "Physical, affective, and psychological determinants of athlete burnout." *The Sport Journal, 1,* 1–14.

Montaner, X., Tárrega, S., Pulgarin, M., and Moix, J. (2022) "Effectiveness of Acceptance and Commitment Therapy (ACT) in professional dementia caregivers burnout." *Clinical Gerontologist, 45,* 4, 915–926.

Moss, J. (2021) *The Burnout Epidemic: The Rise of Chronic Stress and How We Can Fix It.* Boston, MA: Harvard Business Review Press.

Moyser, M. and Burlock, A. (2018) "Time use: Total work burden, unpaid work, and leisure." In *Women in Canada: A Gender-Based Statistical Report.* Statistics Canada. https://www150.statcan.gc.ca/n1/pub/89-503-x/2015001/article/54931-eng.htm.

Murthy, V. (2017) "Work and the loneliness epidemic." *Harvard Business Review,* September 26, 2017.

Murthy, V. (2020) *Together: The Healing Power of Human Connection in a Sometimes Lonely World.* New York, NY: HarperCollins.

Nagoski, E. and Nagoski, A. (2020) *Burnout: The Secret to Unlocking the Stress Cycle.* New York, NY: Ballantine Books.

National Academy of Medicine (2019) *Taking Action Against Clinical Burnout: A Systems Approach to Professional Wellbeing.* Consensus Study Report. Washington DC: The National Academies Press.

Neff, K. (2003) "The development and validation of a scale to measure self-compassion." *Self and Identity, 2,* 223–250.

Neff, K. (2011) *Self-Compassion: The Proven Power of Being Kind to Yourself.* New York, NY: William Morrow Paperbacks.

Nguyen, L.H., Drew, D.A., Graham, M.S., Joshi, A.D. *et al.* (2020) "Risk of COVID-19 among front-line health-care workers and the general community: A prospective cohort study." *The Lancet, 5,* 9, E475–E483.

OECD Policy Responses to Coronavirus (COVID-19) (2021) "Risks that matter 2020: The long reach of COVID-19." www.oecd.org/coronavirus/policy-responses/risks-that-matter-2020-the-long-reach-of-covid-19-44932654.

Olsen, M.E. (1965) "Durkheim's two concepts of anomie." *The Sociological Quarterly 6,* 1, 37–44.

Olson, K., Kemper, K.J., and Mahan, J.D. (2015) "What factors promote resilience and protect against burnout in first-year pediatric and medicine-pediatric residents?" *Journal of Evidence-Based Complementary Alternative Medicine, 20,* 3, 192–198.

Olsson, L.F., Madigan, D.J., Hill, A.P., and Grugan, M.C. (2021) "Do athlete and coach performance perfectionism predict athlete burnout?" *European Journal of Sport Science, 22,* 7, 1073–1084.

Ong, C.W. and Twohig, M.P. (2022) *The Anxious Perfectionist: How to Manage Perfectionism-Driven Anxiety Using Acceptance and Commitment Therapy.* Oakland, CA: New Harbinger Publications.

Opie, T. and Livingston, B.A. (2022) *Shared Sisterhood: How to Take Collective Action for Racial and Gender Equity at Work.* Boston, MA: Harvard Business Review Press.

Pang, A.S.-K. (2016) *Rest: Why You Get More Done When You Work Less.* New York, NY: Basic Books.

Pang, A.S.-K. (2020) *Shorter: Work Better, Smarter, and Less - Here's How.* New York, NY: Hachette Book Group.

Patel, A. and Plowman, S. (2022). "The increasing importance of a best friend at work." *Gallup Workplace,* August 17, 2022.

Paterson, R.J. (2022) *The Assertiveness Workbook: How to Express Your Ideas and Stand Up for Yourself in Work and in Relationships* (second edition). Oakland, CA: New Harbinger Publications.

Payne, J.S. (2022) *Out of the Fire: Healing Black Trauma Caused by Systemic Racism Using Acceptance and Commitment Therapy.* Oakland, CA: New Harbinger Publications.

Perissinotto, C.M., Stijacic Cenzer, I., and Covinsky, K.E. (2012) "Loneliness in older persons: A predictor of functional decline and death." *Archives of Internal Medicine, 172,* 14, 1078–1084.

Platsidou, M. and Salman, L. (2012) "The role of emotional intelligence in predicting burnout and job satisfaction of Greek lawyers." *International Journal of Law, Psychology and Human Life, 1,* 1, 13–22.

Pollan, M. (2020) "Capitalism's favorite drug: The dark history of how coffee took over the world." *The Atlantic,* April, 2020.

Poorman, E. (2019) "Depression and suicide: Occupational hazards of practicing medicine." *Journal of Patient Safety and Risk Management, 24,* 5, 181–183.

Price, D. (2021) *Laziness Does Not Exist: A Defense of the Exhausted, Exploited, and Overworked.* New York, NY: Atria Books.

Puolakanaho, A., Tolvanen, A., Kinnunen, S.M., and Lappalainen, R. (2020) "A psychological flexibility-based intervention for Burnout: A randomized controlled trial." *Journal of Contextual Behavioral Science, 15,* 52–67.

Puranitee, P., Kaewpila, W., Heeneman, S., van Mook, W.N.K.A., and Busari, J.O. (2022) "Promoting a sense of belonging, engagement, and collegiality to reduce burnout: A mixed methods study among undergraduate medical students in a non-Western, Asian context." *BMC Medical Education, 22,* 1, 327.

Purser, R.E. (2019) *McMindfulness: How Mindfulness Became the New Capitalist Spirituality.* London: Repeater.

Raphael, R. (2022) *The Gospel of Wellness: Gyms, Gurus, Goop, and the False Promise of Self-Care.* New York, NY: Henry Holt and Co.

Reeve, A., Moghaddam, N., Tickle, A., and Young, D. (2021) "A brief acceptance and commitment intervention for work-related stress and burnout amongst frontline homelessness staff: A single case experimental design series." *Clinical Psychology & Psychotherapy, 28,* 5, 1001–1019.

Robertson, L.G., Anderson, T.L., Hall, M.E.L., and Kim, C.L. (2019) "Mothers and mental labor: A phenomenological focus group study of family-related thinking work." *Psychology of Women Quarterly, 43,* 2, 184–200.

Rockliff, H., Gilbert, P., McEwan, K., Lightman, S., and Glover, D. (2008) "A pilot exploration of heart rate variability and salivary cortisol responses to compassion-focused imagery." *Clinical Neuropsychiatry, 5,* 3, 132–139.

Rodsky, E. (2019) *Fair Play: A Game-Changing Solution for When You Have Too Much to Do (and More Life to Live).* New York, NY: Penguin.

Rosso, B.D., Dekas, K.H., and Wrzesniewski, A. (2010) "On the meaning of work: A theoretical integration and review." *Research in Organizational Behavior, 30,* 91–127.

Ruisoto, P., Ramírez, M.R., García, P.A., Paladines-Costa, B., Vaca, S.L., and Clemente-Suárez, V.J. (2021) "Social support mediates the effect of burnout on health in health care professionals." *Frontiers in Psychology, 11,* 623587.

Ruiz-Fernández, M.D., Ramos-Pichardo, J.D., Ibáñez-Masero, O., Cabrera-Troya, J., Carmona-Rega, M.I., and Ortega-Galán, Á.M. (2020) "Compassion fatigue, burnout, compassion satisfaction and perceived stress in healthcare professionals during the COVID-19 health crisis in Spain." *Journal of Clinical Nursing, 29,* 21–22, 4321–4330.

Rushton, C.H. (2018) *Moral Resilience: Transforming Moral Suffering in Healthcare.* Oxford: Oxford University Press.

Salzberg, S. (2011) *Real Happiness: A 28-Day Program to Realize the Power of Meditation.* New York, NY: Workman Publishing.

Salzberg, S. (2020) *Real Change: Mindfulness to Heal Ourselves and the World.* New York, NY: Flatiron Books.

Sánchez-Moreno, E., de La Fuente Roldán, I.-N., Gallardo-Peralta, L.P., and de Roda,

A.B.L. (2015) "Burnout, informal social support and psychological distress among social workers." *The British Journal of Social Work, 45*, 8, 2368–2386.

Sanderson, W.C., Arunagiri, V., Funk, A.P., Ginsburg, K.L. *et al.* (2020) "The nature and treatment of pandemic-related psychological distress." *Journal of Contemporary Psychotherapy, 50*, 251–263.

Schaufeli, W.B. and Taris, T.W. (2005) "The conceptualization and measurement of burnout: Common ground and worlds apart." *Work & Stress, 19*, 3, 256–262.

Schernhammer, E.S. and Colditz, G.A. (2004) "Suicide rates among physicians: A quantitative and gender assessment (meta-analysis)." *American Journal of Psychiatry, 161*, 12, 2295–2302.

Schmoldt, R.A., Freeborn, D.K., and Klevit, H.D. (1994). "Physician burnout: Recommendations for HMO managers." *HMO Practice/HMO Group.* 8, 58–63.

Schonfeld, I.S. and Bianchi, R. (2016) "Burnout and depression: Two entities or one?" *Journal of Clinical Psychology, 72*, 1, 22–37.

Shariatpanahi, G., Asadabadi, M., Rahmani, A., Effatpanah, M., and Esslami, G.G. (2022) "The impact of emotional intelligence on burnout aspects in medical students: Iranian Research." *Education Research International.* https://doi.org/10.1155/2022/5745124.

Shechter, A., Diaz, F., Moise, N., Anstey, D.A. *et al.* (2020) "Psychological distress, coping behaviors, and preferences for support among New York healthcare workers during the COVID-19 pandemic." *General Hospital Psychiatry, 66*, 1–8.

Skovholt, T.M. and Trotter-Mathison, M. (2016) *The Resilient Practitioner: Burnout and Compassion Fatigue Prevention and Self-Care Strategies for the Helping Professions* (third edition). New York, NY: Routledge.

Sonenshein, S. (2017) *Stretch: Unlock Power of Less—and Achieve More Than You Ever Imagined.* New York, NY: HarperCollins.

Sorensen, D. (2022) "How to ask for help." *Psyche*, April 20, 2022.

Spinelli, C., Wisener, M., and Khoury, B. (2019) "Mindfulness training for healthcare professionals and trainees: A meta-analysis of randomized controlled trials." *Journal of Psychosomatic Research, 120*, 29–38.

Spitznagel, M.B., Updegraff, A.S.G., Was, C., Martin, J.T. *et al.* (2022) "An acceptance and commitment therapy training program reduces burden transfer, stress, and burnout among veterinary healthcare teams." *American Veterinary Medical Association, 260*, 12, 1554–1561.

Stack, M. (2019) *Women's Work: A Reckoning with Work and Home.* New York, NY: Doubleday.

Stoddard, J. and Afari, N. (2014) *The Big Book of ACT Metaphors: A Practitioner's Guide to Experiential Exercises and Metaphors in Acceptance and Commitment Therapy.* Oakland, CA: New Harbinger Publications.

Stokes-Parish, J., Elliott, R., Rolls, K., and Massey, D. (2020) "Angels and heroes: The unintended consequence of the hero narrative." *Journal of Nursing Scholarship, 52*, 5, 462–466.

Suzman, J. (2020) *Work: A Deep History, from the Stone Age to the Age of Robot.* New York, NY: Penguin Press.

Swensen, S.J. and Shanafelt, T.D. (2020) *Mayo Clinic Strategies to Reduce Burnout: 12 Actions to Create the Ideal Workplace*. New York, NY: Oxford University Press.

Szarko, A.J., Houmanfar, R.A., Smith, G.S., Jacobs, N. *et al.* (2022) "Impact of Acceptance and Commitment Training on psychological flexibility and burnout in medical education." *Journal of Contextual Behavioral Science, 23,* 190–199.

Talbot, S.G. and Dean, W. (2018) "Physicians aren't 'burning out.' They're suffering from moral injury." *STAT*, July 26, 2018.

Tawwab, N.G. (2021). *Set Boundaries, Find Peace: A Guide to Reclaiming Yourself*. New York: TarcherPerigee.

Tedeschi, R.G. and Calhoun, L.G. (2004) "Posttraumatic growth: Conceptual foundations and empirical evidence." *Psychological Inquiry, 15,* 1, 1–18

Tiberius, V. (2023) *What Do You Want Out of Life?: A Philosophical Guide to Figuring Out What Matters*. Princeton, NJ: Princeton University Press.

Tomasello, M. (2014) "The ultra-social animal." *European Journal of Social Psychology, 44,* 3, 187–194.

Trzeciak, S., Mazzarelli, A., and Seppälä, E. (2023) "Leading with compassion has research-backed benefits." *Harvard Business Review*, February 27, 2023.

UKG Workforce Institute (2023) *Mental Health at Work: Managers and Money*. www.ukg.com/resources/article/mental-health-work-managers-and-money.

Van Lange, P.A.M. and Columbus, S. (2021) "Vitamin S: Why is social contact, even with strangers, so important to well-being?" *Current Directions in Psychological Science, 30,* 3, 267–273.

Vanderkam, L. (2018) *Off the Clock*. New York, NY: Portfolio.

Velando-Soriano, A., Ortega-Campos, E., Gómez-Urquiza, J.L., Ramírez-Baena, L., De La Fuente, E.I., and Cañadas-De La Fuente, G.A. (2020) "Impact of social support in preventing burnout syndrome in nurses: A systematic review." *Japan Journal of Nursing Science, 17,* 1, e12269.

Veninga, R.L. and Spradley, J.P. (1981) *The Work/Stress Connection: How to Cope with Job Burnout*. Boston, MA: Little, Brown and Company.

Waldinger, R. and Schultz, M. (2023) *The Good Life: Lessons from the World's Longest Scientific Study of Happiness*. New York, NY: Simon & Schuster.

Wallace, C.L., Wladkowski, S.P., Gibson, A., and White, P. (2020) "Grief during the COVID-19 pandemic: Considerations for palliative care providers." *Journal of Pain Symptom Management, 60,* 1, e70–e76.

Washington, K. (2021) *Already Toast: Caregiving and Burnout in America*. Boston, MA: Beacon Press.

Waytz, A. (2023) "Beware a culture of busyness: Organizations must stop conflating activity with achievement." *Harvard Business Review*, March–April, 2023.

Wegner, D.M. (1994) "Ironic processes of mental control." *Psychological Review, 101,* 1, 34–52.

West, C.P., Dyrbye, L.N., and Shanafelt, T.D. (2018) "Physician burnout: Contributors, consequences and solutions." *Journal of Internal Medicine, 283,* 6, 516–529.

Whillans, A. (2020) *Time Smart: How to Reclaim Your Time and Live a Happier Life*. Boston, MA: Harvard Business Review Press.

Whyte, D. (2001) *Crossing the Unknown Sea: Work as a Pilgrimage of Identity*. New York, NY: Riverhead Books.

Wiens, K. (2017) "Break the cycle of stress and distraction by using your emotional intelligence." *Harvard Business Review*, December 21, 2017.

World Health Organization (2019) "Burn-out an 'Occupational Phenomenon': International Classification of Diseases." May 28, 2019. www.who.int/mental_health/evidence/burn-out/en.

Wrzesniewski, A., Berg, J.M., and Dutton, J.E. (2010) "Managing yourself: Turn the job you have into the job you want." *Harvard Business Review*, June 2010.

Wrzesniewski, A. and Dutton, J.E. (2001) "Crafting a job: Revisioning employees as active crafters of their work." *Academy of Management Review, 26*, 2, 179–201.

Ye, Y., Huang, X., and Liu, Y. (2021) "Social support and academic burnout among university students: A moderated mediation model." *Psychology Research and Behavior Management, 14*, 335–344 https://doi.org/10.2147/PRBM.S300797.

Yerramilli, P. (2020) "I'm a physician and I'm not a hero." KevinMD.com. Accessed on 24/03/23 www.kevinmd.com/2020/03/im-a-physician-and-im-not-a-hero.html.

Yong, E. (2021) "Why health-care workers are quitting in droves." *The Atlantic*, November 16, 2021.

Zapf, D. (2002) "Emotion work and psychological well-being: A review of the literature and some conceptual considerations." *Human Resource Management Review, 12*, 237–268.

Further Reading and Resources

On burnout and stress

Already Toast: Caregiving and Burnout in America by Kate Washington (Beacon Press, 2021).

Black Girl Burnout (podcast).

Burnout: The Secret to Unlocking the Stress Cycle by Emily Nagoski and Amelia Nagoski (Ballantine Books, 2020).

The Burnout Challenge: Managing People's Relationships with Their Jobs by Christina Maslach and Michael P. Leiter (Harvard University Press, 2022).

The Upside of Stress: Why Stress Is Good For You, and How to Get Good at It by Kelly McGonigal (Avery, 2016).

Burnout in context and systemic/social change

Laziness Does Not Exist: A Defense of the Exhausted, Exploited, and Overworked by Devon Price (Atria Books, 2021).

Rest Is Resistance: A Manifesto by Tricia Hersey (Little, Brown Spark, 2022).

Work: A Deep History from the Stone Age to the Age of Robot by James Suzman (Penguin Press, 2020).

Shared Sisterhood: How to Take Collective Action for Racial and Gender Equity at Work by Tina Opie and Beth Livingston (Harvard Business Review Press, 2022).

Emotional intelligence at work

Permission to Feel: Unlocking the Power of Emotions to Help Our Kids, Ourselves, and Our Society Thrive by Marc Brackett (Celadon Books, 2019).
The Power of Emotions at Work: Accessing the Vital Intelligence in Your Workplace by Karla McLaren (Sounds True, 2021).

Leadership and teambuilding

Prosocial: Using Evolutionary Science to Build Productive, Equitable, and Collaborative Groups by Paul Atkins, David Sloan Wilson, and Steven Hayes (Context Press, 2019).
The Empathy Advantage: Leading the Empowered Workforce by Heather McGowan and Chris Shipley (Wiley, 2023).

On ACT and psychological flexibility

ACT Daily Journal: Get Unstuck and Live Fully with Acceptance and Commitment Therapy by Diana Hill and Debbie Sorensen (New Harbinger Publications, 2021).
A Liberated Mind: How to Pivot Toward What Matters by Steven Hayes (Avery, 2019).
Imposter No More: Overcome Self-Doubt and Imposterism to Cultivate a Successful Career by Jill Stoddard. (Balance, 2023).
Psychologists Off the Clock (podcast).

Self-compassion

Self-Compassion: The Proven Power of Being Kind to Yourself by Kristin Neff (William Morrow Paperbacks, 2011).

Values

Finding Your Why and Finding Your Way by Daniel J. Moran and Siri Ming (New Harbinger Publications, 2023).
What Do You Want Out of Life?: A Philosophical Guide to Figuring Out What Matters by Valerie Tiberius (Princeton University Press, 2023).

Mindfulness
Real Change: Mindfulness to Heal Ourselves and the World by Sharon Salzberg (Flatiron Books, 2020).
Real Happiness: A 28-Day Program to Realize the Power of Meditation by Sharon Salzberg (Workman Publishing, 2011).

Habit change
Atomic Habits: An Easy & Proven Way to Build Good Habits & Break Bad Ones by James Clear (Avery, 2018).
How to Change: The Science of Getting from Where You Are to Where You Want to Be by Katy Milkman (Portfolio/Penguin, 2021).

Time management and work-life balance
Four Thousand Weeks: Time Management for Mortals by Oliver Burkeman (Farrar, Straus and Giroux, 2021).
"Work, Parent, Thrive: 12 Science-Backed Strategies to Ditch Guilt, Manage Overwhelm, and Grow Connection" *When Everything Feels Like Too Much* by Yael Schonbrun (Shambhala, 2022).

On the importance of social support
The Good Life: Lessons from the World's Longest Scientific Study of Happiness by Robert Waldinger and Marc Schultz (Simon & Schuster, 2023).
Together: The Healing Power of Human Connection in a Sometimes Lonely World by Vivek Murthy (HarperCollins, 2020).

Speaking up and setting boundaries
The Assertiveness Workbook: How to Express Your Ideas and Stand Up for Yourself in Work and in Relationships (second edition) by Randy J. Paterson (New Harbinger Publications, 2022).
Nonviolent Communication: A Language of Life (third edition) by Marshall Rosenberg (Puddle Dancer Press, 2015).
Set Boundaries, Find Peace: A Guide to Reclaiming Yourself by Nedra Glover Tawwab (Tarcherperigee, 2021).